MySQL® Tutorial

MySQL® Tutorial

Luke Welling and Laura Thomson

800 East 96th Street, Indianapolis, Indiana 46240 USA

MySQL Tutorial

International Standard Book Number: 0-672-32584-5

Library of Congress Catalog Card Number: 2003092540

Printed in the United States of America

First Printing: December 2003

09 08 07 06   10 9 8 7 6

Trademarks

Warning and Disclaimer

Bulk Sales

Pearson offers excellent discounts on this book when ordered in quantity for bulk purchases or special sales. For more information, please contact

U.S. Corporate and Government Sales
1-800-382-3419
corpsales@pearsontechgroup.com

For sales outside of the U.S., please contact

International Sales
1-317-428-3341
international@pearsontechgroup.com

ASSOCIATE PUBLISHER	MANAGING EDITOR	INDEXER	MARKETING MANAGER
Mark Taber	Charlotte Clapp	Sharon Shock	Randi Roger
ACQUISITIONS EDITOR	**SENIOR PROJECT EDITOR**	**PROOFREADER**	**COVER & INTERIOR DESIGNER**
Shelley Johnston	Matthew Purcell	Tonya Fenimore	Gary Adair
DEVELOPMENT EDITOR	**COPY EDITOR**	**TECHNICAL EDITORS**	**PUBLISHING COORDINATOR**
Damon Jordan	Cheri Clark	Zak Greant	Vanessa Evans
		J. Scott Johnson	
		Chris Newman	

MySQL® Press is the exclusive publisher of technology books and materials that have been authorized by MySQL® AB, the company that develops and markets the MySQL database. MySQL Press books are written and reviewed by the world's leading authorities on MySQL technologies, and are edited, produced, and distributed by the Que/Sams Publishing group of Pearson Education, the worldwide leader in integrated education and computer technology publishing. For more information on MySQL Press and MySQL Press books, please go to **www.mysqlpress.com**.

MYSQL HQ
MySQL AB
Bangårdsgatan 8
S-753 20 Uppsala
Sweden

GERMANY, AUSTRIA AND SWITZERLAND
MySQL GmbH
Schlosserstraße 4
D-72622 Nürtingen
Germany

FRANCE
MySQL AB (France)
123, rue du Faubourg St. Antoine
75011, Paris
France

UNITED STATES
MySQL Inc.
2510 Fairview Avenue East
Seattle, WA 98102
USA

FINLAND
MySQL Finland Oy
Tekniikantie 21
FIN-02150 Espoo
Finland

MySQL® AB develops, markets, and supports a family of high-performance, affordable database servers and tools. With headquarters in Sweden, and with offices and employees located throughout the world, MySQL's mission is to make superior data management available and affordable for all and to contribute to building mission-critical, high-volume systems and products worldwide. MySQL AB is the sole owner of the MySQL server source code, the MySQL trademark, and the mysql.com domain. For more information on MySQL AB and MySQL AB products, please go to **www.mysql.com**.

*This book is dedicated to our families: both
the human and four-legged members.*

About the Authors

Luke Welling is a senior web developer at MySQL AB. He chooses to use Open Source software whenever practical and evangelizes the advantages of this approach as widely as possible. He has spoken to audiences in Australia, North America, and Europe about MySQL, PHP, and other Open Source topics. He has taught a wide variety of technical topics to university students and professionals, but he specializes in Internet-related topics.

Laura Thomson is a lecturer in the School of Computer Science and Information Technology at RMIT University in Melbourne, Australia. She has taught a wide variety of courses with a Web and Internet focus and is currently completing a Ph.D. in Web Mining. She speaks at conferences around the globe and has delivered training at organizations as diverse as Ericsson and Lonely Planet. Previously, Laura has worked for Telstra and the Boston Consulting Group. She holds a first-class honors degree in Computer Systems Engineering and a degree (with distinction) in Computer Science. In her spare time, she rides her horses, feeds her menagerie of animals, and occasionally speaks to Luke about something nontechnical.

Acknowledgments

We would like to thank all the lovely people at Sams for being supportive, enthusiastic, and really good fun. Thanks especially to Shelley (of course), Damon, and Mark.

Contents At a Glance

Introduction   1

PART I: **MySQL Basics**

1 Installing MySQL   9
2 Quick Tour   17

PART II: **Designing and Creating Databases with MySQL**

3 Database Design Crash Course   27
4 Creating Databases, Tables, and Indexes   41

PART III: **Using MySQL**

5 Inserting, Deleting, and Updating Data   65
6 Querying MySQL   81
7 Advanced Queries   95
8 Using MySQL Built-in Functions with SELECT   111

PART IV: **MySQL Table Types and Transactions**

9 Understanding MySQL's Table Types   131
10 Using Transactions with InnoDB Tables   147

PART V: **Administering MySQL**

11 Managing User Privileges   161
12 Configuring MySQL   173
13 Administering Your Database   181
14 Backup and Disaster Recovery   191
15 Securing Your MySQL Installation   205
16 Replicating Your Database   213

PART VI: **Optimizing MySQL**

17 Optimizing Your MySQL Server Configuration   225
18 Optimizing Your Database   231
19 Optimizing Your Queries   239
    Index   247

Table of Contents

Introduction   1

PART I: MySQL Basics

1   Installing MySQL   9

Installing on Linux 10
Installing on Windows 10
Installing on OS X 12
Configuring Your System 13
Checking Your System Works 14
Setting the Root Password 15
Deleting Anonymous Accounts 15
Creating an Account for Basic Use 15
Summary 16

2   Quick Tour   17

MySQL Directory Structure 17
Overview of Executables 18
Overview of User Interfaces 19
Quick Introduction to the MySQL Monitor 20
Summary 21

PART II: Designing and Creating Databases with MySQL

3   Database Design Crash Course   27

Database Concepts and Terminology 27
    Entities and Relationships 27
    Relations or Tables 29
    Columns or Attributes 29
    Rows, Records, Tuples 29
    Keys 29
    Functional Dependencies 30
    Schemas 30
Database Design Principles 30
    Redundancy Versus Loss of Data 30
    Anomalies 31
    Null Values 32

Normalization 32
    First Normal Form 32
    Second Normal Form 34
    Third Normal Form 35
    Boyce-Codd Normal Form 36
    Higher Normal Forms 36
Summary 36

4 Creating Databases, Tables, and Indexes   41

Case Sensitivity 42
Identifiers in MySQL 42
Creating a Database 43
Selecting a Database 43
Creating Tables 43
    Table Creation Example 44
    CREATE TABLE Statement 48
Column and Data Types in MySQL 51
    Numerical Types 51
    String and Text Types 52
    Date and Time Types 54
Creating Indexes 54
Deleting Databases, Tables, and Indexes 55
Altering Existing Table Structures 55
Summary 57

PART III: Using MySQL

5 Inserting, Deleting, and Updating Data   65

Using INSERT 65
Using REPLACE 70
Using DELETE 70
Using TRUNCATE 72
Using UPDATE 72
Uploading Data with LOAD DATA INFILE 73
Summary 75

6 Querying MySQL   81

Overview of SELECT 82
Simple Queries 82
Selecting Particular Columns 83
Specifying Absolute Databases and Tables 83
Aliases 84
Using the WHERE Clause to Select Particular Rows 85
Removing Duplicates with DISTINCT 87
Using the GROUP BY Clause 88
Selecting Particular Groups with HAVING 89
Sorting Search Results with ORDER BY 90
Limiting Search Results with LIMIT 90
Summary 91

7 Advanced Queries   95

Using Joins to Run Queries over Multiple Tables 95
Joining Two Tables 95
Joining Multiple Tables 97
Joining a Table to Itself—Self Joins 99
Understanding the Different Join Types 100
Understanding the Basic Join 100
Understanding LEFT and RIGHT Joins 100
Writing Subqueries 101
Using Derived Table Subqueries 102
Using Single-Value Subqueries 102
Using Boolean Expression Subqueries 103
Using SELECT Statement Options 105
Summary 106

8 Using MySQL Built-In Functions with SELECT   111

Operators 112
Arithmetic Operators 112
Comparison Operators 112
Logical Operators 114
Control Flow Functions 115
String Functions 116
String Processing Functions 116
String Comparison Functions 117

Numeric Functions 120
Date and Time Functions 121
Cast Functions 123
Other Functions 123
Functions for Use with GROUP BY Clauses 124
Summary 125

PART IV: **MySQL Table Types and Transactions**

9 **Understanding MySQL's Table Types   131**

ISAM Tables 132
MyISAM Tables 133
    Compressing MyISAM Tables 134
    Full-Text Searching on MyISAM Tables 135
InnoDB Tables 137
BerkeleyDB (BDB) Tables 138
MERGE Tables 139
HEAP Tables 141
Summary 141

10 **Using Transactions with InnoDB Tables   147**

What Are Transactions? 147
Using Transactions in MySQL 150
    Setting the Autocommit Mode 151
    Using Locks 152
The InnoDB Transaction Model 153
    ACID Compliance 153
    Transaction Isolation 154
Summary 156

PART V: **Administering MySQL**

11 **Managing User Privileges   161**

Creating User Accounts with GRANT and REVOKE 161
    Granting Privileges 162
Privilege Levels 163
    User-Level Privileges 163
    Administrator-Level Privileges 164

Evaluating Privileges 164
Using the REVOKE Statement 165
Understanding the Privilege Tables 165
    Understanding the User Table 166
    Understanding the db Table 167
    Understanding the Host Table 167
    Understanding the tablesPriv Table 168
    Understanding the columnsPriv Table 169
Summary 169

12 Configuring MySQL   173

Setting MySQL Configuration Options 173
    Setting Options for mysqld 175
Setting InnoDB Configuration Options 176
Multi-Install Configuration Options 177
Configuring for Internationalization 178
Summary 178

13 Administering Your Database   181

Starting Up and Shutting Down the MySQL Server 181
Getting Information About the Server and Databases 183
    Retrieving Database Information 183
    Viewing Server Status and Variables 184
    Viewing Process Information 185
    Viewing Grant and Privilege Information 185
    Viewing Reference Information About Tables 185
Setting Variables 186
Killing Threads 186
Clearing Caches 186
Understanding the Log Files 187
    mysqladmin Option Summary 188
Summary 188

14 Backup and Disaster Recovery   191

Backing Up and Restoring Your Database 191
    Backing Up and Restoring with mysqldump 192
    Backing Up and Restoring with mysqlhotcopy 196

Backing Up and Restoring Manually 197

Backing Up and Restoring with BACKUP TABLE and RESTORE
TABLE 198

Restoring from the Binary Log 198

Testing Your Backup 199

Checking and Repairing Tables 199

Checking and Repairing Tables with CHECK and REPAIR 200

Checking and Repairing Tables with myisamchk 200

Checking and Repairing Tables with mysqlcheck 201

Summary 202

15 Securing Your MySQL Installation   205

How the Privilege System Works in Practice 205

Securing Accounts 206

Setting the Password for the Root Account 206

Deleting Anonymous Accounts 206

Dangerous Privileges 207

Passwords and Encryption 207

Securing Your Installation Files 207

Don't Run mysqld as Root 207

Access and Privileges Under Your Operating System 208

Filtering User Data 208

Other Tips 208

Using SSL Connections 208

Securing Your Installation Physically 209

Summary 209

16 Replicating Your Database   213

Replication Principles 213

A Note on Versions 214

Setting Up and Configuring for Replication 215

Create a Replication User 215

Check Master Configuration 215

Create a Master Snapshot 216

Configure Slaves 217

Start Slaves 218

Advanced Topologies 219

Replication Future 220

Summary 220

PART VI: **Optimizing MySQL**

17 **Optimizing Your MySQL Server Configuration   225**

Compiling and Linking for Speed 225

Tuning Server Parameters 226

Tuning Other Factors 228

Summary 228

18 **Optimizing Your Database   231**

What's Slow in MySQL Databases? 231

Making the Right Design Choices 232

Indexing for Optimization 233

ANALYZE TABLE 234

Using OPTIMIZE TABLE 234

Summary 234

19 **Optimizing Your Queries   239**

Finding Slow Queries 239

Benchmarking Your Queries 240

Using the Slow Query Log 240

Using EXPLAIN to See How Queries Are Executed 241

Understanding MySQL's Built-In Query Optimization 243

Optimization Tips 244

Summary 244

Index 247

Introduction

Welcome to MySQL Tutorial. This book is a fast-paced tutorial to get you up to speed with MySQL quickly. It covers MySQL both from an end user's perspective and from an administrator's perspective.

In this introduction, we will review the following:

- Why use MySQL?
- Why MySQL instead of another database?
- What's different in MySQL 4.0 and 4.1?
- What features are still to come in future versions?
- Who should read this book?
- How this book works
- A note on MySQL licensing

Why Use MySQL?

MySQL is an excellent database server product. There are many reasons you should consider using MySQL for your database server.

MySQL is fast and stable. This is the key to its success. In February 2002, *eWeek* (www.eweek.com) performed a benchmarking study of the major database systems including Oracle, Microsoft SQL Server, DB2, and MySQL. The study rated MySQL and Oracle 9 as the best overall performers. This study was done using only the alpha of MySQL 4.0, but MySQL 4.1 is even faster.

MySQL is available as free software and as commercial software. It is available under a dual licensing scheme. All MySQL software is available under the GNU General Public License (GPL), but in situations in which you need or want a commercial license, you can buy one.

MySQL supports the vast majority of features considered important by the database community, such as transactions, row-level locking, foreign keys, subqueries, and full text searching. Version 5.0 will add stored procedures to the list.

MySQL scales well. It is used by some very demanding customers including Yahoo! Finance, Slashdot, and the U.S. Census Bureau.

MySQL is a great tool for learning about databases in general due to the ease of installation and use and the small hard disk and memory footprint.

Overall, MySQL is an excellent choice for your database application.

Why MySQL Instead of Another Database?

Too many databases are available to compare MySQL to each one in detail, but MySQL offers a combination of performance, price, and features that others will find hard to match.

Performance

MySQL is undeniably fast. Oracle, Microsoft, and IBM all claim to sell the fastest database in the world, which, depending on your level of credulity, demonstrates either that a benchmark can be made to prove anything its sponsor requires or that different products excel under different conditions.

On the MySQL Web site, you can read benchmarks comparing MySQL and various other databases. These benchmarks generally show MySQL solidly outperforming competitors. Although you are probably wise to take all benchmarks, especially vendor-designed benchmarks, with a grain or two of salt, all available evidence including independent tests indicates that MySQL is among the fastest products available.

The benchmark results can be found at

`www.mysql.com/information/benchmarks.html`

and the tests are included in the source download in case you want to make comparisons in your own environment.

The benchmarking exercise undertaken by *eWeek* magazine in 2002 showed MySQL performing as well as Oracle in backing a Web-based Java application running on a quad processor Windows machine. These two products outperformed IBM's DB2, Microsoft's SQL Server, and Sybase's ASE. We will come back to price in a moment, but it is worth noting that in this benchmark, one of the leading performers was free, whereas the other had a price of $160,000 ($40,000 per processor). See `www.eweek.com/article2/0,3959,293,00.asp` for details.

Speed has always been a key MySQL design consideration. New features are added to MySQL only when this can be done without harming performance. Sometimes this means that features are added more slowly than users would like, but it has ensured that MySQL has always been fast. Your own testing or experience will probably confirm this assertion.

Price

Price is perhaps the easiest point to compare. For many purposes, MySQL is a free application. The GPL allows you to use the software, alter the source code, and redistribute MySQL to other people who will also be bound by the GPL. Under some circumstances, such as if you want to redistribute MySQL as part of a commercial product, you will need to purchase a commercial license. A single server license costs $220 or $440 (at the time of writing), depending on whether you want to use the InnoDB table type. In other words, MySQL uses a dual licensing scheme where the free use is channeled through the GPL and the commercial use is channeled through industry-standard EULAs (End-User License Agreements) and OEM (Original Equipment Manufacturer) agreements. MySQL AB's general rule is, "if you are free, so are we; if you are commercial, so are we."

The major competitors are commercial, with complex pricing schemes that depend on the intended use, number of processors in each server, and number of users that will connect. The Oracle Database, Microsoft SQL Server, and IBM DB2 Sybase can all cost tens of thousands of dollars in moderate scenarios and hundreds of thousands of dollars on a server with many processors and many connected clients.

MySQL is sometimes compared to other Open Source databases, such as PostgreSQL and Firebird. Of these Open Source databases, MySQL is the only product with one company behind it, owning all intellectual property rights and offering full commercial licenses including liability and indemnifications required by large user organizations.

Another category of software that MySQL is at times compared with are the inexpensive non-client-server databases, targeted at home or small business users (such as Microsoft Access and Filemaker Pro). While often having an easy-to-use graphical user interface (GUI), the programs in this category lack important functionality, as well as the stability, scalability, and speed needed for mission critical applications.

Stability

The developers at MySQL have always regarded stability to be of prime importance. All MySQL versions released in binary form—even alpha releases—must pass the MySQL Test Suite. This process tests functions and other features, as well as the results of operations where a bug has been fixed in the past; thereby, ensuring that bugs can never be accidentally re-introduced.

Developers must also give the fixing of a bug higher priority than their other development tasks. Basically, their other work stops until any bugs related to their field of expertise are fixed. The rule is that MySQL releases should be free of all known and reproducible bugs. Naturally, some things cannot be resolved without causing problems elsewhere. This is particularly the case with production versions that should not be subject to major changes that can influence their stability. In these instances, the issue is documented and fixed in all later versions.

Finally, quality is ensured through the MySQL customers and community. With over four million users around the world working in a wide variety of environments, this provides unparalleled opportunity for finding bugs even in early stages of development. The bug reporting and handling system at MySQL is public, so people can see what others have reported and add their own comments.

Ease of Use

Another key feature of MySQL is its ease of use. No complicated configuration procedure is required in order to get started. MySQL Server works adequately straight out of the box. The defaults are set for minimal use of disk and memory resources. For optimal performance and for specific production requirements such as logging, tuning of this default setup will naturally be required. Sample configuration files are included to help with this.

Features

Feature comparison depends greatly on which features you regard as important. MySQL has some features, such as full text search, replication, and support for massive tables, that are missing or immature in other low-cost offerings. It is, however, missing features such as stored procedures and views that are standard in the high-cost options and available in some of the low-cost products. Some of these omissions are planned for upcoming versions (such as stored procedures); others (such as views) will take longer. Some MySQL features (such as row level locking) are missing even from most of the top-priced systems.

The feature comparison page on MySQL's Web site at `http://www.mysql.com/information/features.html` allows you to do a very fine-grained comparison between MySQL and around 20 competitors to see what is supported in different offerings. What follows, though, is a brief list of features MySQL has that are not offered by all competitors, as well as a list of features MySQL lacks that exist elsewhere.

MySQL 4.1 offers

- ACID-compliant transactions
- Cross-platform support
- Replication
- Support for huge tables and databases
- Full text search
- Subqueries
- Support for most SQL 92 syntax

MySQL does not currently include

- Views
- Stored procedures
- Triggers

What's Different in MySQL 4.0 and 4.1?

MySQL 3.23 was the production version for a long time. MySQL 4.0.13 was released as the production version of 4.0 in March 2003. The alpha of 4.1 was released in April.

If you have used 3.23, these are the major changes you'll note in 4.0:

- The InnoDB storage engine is included in the standard binary. This was included in some later versions of 3.23. The InnoDB engine is ACID compliant, supporting transactions, foreign keys, and row-level locking.
- MySQL now uses a query cache, storing the results returned by queries for later reuse and, hence, greatly improving performance for common queries.
- Full-text indexing and searching, which were added in 3.23.23, have been improved with the addition of Boolean mode.
- MERGE tables now support INSERT and AUTO_INCREMENT.

- The result sets from SELECT queries can now be merged with UNION.
- You can now delete rows from multiple tables with a single DELETE statement.
- User privilege management has been refined. More privileges have been added to give you a finer grain of control, and you can also now limit a user's resource use.
- You can now make changes to server configuration without having to restart the server.
- A new C language library, libmysqld, is now available to allow you to embed MySQL servers in your programs.
- Replication, which has been available since 3.23.15, has been improved in various ways, mostly bug fixes. For example, you can now set up a slave using LOAD DATA FROM MASTER, rather than having to use mysqldump or a tool like mysqlsnapshot.

A lot of other small changes and improvements have been made.

In 4.1, there are some additional improvements. The most important change is the addition of subqueries and derived tables. You also get Unicode support, support for OpenGIS geographical data storage, and a host of other minor improvements.

What Features Are Still to Come in Future Versions?

Version 5.0 is currently in the pre-alpha stage, but you can download the source code and experiment with it if you want. The biggest change in version 5.0 is the addition of stored procedures, which have already been implemented in this pre-alpha. Other changes are also planned, including support for cursors, RTREE indexes, true VARCHARs, and a host of other minor features.

Version 5.1 should support foreign keys for all table types (among a host of other features). Views should be supported in one of the 5.x versions.

Who Should Read This Book?

This book is unique because it consists of a series of short, concise chapters, each on a tightly targeted topic, with a task-oriented focus. Each chapter ends with a series of review questions and exercises so that you can test your understanding of the concepts in that chapter.

In short, we are aiming this book to be a tutorial for smart people. This book is not a reference manual. For that, we refer you to the excellent online MySQL manual. There is no point in reinventing the wheel.

We will focus on five key areas: installing and configuring MySQL, designing and creating databases with MySQL, using MySQL, administering MySQL, and optimizing MySQL. We will cover all the core skills necessary to use MySQL on a professional basis.

You can use this book when you need to learn how to perform MySQL-related tasks for a new project, a new job, or a course when you do not have time to plow through a thousand-page book. This book has a task-oriented focus to help you get the job done.

How This Book Works

This book is divided into five parts:

Part I, "MySQL Basics," will teach you how to install and configure MySQL on your system and will give you a tour of your installation.

Part II, "Designing and Creating Databases with MySQL," will take you through the process of database design and creation. Readers who have done database design before can skim through this part of the book, but if databases are new to you, we suggest that you read it in detail.

Part III, "Using MySQL," takes you through how to query MySQL on a day-to-day basis.

Part IV, "MySQL Table Types and Transactions," explains how to use the different storage engine types in MySQL, with a special focus on the InnoDB engine and how it can be used for transactions.

Part V, "Administering MySQL," explains the basic tasks needed to perform DBA duties with MySQL, including user management, configuration, database maintenance, backup and recovery, database security, and replication.

Part VI, "Optimizing MySQL," will help you to get the most out of your MySQL database by optimizing your server setup, database, and queries for your specific situation.

At the end of each chapter, you'll find a set of review questions and practical exercises for you to practice the skills from that particular chapter.

A Note on MySQL Licensing

The company MySQL AB, run by MySQL's developers and founders, owns the MySQL code and documentation.

Most parts of the MySQL source code are available under the GNU General Public License. What this means in practice is that you can freely use, copy, distribute, and modify the source code for MySQL. If you copy or distribute the code (or modify and then copy and distribute the code), you must do so again under the GPL. If you distribute binaries, you must also include the source code.

You can read the full text of the GNU GPL in your MySQL distribution, online in the MySQL manual, or online at the Free Software Foundation:

```
http://www.gnu.org/licenses/
```

More information on the GPL is provided at

```
http://www.gnu.org/licenses/gpl-faq.html
```

If this does not suit your purposes—if, for example, you want to modify MySQL and sell the modified binary without access to the source code—you must purchase a commercial license from MySQL AB. You can also choose to purchase a commercial license from MySQL AB if you want to support the development of MySQL.

One important note is that the MySQL documentation is not available under the GPL, but it can be printed for personal use.

MySQL Basics

1 Installing MySQL

2 Quick Tour

1

Installing MySQL

In this chapter, we will see how to install MySQL and set it up for normal use. In this chapter, we will cover the following:

- Installing on Linux
- Installing on Windows
- Installing on OS X
- Configuring your system
- Setting the root password
- Deleting anonymous accounts

We will begin by installing MySQL on your system. If you already have a copy of MySQL 4.1 or above installed, you can skip ahead to the section "Setting the Root Password."

You should first download the version of MySQL that is appropriate for your system. MySQL is available either as source code or as a binary distribution for most systems. If you are learning to use MySQL, we recommend that you download the binary for your system because it is much easier to install. Additionally, MySQL's binaries are tuned for optimal, stable performance.

For each platform, MySQL is available in three versions: Standard, Max, and Debug. For the examples in this book, you will need the Max version. This comes with various useful options enabled, such as InnoDB transaction-safe tables, which we will use extensively.

MySQL is available in several versions at a time: the current version, the most recent version, and a couple of development versions in different stages. This book was written for MySQL 4.1.

You can download MySQL from

`www.mysql.com/downloads/index.html`

We will discuss how to install MySQL binaries on Linux, Windows, and OS X. MySQL is available for many other systems, but if you have one of these others, you will have to consult the MySQL manual for details on installation.

Installing on Linux

Depending on your Linux version and how recently you installed it, you will quite likely already have a version of MySQL on your system, but it is also very likely that you won't have the newest version.

We recommend that you install MySQL on Linux from a MySQL-provided RPM— assuming that your system supports this package management format. We suggest that you use the versions of the RPMs available from MySQL, instead of any that come from the vendor of your Linux distribution, particularly if you are just beginning with MySQL. The MySQL binaries are updated more promptly than any distribution, so they include newer improvements and bug fixes. Also, your directory structure will be set up as documented in the MySQL manual, which can make finding things easier to begin with.

Several RPM files come in the distribution. The ones you will need in order to run the MySQL server and client are MySQL-server-*VERSION*.i386.rpm, MySQL-Max-*VERSION*.i386.rpm, and MySQL-client-*VERSION*.i386.rpm. (The word *VERSION* will be replaced with the appropriate version number.)

You can install the server and client by typing this in your shell:

```
rpm -i MySQL-server-VERSION.i386.rpm MySQL-client-VERSION.i386.rpm
```

This will also start mysqld, the MySQL server, and create the appropriate entries in /etc/init.d/ to start the server automatically for you when your system is started.

If you want to install MySQL in some other way—that is, not from an RPM—refer to the manual for detailed instructions.

Please understand that installing MySQL can be quite complex, and your experiences may differ due to previously installed versions of MySQL or your version of Linux.

Installing on Windows

To install MySQL on recent versions of Windows, you will need to be logged in as an administrator.

If you already have a version of MySQL installed, you will need to stop the server before installing a new version. You can do this with the following:

```
mysqladmin -u root -p shutdown
```

If you have MySQL installed as a service, you will need to remove the service. You can do this from the command prompt by typing this:

```
mysqld --remove
```

You may need to replace mysqld with the name of the server binary you originally installed as a service.

If you prefer a graphical tool, you can also remove the service from the Services Manager, located under Administrative Tools Services on Control Panel, or on some systems under Microsoft Management Console.

Please understand that installing MySQL can be quite complex, and your experiences may differ due to previously installed versions of MySQL or your version of Windows. Begin installing MySQL by unzipping your download file.

Depending on when you read this, the contents of this file will vary. At the time of writing, MySQL was installed by running setup.exe. However, MySQL AB, the company that makes MySQL, is planning an MSI installer. If you see a .msi file instead of setup.exe, you can install MySQL by double-clicking on the MSI file.

The setup program will give you the option to install MySQL in the default location (c:\mysql) or elsewhere. This book assumes that you'll install it in the default location.

After MySQL is installed, you will need to create an options file to set up your initial MySQL configuration. You should do this before starting the server for the first time. Details of the configuration can be found in the section "Configuring Your System," later in this chapter.

After performing your configuration, it is usually a good idea to start your server for the first time from the command line. (In a moment, we will look at how to install it as a service, but let's check whether it's working first.)

Open a command-prompt window and go to the directory where the MySQL server is located. If you have the standard installation, this will be c:\mysql\bin.

Type the following:

```
mysqld-max --standalone
```

This should give you a set of startup messages. Assuming that everything goes well, you can then install MySQL as a service.

Type the name of the server executable you plan to use followed by `--install`. For example:

```
mysqld-max --install
```

The `mysqld-max` executable is the one we recommend for use with this book.

There is one final thing you should do to make your MySQL installation fully functional. Some of the associated programs that come with MySQL are actually scripts written in the Perl language, so you will need a Perl engine to run them. Download and install ActivePerl from ActiveState at the following URL:

```
www.activestate.com/Products/ActivePerl/
```

ActivePerl comes as an MSI file. Download this file and install ActivePerl by double-clicking on it. You can stick with all the default options that the installer gives you for use with MySQL.

Installing on OS X

You can install MySQL on OS X from a package, assuming that you have OS X version 10.2 or newer.

If you already have a version of the MySQL server running, you will need to shut it down before installing a new one. You can do this by typing the following at a command prompt:

```
mysqladmin -u root -p shutdown
```

To run the server, you will need to have an account called mysql. If you have OS X 10.2 or above, this account will already exist.

The file you download from MySQL is a .dmg file—that is, a disk image file. Begin by opening the Finder and double-clicking on the .dmg file.

You will now see the contents of the disk image file. Find the PKG file and double-click on it. For the purposes of this book, you can go along with all the default options that the installer gives you.

You can set up MySQL to start automatically on system startup by adding a StartupItem. You can do this by double-clicking on the file called MySQLStartupItem.pkg that should be located in your .dmg file.

After performing the steps contained in the section "Configuring Your System," you can start the MySQL server by typing the following if you have installed the StartupItem:

```
sudo /Library/StartupItems/MySQL/MySQL start
```

If you have not installed the StartupItem, you can start the server with the following series of commands:

```
cd /usr/local/mysql
sudo ./bin/mysqld_safe
```

Now press Ctrl+Z. Finally, type the following command:

```
bg
```

If you have not installed the StartupItem, you will need to repeat these steps each time you restart your system and want to use MySQL.

Please understand that installing MySQL can be quite complex and your experiences may differ due to previously installed versions of MySQL or your version of OS X.

Configuring Your System

The initial MySQL configuration, as installed, will work as-is; however, some useful features are turned off by default, and it starts out insecure.

In this book, we recommend that you change the following configuration options:

- We will be using InnoDB tables, so we need to perform a basic setup for these tables.

- We recommend that you turn on binary logging in all situations. This is highly useful for disaster recovery.

- We recommend that you turn on slow query logging. This tracks slow queries (as you might expect from the name) and will help you optimize your applications.

MySQL uses options files to store configuration values. On Windows, your global options file can be located either in your Windows directory and named my.ini or in c:\my.cnf. We recommend using my.ini because .cnf is sometimes used as a file extension by other applications.

Under Unix-like operating systems, the global options file is typically located in /etc/my.cnf. If you want to run more than one server per machine, you can keep server-specific information in your data directory in my.cnf for each server. You can also allow individual users to have separate options in their own account—these should be located in ~/.my.cnf (note the . before the filename).

Depending on your setup, you may or may not have an options file to begin with. Open up the file in your favorite text editor—Notepad will do if you are using Windows—or create it if it does not exist.

We suggest an initial options file as shown in Listing 1.1.

LISTING 1.1 **Suggested Options File**

```
[mysqld]
# turn on binary logging and slow query logging
log-bin
log-slow-queries

# InnoDB config
# This is the basic config as suggested in the manual
# Datafile(s) must be able to
# hold your data and indexes.
# Make sure you have enough
# free disk space.
innodb_data_file_path = ibdata1:10M:autoextend
# Set buffer pool size to
# 50 - 80 % of your computer's
# memory
set-variable = innodb_buffer_pool_size=70M
set-variable = innodb_additional_mem_pool_size=10M
```

LISTING 1.1   **Continued**

```
# Set the log file size to about
# 25 % of the buffer pool size
set-variable = innodb_log_file_size=20M
set-variable = innodb_log_buffer_size=8M
# Set ..flush_log_at_trx_commit
# to 0 if you can afford losing
# some last transactions
innodb_flush_log_at_trx_commit=1
```

Most of this options file is based on the very simple InnoDB configuration file suggested in the MySQL manual. One point to note is that if you have an existing installation of MySQL with InnoDB and are adding this options file to it, you may have to comment out the line

```
set-variable = innodb_log_file_size=20M
```

by placing a # at the start of the line. (If you have an existing log file of a different size, MySQL will become confused.)

We will look further at configuration in Chapter 12, "Configuring MySQL."

Checking Your System Works

After you have installed MySQL, set it up to run automatically on startup, and configured it, you should be able to connect to it.

You can do this by typing the following:

```
mysql -u root
```

You may need to supply a path to the mysql executable (for example, on Windows, typically c:\mysql\bin\mysql -u root) or change your PATH.

This should log you in as the root (administrator) user to the MySQL monitor (a command-line interface to MySQL). You should see a welcome message similar to this:

```
Welcome to the MySQL monitor.  Commands end with ; or \g.
Your MySQL connection id is 4 to server version: 4.1.0-alpha-max-debug-log
Type 'help;' or '\h' for help. Type '\c' to clear the buffer.
mysql>
```

Things that are likely to be different on your system are the connection id and the server version number. Don't worry about this.

If you get a message similar to

```
ERROR 2003: Can't connect to MySQL server on 'localhost' (10061)
```

it means the MySQL server is not running. You may want to restart your system so that the server has a chance to start automatically, or you can start the server manually by typing

```
mysqld --standalone
```

at a command prompt. (It's easiest to do this in one window and then open another window to log in.)

To log back out of the MySQL monitor, you can type this:

```
\q
```

(That's a backslash followed by q followed by Enter.)

Don't log out yet, though. (If you have already done so, just go ahead and log back in.) There are a couple more administrative things you need to do before you can really begin using your MySQL installation. These things are important, so you'll want to continue following along in this chapter.

Setting the Root Password

As you probably noticed when you logged in just now, you had to supply a username—root—but not a password. The initial installation of MySQL has no root password set. It's really important to set this password for obvious security reasons. In the MySQL monitor, type the following:

```
set password for root@localhost=password('your password');
```

Obviously, you should replace *your password* with whatever you would like the root password to be.

Log out (\q) and then log back in. This time, you need to log in like this:

```
mysql -u root -p
```

MySQL then prompts you for your password. The -u means username, and the -p means log in with password.

Deleting Anonymous Accounts

MySQL creates some anonymous accounts that require no username to log in. We recommend that you delete these. The reasons behind this are covered in detail in Chapter 15, "Securing Your MySQL Installation," in the section "Deleting Anonymous Accounts." You can get rid of these accounts by typing this:

```
use mysql;
delete from user where User='';
delete from db where User='';
flush privileges;
```

Creating an Account for Basic Use

It is usually a good idea to use some account other than root for basic day-to-day work for security reasons.

We will briefly cover how to create a separate account now. For full details of how user accounts work in MySQL, read Chapter 11, "Managing User Privileges."

Create an account for day-to-day use by typing the following:

```
grant create, create temporary tables, delete, execute, index, insert,
 lock tables, select, show databases, update
on *.*
to username identified by 'password';
```

Obviously, you should substitute your own username and password into this command.

You should now log out and log back in with the username and password you set. You will need to use a root account for some of the things we will do in the later chapters of this book, but this account we have just created has fewer privileges than root, so it is safer for day-to-day use.

Summary

By this stage, you should have a working MySQL installation ready to follow along in the rest of the book. You should have done the following:

- Downloaded the latest binary version of MySQL for your operating system from mysql.com.
- Installed it—either via the installation program (on Windows or OS X) or via RPM.
- Set up the server to run automatically on system startup, if so desired.
- Created an options file.
- Logged in and out for the first time.
- Set the root password.
- Deleted anonymous accounts.
- Created a username and password for your own programming tasks.

Exercises

Install MySQL on a local system according to the steps in this chapter, if you have not done so already.

Next

In Chapter 2, "Quick Tour," we will look at the components of your MySQL installation and review user interfaces and basic MySQL usage.

## 2

Quick Tour

This chapter introduces the structure and tools associated with MySQL. We will take a quick tour to learn what the various MySQL tools are, where the binary and data files live, what command-line tools are available, and what the most commonly used client-side user interfaces are. We will cover the following:

- MySQL directory structure
- Overview of executables
- Overview of user interfaces
- Quick introduction to the MySQL monitor

MySQL Directory Structure

We will assume in this discussion that you have installed MySQL in the default location on your operating system. If you have installed it elsewhere, the basic directory structure will still be the same, but the base locations will be different.

If your system came with a vendor-supplied version of MySQL, you may have a different structure. For example, if you have Red Hat 9, you will find that it has reorganized the files to fit into its overall filing system. If you have installed MySQL from a MySQL-supplied RPM, the files should be in the locations documented here.

You should also note that the directory structure will vary slightly depending on which optional items you installed and whether you installed a binary distribution or a source distribution. In this book, we assume that you installed a binary distribution as recommended in Chapter 1, "Installing MySQL."

If you have a Unix-like operating system, the default location for the MySQL files is in /usr/local/mysql. If you have Windows, the default location is C:\mysql.

At that location, you will find a set of directories, including the following (assuming that you installed from a binary distribution):

- bin: This directory contains the MySQL server and client programs and several other useful compiled programs. The contents of this directory are covered in the next section of this chapter.

- scripts: This directory contains a set of Perl scripts that perform useful tasks. We will look at these in the next section of this chapter.

- data: This is where your actual database data resides.

- docs (Linux) or Docs (Windows): You will find the MySQL documentation in this directory, in HTML format.

- sql-bench (Linux) or bench (Windows): This directory contains a benchmarking suite.

There are also a couple of other directories that the average user will rarely go into: include (containing header files), lib (containing libraries used by MySQL), share (containing MySQL's error messages), and examples (only in Windows, containing examples of using the libmysql DLL). You may need to know where these directories are if you install other software (such as PHP) that links to MySQL, but you are unlikely to interact with them directly.

Overview of Executables

The MySQL executables are in the bin and scripts directories. Let's begin by looking in the bin directory.

You will find the mysqld executable and any variations for your operating system in here. This is the MySQL server program, the one you set up to run automatically when you started your system in Chapter 1.

You will also find mysql, the MySQL monitor, here. This is the basic command-line client.

As well as these two main programs, you will find several others. We will cover the usage of many of these through the course of this book. Some particularly important programs are listed here:

- mysqladmin: Used to perform many administrative functions.

- myisamchk: Used to check and repair damaged MyISAM tables.

- mysqldump: Used to back up your databases.

- mysqlbinlog: Used to read the contents of the binary log, essential for disaster recovery.

- mysqlshow: Used to get information about databases and tables.

We will use mysqld and mysql throughout the course of this book, and we'll revisit these other programs in Part V, "Administering MySQL."

Now, look in the scripts directory. The programs in this directory are interpreted Perl scripts, rather than compiled programs as in the bin directory. Again, we will cover the usage of some of these as you work your way through this book. The main one we will use in this book is mysqlhotcopy, which is used for backing up databases. (This is covered in Chapter 14, "Backup and Disaster Recovery.")

Overview of User Interfaces

You have various options as to the user interface or client to MySQL that you choose to use. The three most popular user interfaces are the command-line interface mysql (also known as the MySQL monitor), MySQL Control Center (MySQLCC for short), and phpMyAdmin.

The MySQL monitor comes with your basic installation. It is a command-line interface. This is always available as an option, it is simple to use, and it works on all platforms.

The MySQL Control Center (MySQLCC) is a graphical user interface. It is written using the Qt windowing toolkit, which is cross-platform. At the time of writing, MySQLCC was available for Unix and Windows, and it is planned to be available for OS X in the future.

phpMyAdmin is a Web-based interface for using MySQL. It is very popular with ISPs that supply MySQL for use in developing Web applications.

If you have MySQL installed, you already have the MySQL monitor. MySQLCC is an official MySQL product, but depending on which MySQL version you have, it may be a separate download. You can get it from

`www.mysql.com/downloads/mysqlcc.html`

MySQLCC is extremely simple to install, and you can find instructions for this at

`www.mysql.com/products/mysqlcc/install.html`

phpMyAdmin can be downloaded from

`www.phpmyadmin.net/`

If you want to install phpMyAdmin yourself, you will first need a working Web server and PHP installation.

For the purposes of this book, it does not matter which user interface you choose to use. The functionality is basically the same for all of them. You enter queries as text, and the results are displayed as text, regardless of which user interface you use.

The examples given were usually tested using the MySQL monitor, but you can use whatever you like—mysql, MySQLCC, phpMyAdmin, or any other front end you find on the Net. For some tasks, you will need to exit from your user interface and use a command line.

Quick Introduction to the MySQL Monitor

We will now cover the basic use of the MySQL monitor. We covered logging in to mysql in Chapter 1. Just as a reminder, you can connect to MySQL using

```
mysql -u username -p
```

The client program has some other switches you may find useful. If you are connecting to a MySQL database on another machine, you can use the -h switch to specify the host; for example:

```
mysql -h hostname -u username -p
```

A really useful option to mysql is the --i-am-a-dummy option. You can also invoke this option in a less pejorative way using --safe-updates. For example:

```
mysql --i-am-a-dummy -u root -p
```

The effect of this switch is to limit the damage you can do with a single command. This is an especially useful option (available for the command-line tool only) while you are first learning to use MySQL. You might like to use it while working your way through this book. (Specifically, this switch stops you from updating or deleting rows unless you specify a key value for those rows. If you don't know what this means yet, don't worry. All will become clear in Part III, "Using MySQL.")

After you're logged in, you can see what databases exist on the system by using the SHOW command:

```
show databases;
```

For most of you, this will be a short list at this stage. You should see the database called mysql in the list. This is the system database that holds information about user accounts and privileges. We'll discuss it later in the book.

Notice that the command has a semicolon at the end of the line. Most commands you type in the monitor need to be terminated with a semicolon; otherwise, MySQL will not execute them. Try typing

```
show databases
```

and pressing Enter. MySQL just sits there and waits. You can now type a semicolon and press Enter, and the command is executed. This allows you to split complex commands over multiple lines for readability. You can also type \g (backslash g) instead of the semicolon, but most people use the semicolon.

You can select a database from this list and type this:

```
use databasename;
```

(Substitute the name of the database you want to use.)

This tells MySQL that you want to work with a particular database. Pick one and do this. (You may not have sufficient privileges to select any of the databases. If you get a message to this effect, pick a different database and try again.)

After you have selected a database, you can see what tables are in it by typing

```
show tables;
```

You can get information on a particular table by typing

```
describe tablename;
```

You can log out of the monitor by typing

```
\q
```

You will notice that this command does *not* end with a semicolon. There is a set of commands that begin with \ (backslash). None of them need a terminating semicolon. You can get a list of these commands by typing

```
\h
```

(The h is for help.)

You can type commands and SQL statements directly into the monitor. However, you can also put these commands and statements into a file and run them all at once, like a script. We will do this later in the book, when creating databases in Chapter 4, "Creating Databases, Tables, and Indexes," for example.

If you are logged in to the MySQL monitor, you can run a file of commands by typing

```
source filename
```

If you are not logged into the monitor, you can execute a file of commands by using file redirection; for example:

```
mysql -u username -p < filename
```

You now know the basics of how to use the mysql client program.

Summary

- The most important directories in your MySQL installation are bin (executable programs), data (database data), and docs (documentation).
- The two programs you will use the most are mysqld, the MySQL server, and mysql, the command-line client.
- You have a choice of several user interfaces/client programs. We discussed mysql (command-line), MySQLCC (GUI), and phpMyAdmin (Web-based).
- The mysql command-line program has many useful command-line switches and options. We have discussed -u (to specify username), -p (to log in with a password), -h (to specify the host), and --i-am-a-dummy (for damage-control mode).
- When logged in, you can use SHOW DATABASES or SHOW TABLES to get a list of what is in the system and DESCRIBE tablename to get information about a particular table.

- You can log out with \q.
- You can terminate commands with ; or \g to send them to the server for execution.
- You can execute a file of commands from inside the client with source *filename* and from outside the client by using file redirection.

Quiz

1. You would find the MySQL server program in
   a) the docs or Docs directory
   b) the lib directory
   c) the scripts directory
   d) the bin directory

2. You would find the MySQL documentation in
   a) the docs or Docs directory
   b) the lib directory
   c) the scripts directory
   d) the bin directory

3. You would find mysqlhotcopy in
   a) the docs or Docs directory
   b) the lib directory
   c) the scripts directory
   d) the bin directory

4. Commands in the MySQL monitor
   a) should be terminated with a semicolon
   b) should be terminated with \g
   c) either a) or b)
   d) none of the above

5. The --i-am-a-dummy option to the mysql executable
   a) means what it says
   b) prevents me from doing too much damage while learning SQL
   c) prevents me from doing anything at all other than logging in and out
   d) none of the above

Exercises

Download and install a graphical or Web-based user interface such as MySQLCC. Work out how to log in and get a list of available databases using the client program you have chosen.

Answers

Quiz

1. d
2. a
3. c
4. c
5. b

Next

In Chapter 3, "Database Design Crash Course," we will look at general database concepts, terminology, and design principles including normalization. If you are not new to databases but are new to MySQL, you can skim this chapter.

Designing and Creating Databases with MySQL

II

3 Database Design Crash Course

4 Creating Databases, Tables, and Indexes

Database Design Crash Course

In this chapter we will review the basic principles of database design and normalization. A well-designed database minimizes redundancy without losing any data. That is, we aim to use the least amount of storage space for our database while still maintaining all links between data.

We will cover the following:

- Database concepts and terminology
- Database design principles
- Normalization and the normal forms
- Database design exercises

Database Concepts and Terminology

To understand the principles we will look at in this chapter, we need to establish some basic concepts and terminology.

Entities and Relationships

The very basics of what we are trying to model are entities and relationships. Entities are the things in the real world that we will store information about in the database. For example, we might choose to store information about employees and the departments they work for. In this case, an employee would be one entity and a department would be another. Relationships are the links between these entities. For example, an employee works for a department. Works-for is the relationship between the employee and department entities.

Relationships come in different degrees. They can be one-to-one, one-to-many (or many-to-one depending on the direction you are looking at it from), or many-to-many. A one-to-one relationship connects exactly two entities. If employees in this organization had a cubicle each, this would be a one-to-one relationship. The works-for relationship is usually a many-to-one relationship in this example. That is, many employees work for a single department, but each employee works for only one department. These two relationships are shown in Figure 3.1.

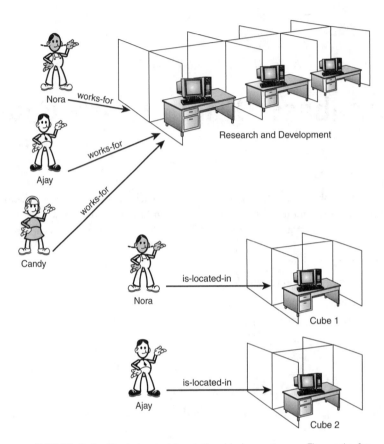

FIGURE 3.1   The is-located-in relationship is one-to-one. The works-for
relationship is many-to-one.

Note that the entities, the relationships, and the degree of the relationships depend on your environment and the business rules you are trying to model. For example, in some companies, employees may work for more than one department. In that case, the works-for relationship would be many-to-many. If anybody shares a cubicle or anybody has an office instead, the is-located-in relationship is not one-to-one.

When you are coming up with a database design, you must take these rules into account for the system you are modeling. No two systems will be exactly the same.

Relations or Tables

MySQL is a relational database management system (RDBMS)—that is, it supports databases that consist of a set of relations. A relation in this sense is not your auntie, but a table of data. Note that the terms *table* and *relation* mean the same thing. In this book, we will use the more common term *table*. If you have ever used a spreadsheet, each sheet is typically a table of data. A sample table is shown in Figure 3.2.

employee

employeeID	name	job	departmentID
7513	Nora Edwards	Programmer	128
9842	Ben Smith	DBA	42
6651	Ajay Patel	Programmer	128
9006	Candy Burnett	Systems Administrator	128

FIGURE 3.2   The employee table stores employee IDs, names, jobs,
and the department each employee works for.

As you can see, this particular table holds data about employees at a particular company. (We have not shown data for all the employees, just some examples.)

Columns or Attributes

In database tables, each column or attribute describes some piece of data that each record in the table has. The terms *column* and *attribute* are used fairly interchangeably, but a column is really part of a table, whereas an attribute relates to the real-world entity that the table is modeling. In Figure 3.2 you can see that each employee has an employeeID, a name, a job, and a departmentID. These are the columns of the employee table, sometimes also called the attributes of the employee table.

Rows, Records, Tuples

Look again at the employee table. Each row in the table represents a single employee record. You may hear these called rows, records, or tuples. Each row in the table consists of a value for each column in the table.

Keys

A *superkey* is a column (or set of columns) that can be used to identify a row in a table. A *key* is a minimal superkey. For example, look at the employee table. We could use the employeeID and the name together to identify any row in the table. We could also use the set of all the columns (employeeID, name, job, departmentID). These are both superkeys.

However, we don't need all those columns to identify a row. We need only (for example) the employeeID. This is a minimal superkey—that is, a minimized set of columns that can be used to identify a single row. So, employeeID is a key.

Look at the employee table again. We could identify an employee by name or by employeeID. These are both keys. We call these *candidate keys* because they are candidates from which we will choose the *primary key*. The primary key is the column or set of columns that we will use to identify a single row from within a table. In this case we will make employeeID the primary key. This will make a better key than name because it is common to have two people with the same name.

Foreign keys represent the links between tables. For example, if you look back at Figure 3.2, you can see that the departmentID column holds a department number. This is a foreign key: The full set of information about each department will be held in a separate table, with the departmentID as the primary key in that table.

Functional Dependencies

The term *functional dependency* comes up less often than the ones previously mentioned, but we will need to understand it to understand the normalization process that we will discuss in a minute.

If there is a functional dependency between column A and column B in a given table, which may be written A → B, then the value of column A determines the value of column B. For example, in the employee table, the employeeID functionally determines the name (and all the other attributes in this particular example).

Schemas

The term *schema* or *database schema* simply means the structure or design of the database—that is, the form of the database without any data in it. If you like, the schema is a blueprint for the data in the database.

We can describe the schema for a single table in the following way:

employee(<u>employeeID</u>, name, job, departmentID)

In this book, we will follow the convention of using a solid underline for the attributes that represent the primary key and a broken underline for any attributes that represent foreign keys. Primary keys that are also foreign keys will have both a solid and a broken underline.

Database Design Principles

When we design a database, we need to take two important things into account:

- What information needs to be stored? That is, what things or entities do we need to store information about?
- What questions will we ask of the database? (These are called *queries*.)

When thinking about these questions, we must bear in mind the business rules of the business we are trying to model—that is, what the things are that we need to store data about and what specifically the links are between them.

Along with these questions, we need to structure our database in such a way that it avoids structural problems such as redundancy and data anomalies.

Redundancy Versus Loss of Data

When designing our schema, we want to do so in such a way that we minimize redundancy of data without losing any data. By redundancy, I mean data that is repeated in different rows of a table or in different tables in the database.

Imagine that rather than having an employee table and a department table, we have a single table called `employeeDepartment`. We can accomplish this by adding a single `departmentName` column to the `employee` table so that the schema looks like this:

employeeDepartment(<u>employeeID</u>, name, job, departmentID, departmentName)

For each employee who works in the Department with the number 128, Research and Development, we will repeat the data "128, Research and Development," as shown in Figure 3.3. This will be the same for each department in the company.

employeeDepartment

employeeID	name	job	departmentID	departmentName
7513	Nora Edwards	Programmer	128	Research and Development
9842	Ben Smith	DBA	42	Finance
6651	Ajay Patel	Programmer	128	Research and Development
9006	Candy Burnett	Systems Administrator	128	Research and Development

FIGURE 3.3   This schema design leads to redundantly storing the department name over and over.

We can change this design as shown here:

employee(employeeID, name, job, departmentID)
department(departmentID, name)

In this case, each department name is stored in the database only once, rather than many times, minimizing storage space and avoiding some problems.

Note that we must leave the departmentID in the employee table; otherwise, we lose information from the schema, and in this case, we would lose the link between an employee and the department the employee works for. In improving the schema, we must always bear these twin goals in mind—that is, reducing repetition of data without losing any information.

Anomalies

Anomalies present a slightly more complex concept. Anomalies are problems that arise in the data due to a flaw in the database design. There are three types of anomalies that may arise, and we will consider how they occur with the flawed schema shown in Figure 3.3.

Insertion Anomalies

Insertion anomalies occur when we try to insert data into a flawed table. Imagine that we have a new employee starting at the company. When we insert the employee's details into the employeeDepartment table, we must insert both his department id and his department name. What happens if we insert data that does not match what is already in the table, for example, by entering an employee as working for Department 42, Development? It will not be obvious which of the rows in the database is correct. This is an insertion anomaly.

Deletion Anomalies

Deletion anomalies occur when we delete data from a flawed schema. Imagine that all the employees of Department 128 leave on the same day (walking out in disgust, perhaps). When we delete these employee records, we no longer have any record that Department 128 exists or what its name is. This is a deletion anomaly.

Update Anomalies

Update anomalies occur when we change data in a flawed schema. Imagine that Department 128 decides to change its name to Emerging Technologies. We must change this data for every employee who works for this department. We might easily miss one. If we do miss one (or more), this is an update anomaly.

Null Values

A final rule for good database design is that we should avoid schema designs that have large numbers of empty attributes. For example, if we want to note that one in every hundred or so of our employees has some special qualification, we would not add a column to the employee table to store this information because for 99 employees, this would be NULL. We would instead add a new table storing only employeeIDs and qualifications for those employees who have those qualifications.

Normalization

Normalization is a process we can use to remove design flaws from a database. In normalization, we describe a number of normal forms, which are sets of rules describing what we should and should not do in our table structures. The normalization process consists of breaking tables into smaller tables that form a better design.

To follow the normalization process, we take our database design through the different forms in order. Generally, each form subsumes the one below it. For example, for a database schema to be in second normal form, it must also be in first normal form. For a schema to be in third normal form, it must be in second normal form and so on. At each stage, we add more rules that the schema must satisfy.

First Normal Form

The first normal form, sometimes called 1NF, states that each attribute or column value must be atomic. That is, each attribute must contain a single value, not a set of values or another database row.

Consider the table shown in Figure 3.4.

employee

employeeID	name	job	departmentID	skills
7513	Nora Edwards	Programmer	128	C, Perl, Java
9842	Ben Smith	DBA	42	DB2
6651	Ajay Patel	Programmer	128	VB, Java
9006	Candy Burnett	Systems Administrator	128	NT, Linux

FIGURE 3.4   This schema design is not in first normal form because it contains sets of values in the skill column.

This is an unnormalized version of the employee table we looked at earlier. As you can see, it has one extra column, called skill, which lists the skills of each employee.

Each value in this column contains a set of values—that is, rather than containing an atomic value such as `Java`, it contains a list of values such as `C`, `Perl`, `Java`. This violates the rules of first normal form.

To put this schema in first normal form, we need to turn the values in the skill column into atomic values. There are a couple of ways we can do this. The first, and perhaps most obvious, way is shown in Figure 3.5.

employee

employeeID	Name	job	departmentID	skill
7513	Nora Edwards	Programmer	128	C
7513	Nora Edwards	Programmer	128	Perl
7513	Nora Edwards	Programmer	128	Java
9842	Ben Smith	DBA	42	DB2
6651	Ajay Patel	Programmer	128	VB
6651	Ajay Patel	Programmer	128	Java
9006	Candy Burnett	Systems Administrator	128	NT
9006	Candy Burnett	Systems Administrator	128	Linux

FIGURE 3.5   All values are now atomic.

Here we have made one row per skill. This schema is now in first normal form.

Obviously, this arrangement is far from ideal because we have a great deal of redundancy—for each skill-employee combination, we store all the employee details.

A better solution, and the right way to put this data into first normal form, is shown in Figure 3.6.

employee

employeeID	name	job	departmentID
7513	Nora Edwards	Programmer	128
9842	Ben Smith	DBA	42
6651	Ajay Patel	Programmer	128
9006	Candy Burnett	Systems Administrator	128

employeeSkills

employeeID	skill
7513	C
7513	Perl
7513	Java
9842	DB2
6651	VB
6651	Java
9006	NT
9006	Linux

FIGURE 3.6   We solve the same problem the right way by creating a second table.

In this example, we have split the skills off to form a separate table that only links employee ids and individual skills. This gets rid of the redundancy problem.

You might ask how we would know to arrive at the second solution. There are two answers. One is experience. The second is that if we take the schema in Figure 3.5 and continue with the normalization process, we will end up with the schema in Figure 3.6. The benefit of experience allows us to look ahead and just go straight to this design, but it is perfectly valid to continue with the process.

Second Normal Form

After we have a schema in first normal form, we can move to the higher forms, which are slightly harder to understand.

A schema is said to be in second normal form (also called 2NF) if all attributes that are not part of the primary key are fully functionally dependent on the primary key, and the schema is already in first normal form. What does this mean? It means that each non-key attribute must be functionally dependent on all parts of the key. That is, if the primary key is made up of multiple columns, every other attribute in the table must be dependent *on the combination of these columns*.

Let's look at an example to try to make things clearer.

Look at Figure 3.5. This is the schema that has one line in the employee table per skill. This table is in first normal form, but it is not in second normal form. Why not?

What is the primary key for this table? We know that the primary key must uniquely identify a single row in a table. In this case, the only way we can do this is by using the combination of the employeeID and the skill. With the skills set up in this way, the employeeID is not enough to uniquely identify a row—for example, the employeeID 7513 identifies three rows. However, the combination of employeeID and skill will identify a single row, so we use these two together as our primary key. This gives us the following schema:

employee(<u>employeeID</u>, name, job, <u>departmentID</u>, <u>skill</u>)

We must next ask ourselves, "What are the functional dependencies here?" We have
employeeID, skill → name, job, departmentID

but we also have
employeeID → name, job, departmentID

In other words, we can determine the name, job, and departmentID from the employeeID alone. This means that these attributes are partially functionally dependent on the primary key, rather than fully functionally dependent on the primary key. That is, you can determine these attributes from a part of the primary key without needing the whole primary key. Hence, this schema is not in second normal form.

The next question is, "How can we put it into second normal form?"

We need to decompose the table into tables in which all the non-key attributes are fully functionally dependent on the key. It is fairly obvious that we can achieve this by breaking the table into two tables, to wit:

employee(<u>employeeID</u>, name, job, <u>departmentID</u>)
employeeSkills(<u>employeeID</u>, <u>skill</u>)

This is the schema that we had back in Figure 3.6.

As already discussed, this schema is in first normal form because the values are all atomic. It is also in second normal form because each non-key attribute is now functionally dependent on all parts of the keys.

Third Normal Form

You may sometimes hear the saying "Normalization is about the key, the whole key, and nothing but the key." Second normal form tells us that attributes must depend on the whole key. Third normal form tells us that attributes must depend on nothing but the key.

Formally, for a schema to be in third normal form (3NF), we must remove all transitive dependencies, and the schema must already be in second normal form. Okay, so what's a transitive dependency?

Look back at Figure 3.3. This has the following schema:

employeeDepartment(<u>employeeID</u>, name, job, departmentID, departmentName)

This schema contains the following functional dependencies:

employeeID → name, job, departmentID, departmentName
departmentID → departmentName

The primary key is employeeID, and all the attributes are fully functionally dependent on it—this is easy to see because there is only one attribute in the primary key!

However, we can see that we have

employeeID → departmentName
employeeID → departmentID
and
departmentID → departmentName

Note also that the attribute departmentID is not a key.

This relationship means that the functional dependency employeeID → departmentName is a transitive dependency. Effectively, it has a middle step (the departmentID → departmentName dependency).

To get to third normal form, we need to remove this transitive dependency.

As with the previous normal forms, to convert to third normal form we decompose this table into multiple tables. Again, in this case, it is pretty obvious what we should do. We convert the schema to two tables, employee and department, like this:

employee(<u>employeeID</u>, name, job, <u>departmentID</u>)
department(<u>departmentID</u>, departmentName)

This brings us back to the schema for employee that we had in Figure 3.2 to begin with. It is in third normal form.

Another way of describing third normal form is to say that formally, if a schema is in third normal form, then for every functional dependency in every table, either

- The left side of the functional dependency is a superkey (that is, a key that is not necessarily minimal).

or

- The right side of the functional dependency is part of any key of that table.

The second part doesn't come up terribly often! In most cases, all the functional dependencies will be covered by the first rule.

Boyce-Codd Normal Form

The final normal form we will consider—briefly—is Boyce-Codd normal form, sometimes called BCNF. This is a variation on third normal form. We looked at two rules previously. For a relation to be in BCNF, it must be in third normal form and come under the first of the two rules. That is, all the functional dependencies must have a superkey on the left side.

This is most frequently the case without our having to take any extra steps, as in this example. If we have a dependency that breaks this rule, we must again decompose as we did to get into 1NF, 2NF, and 3NF.

Higher Normal Forms

There are higher normal forms (fourth, fifth, and so on), but these are more useful for academic pursuits than practical database design. 3NF (or BCNF) is sufficient to avoid the data redundancy problems you will encounter.

Summary

To round up, here's what we covered in this chapter.

Concepts

- Entities are things, and relationships are the links between them.
- Relations or tables hold a set of data in tabular form.
- Columns belonging to tables describe the attributes that each data item possesses.
- Rows in tables hold data items with values for each column in a table.
- Keys are used to identify a single row.
- Functional dependencies identify which attributes determine the values of other attributes.
- Schemas are the blueprints for a database.

Design Principles

- Minimize redundancy without losing data.
- Insertion, deletion, and update anomalies are problems that occur when trying to insert, delete, or update data in a table with a flawed structure.
- Avoid designs that will lead to large quantities of null values.

Normalization

- Normalization is a formal process for improving database design.
- First normal form (1NF) means atomic column or attribute values.
- Second normal form (2NF) means that all attributes outside the key must depend on the whole key.
- Third normal form (3NF) means no transitive dependencies.
- Boyce-Codd normal form (BCNF) means that all attributes must be functionally determined by a superkey.

Quiz

1. A superkey is

   a) A minimal key

   b) A foreign key

   c) A set of attributes that can be used to identify a single row in a table

   d) A minimal set of attributes that can be used to identify a single row in a table

2. If a table is in second normal form

   a) It is also in first normal form

   b) It is also in third normal form

   c) It does not contain any transitive dependencies

   d) It contains attributes that are not fully functionally dependent on the key

3. If a table is in third normal form

   a) It is also in Boyce-Codd normal form

   b) It contains non-atomic attributes

   c) It does not contain any transitive dependencies

   d) It contains attributes that are not fully functionally dependent on the key

4. The three kinds of anomalies are

   a) insertion, selection, deletion

   b) insertion, update, deletion

   c) selection, update, deletion

5. A tuple is

   a) a column

   b) a row

   c) a candidate key

   d) the birthplace of Elvis Presley

   e) a foreign key

Exercises

1. Normalize the following schema into third normal form:

   Orders(customerID, customerName, customerAddress, orderID, orderDate, itemID, itemName, itemQuantity)

2. Try to design a schema that is in 3NF but not in BCNF.

Answers

Quiz

   1. C

   2. A

   3. C

   4. B

   5. B (Elvis was born in Tupelo)

Exercises

1.

   Customers(<u>customerID</u>, customerName, customerAddress)

   Orders(<u>orderID</u>, orderDate, <u>customerID</u>)

   OrderItems(<u>orderID</u>, <u>itemID</u>, itemQuantity)

   Items(<u>itemID</u>, itemName)

2. There are many possible answers—just check that yours corresponds to the appropriate normalization rules.

Next

In Chapter 4, "Creating Databases, Tables, and Indexes," we will take a database schema and turn it into an actual MySQL database.

## 4

Creating Databases, Tables, and Indexes

In this chapter you'll learn how to create all the basic MySQL structures: databases, tables, and indexes. We'll cover the following:

- Creating a database
- Selecting a database
- Creating tables
- Column and data types in MySQL
- Creating indexes
- Deleting databases, tables, and indexes
- Altering existing table structures

We will use a simple sample database for the examples in this chapter—this is the employee database we talked about in the preceding chapter. This is the database schema:

```
employee(employeeID, name, job, departmentID)
department(departmentID, name)
employeeSkills(employeeID, skill)
client(clientID, name, address, contactPerson, contactNumber)
assignment(clientID, employeeID, workdate, hours)
```

You can follow along in this chapter by entering the commands to create this database into MySQL. You can, of course, create databases, tables, and indexes easily from any of the MySQL IDEs, but in these examples, we will use the MySQL monitor to create the database. We will do it this way here to give you a greater understanding of database, table, and index structures.

You should begin by logging in to the MySQL monitor as you did in Chapter 1, "Installing MySQL," and Chapter 2, "Quick Tour."

In this chapter we will use the data definition language aspects of SQL to create databases, tables, and indexes. What does this mean? SQL stands for Structured Query Language, which is the language we use for creating and querying relational databases. It consists of two semantically separate parts: a Data Definition Language (or DDL) for creating database structures and a Data Manipulation Language (or DML) for querying the database.

Let's go ahead and look at how to create databases, tables, and indexes with MySQL.

Case Sensitivity

As we begin using SQL and creating MySQL identifiers, we should briefly talk about case sensitivity in MySQL.

SQL keywords are *not* case sensitive. This is standard across database systems.

Case sensitivity for identifiers depends on the database system you are using. In MySQL, whether database and table names are case sensitive depends on your operating system. The reason for this is that generally each database will have an underlying directory in your operating system, and each table will have an underlying file. These directory names and filenames follow different rules depending on the operating system.

What this means in practice is that if you are using Windows, database and table names are not case sensitive, but if you are using a Unix-like operating system, they are. This can be a bit of a minefield, especially when you consider that in MacOS X, you can set up your file systems to be either case insensitive (HFS+, the default,) or case sensitive (UFS).

To reduce confusion, it is good practice to treat all identifiers as case sensitive, even if you are working on a Windows system. This will allow you to move to another platform easily. Deliberately using two forms of the same identifier, such as Employee and employee, would create confusion for any humans reading the code, so this is a bad idea.

Column names, indexes, and aliases (which we will discuss later) are never case sensitive in MySQL.

Identifiers in MySQL

An identifier is simply the name of an alias, a database, a table, a column, or an index. It is how you uniquely identify that object. Before you can begin creating your own databases and tables, we should discuss what identifiers are valid in MySQL.

Generally speaking, identifiers can contain any characters, with these exceptions:

- They can't contain quote characters, ACSII(0) and ASCII(255).

- Database names can contain any characters that are allowed in a directory name, but not the characters that have special meaning in a directory name (/, \, and .) for obvious reasons.

- Table names can contain any characters that are allowed in filenames, except for . and /.

All identifiers except aliases can be up to 64 characters long. Alias names (covered in Chapter 7, "Advanced Queries") can be up to 255 characters long.

One strange rule about identifiers in MySQL is that you can use reserved words as identifiers, as long as they have quotes around them. For example, you could have a table called TABLE. Of course, just because you can doesn't mean you should, and this is a practice best avoided. Even if it does not confuse you when working with the system, it may confuse the program mysqldump, which is often used for backups.

There is a short list of reserved words that MySQL will allow you to have as identifiers without quoting. This is contrary to the ANSI standard for SQL, but it is fairly common in day-to-day use. The most common examples you will see are DATE and TIMESTAMP used as column names.

Creating a Database

After design, the first step in creating a database is, logically enough, to tell MySQL that we want to create a new database. We do this with the CREATE DATABASE SQL statement, as follows:

```
create database employee;
```

You can check to see that this statement worked by executing the command

```
show databases;
```

You should now see the employee database listed among the databases in the system.

We now have an empty database, waiting for some tables to be created.

Selecting a Database

Before we can create any tables or do anything else with the employee database, we need to tell MySQL that we want to work with our new database. We do this with the use statement, as follows:

```
use employee;
```

The employee database is now selected, and all actions we take from now on will be applied to this database by default.

Creating Tables

To create the tables in the employee database, we use the CREATE TABLE SQL statement. The usual form of this statement is

```
create table tablename ( table definition ) [type=table_type];
```

That is, we begin with the words create table, followed by the name we would like the table to have, followed by a set of column definitions. At the end of the statement, we can optionally specify the storage engine type we would like to use.

Table Creation Example

We will look at an example of table creation to illustrate this point. Listing 4.1 shows a set of SQL statements that can be used to create the employee database. You can type these by hand or download the file (along with some sample data for the database) from this book's Web site.

LISTING 4.1   **SQL to Create the Employee Database**

```
drop database if exists employee;
create database employee;

use employee;

create table department
(
  departmentID int not null auto_increment primary key,
  name varchar(30)
) type=InnoDB;

create table employee
(
  employeeID int not null auto_increment primary key,
  name varchar(80),
  job varchar(30),
  departmentID int not null references department(departmentID)
) type=InnoDB;

create table employeeSkills
(
  employeeID int not null references employee(employeeID),
  skill varchar(15) not null,
  primary key (employeeID, skill)
) type=InnoDB;

create table client
(
  clientID int not null auto_increment primary key,
  name varchar(40),
  address varchar(100),
  contactPerson varchar(80),
  contactNumber char(12)
) type=InnoDB;
```

LISTING 4.1 **Continued**

```
create table assignment
(
  clientID int not null references client(clientID),
  employeeID int not null references employee(employeeID),
  workdate date not null,
  hours float,
  primary key (clientID, employeeID, workdate)
) type=InnoDB;
```

Let's go though the SQL statements in this file one by one.

We begin with

```
drop database if exists employee;
```

This statement checks whether an employee database already exists and deletes it if it does, cleaning the slate if you like. This is not strictly necessary and could even be dangerous, but we do it here to make sure that this database creation script should work, even if you have already been experimenting with an employee database.

Note that if you use MySQL in a hosted environment, your hosting company can disable the drop database command. In this case, simply eliminate that line of the script (but make sure that there isn't a database called employee).

We then create the database and select it for use, as we have seen already:

```
create database employee;
use employee;
```

Now, we begin creating tables inside this database. We begin by creating the department table, as follows:

```
create table department
(
  departmentID int not null auto_increment primary key,
  name varchar(20)
) type=InnoDB;
```

This table has two columns, departmentID, which is the primary key, and the department name. To declare the columns in the table, we give a comma-separated list of the column declarations enclosed in parentheses. Note that attributes of a column do not need to be comma separated—only the columns themselves do.

This is our first multiline SQL statement. Whitespace is not important in SQL, so we can lay out our queries in any way we like. Typically, with CREATE statements, you tend to put one item on each line to increase readability. The SQL interpreter will not try to interpret your statement until you have typed the final semicolon (;) and pressed Enter. (You can also choose to end your statements with \g, but the semicolon is far more commonly used.)

In this table, we are declaring two columns. Each column declaration begins with the name of the column, which is followed by information about the type of that column. Look at the second column first in this example because it's a little easier to understand. The declaration

```
name varchar(20)
```

tells us that the column is called `name` and that its type is `varchar(20)`. The `varchar` type is a variable-length string, in this case up to 20 characters. We could also have used `char`, which is a fixed-length string. Choosing `varchar` or `char` does not make a difference in terms of using the data, just in how the data is stored in memory. A `varchar(20)` takes up only as much room as the number of characters stored in it, whereas a `char(20)` is always 20 characters wide, regardless of what is stored in it. We will talk about the relative advantages and disadvantages of this later in this chapter in the section "Column Types."

Now, look back at the first column definition. It looks like this:

```
departmentID int not null auto_increment primary key,
```

The name of this column is `departmentID`, and it is of type `int` (integer). This is a unique number that we will use to identify each department in the company.

After the type, there is some further information about the column.

First, we have specified that this column is `not null`—in other words, for every row in this table, this column must have a value in it.

Secondly, we have specified that this column is an `auto_increment` column. This is a nice feature in MySQL. When we insert data into this table, if we do not specify a department number, MySQL will allocate a unique number that will be the next number in the `auto_increment` sequence. This makes life easy for us.

Finally, we have specified that this column is to be the `primary key` for this table. If the primary key consists of a single column, we can specify it like this. For multicolumn primary keys, we must use a different approach, which we will look at in a moment.

That's the table definition. Now, look at the very end of the SQL statement. After the end parenthesis, you will see the following line:

```
type=InnoDB
```

This specifies that this table should use the InnoDB storage engine. If you look through the table definitions, you will see that in this case, we have declared all the tables as InnoDB tables.

What does this mean? MySQL supports various storage engines, and we will discuss them all in detail in Chapter 9, "Understanding MySQL's Table Types." The default type is MyISAM. If we want to use MyISAM tables, we don't need to add the `type` clause at the end of the `create database` statement.

In this case, we are using InnoDB because we are going to work through some examples using foreign keys. The InnoDB storage engine supports foreign keys and transactions, whereas the MyISAM table type does not. The MyISAM table type is often faster than the InnoDB table type. We need to decide what type is best for each table.

We could make the tables of different types having, for example, some InnoDB tables and some MyISAM tables (and perhaps some of the other types, if needed), but we are keeping it simple in this example and using InnoDB for all our tables.

Look now at the second `create table` statement:

```
create table employee
(
  employeeID int not null auto_increment primary key,
  name varchar(80),
  job varchar(15),
  departmentID int not null references department(departmentID)
) type=InnoDB;
```

There is only one new piece of syntax in this statement. The last column in the employee table is the id of the department for which the employees work. This is a foreign key. We declare this in the table definition by adding the `references` clause as follows:

```
departmentID int not null references department(departmentID)
```

This tells us that the `departmentID` in the employee table should be referenced back to the `departmentID` column in the department table.

Note that we can use this foreign key syntax because the employee table is an InnoDB table. When we use MyISAM tables, we cannot use foreign keys. Foreign keys in MyISAM tables are planned for a future version of MySQL, probably version 5.1 according to the development schedule.

Now, look at the third `create table` statement:

```
create table employeeSkills
(
  employeeID int not null references employee(employeeID),
  skill varchar(15) not null,
  primary key (employeeID, skill)
) type=InnoDB;
```

Again, in this table, we have a foreign key, in this case the `employeeID`. The interesting thing about this table definition is that this table has a two-column primary key. You can see that we declare the two columns in the table, `employeeID` and `skill`, and then declare the primary key separately with the following line:

```
primary key (employeeID, skill)
```

The other table definitions don't contain any new syntax, so we won't go through them in detail. You will note that we have used a couple of other data types: in the assignment table, the number of hours is a `float`, or floating-point number, and the workdate is of type `date`. We will revisit the column types in more detail later in this chapter.

You can check whether the tables in your database have been set up correctly using the command

```
show tables;
```

You should get the following output:

```
+--------------------+
| Tables_in_employee |
+--------------------+
| assignment         |
| client             |
| department         |
| employee           |
| employeeSkills     |
+--------------------+
```

You can get more information about the structure of each table by using the `describe` command, for example,

```
describe department;
```

This should give you something like the following output:

```
+--------------+-------------+-------------------+------+-----+---------+----------------+
| Field        | Type        | Collation         | Null | Key | Default | Extra          |
+--------------+-------------+-------------------+------+-----+---------+----------------+
| departmentID | int(11)     | binary            |      | PRI | NULL    | auto_increment |
| name         | varchar(20) | latin1_swedish_ci | YES  |     | NULL    |  _____         |
+--------------+-------------+-------------------+------+-----+---------+----------------+
```

You might want to check the other tables at this point.

CREATE TABLE Statement

Now that we've looked at an example, let's go over the complete syntax for the CREATE TABLE statement. The MySQL manual tells us that the general form of this statement is as follows:

```
CREATE [TEMPORARY] TABLE [IF NOT EXISTS] tbl_name [(create_definition,...)]
[table_options] [select_statement]
```

or

```
CREATE [TEMPORARY] TABLE [IF NOT EXISTS] tbl_name LIKE old_table_name;
```

```
create_definition:
  col_name type [NOT NULL | NULL] [DEFAULT default_value] [auto_increment]
          [PRIMARY KEY] [reference_definition]
  or    PRIMARY KEY (index_col_name,...)
  or    KEY [index_name] (index_col_name,...)
  or    INDEX [index_name] (index_col_name,...)
  or    UNIQUE [INDEX] [index_name] (index_col_name,...)
```

```
or    FULLTEXT [INDEX] [index_name] (index_col_name,...)
or    [CONSTRAINT symbol] FOREIGN KEY [index_name] (index_col_name,...)
         [reference_definition]
or    CHECK (expr)
```

Let's go through the various options we can see in this general form.

The TEMPORARY keyword is used to create a table that will be visible only in your current database session, and that will be automatically deleted when your connection is closed.

We can use the IF NOT EXISTS clause, logically enough, to create a table only if there is not already a table with this table name.

We can use the LIKE old_table_name clause to create a new table with the same schema as old_table_name.

Inside the parentheses of the CREATE TABLE statement, we declare the columns that we want, their types, and any other information about the structure of the table. The simplest column definition is a column name followed by a column type. In the next section of this chapter, we will look at valid column types.

Other options we can add to each column declaration include the following:

- We can declare each column as NOT NULL or NULL, meaning either that the column cannot contain a NULL (NOT NULL) or that it may contain NULLs (NULL). The default is that columns may contain NULLs.

- We can declare a default value for a column using the DEFAULT keyword followed by the default value we want.

- We can use the auto_increment keyword, as we did in the previous example, to generate a sequence number. The value automatically generated will be one greater than the current largest value in the table. The first row inserted will have the sequence number 1. You can have only one auto_increment column per table, and it must be indexed. You will note that in the previous examples, we did not manually create any indexes; however, some were automatically created for us. Indexes are automatically created for columns that are declared as PRIMARY KEY, which all our auto_increment columns were in this example.

- We can declare that this particular column is the PRIMARY KEY for the table.

- We can specify that this particular column is a foreign key using the REFERENCES clause, as we did in the example.

As well as declaring column names and types, we can declare some other column information in this part of the CREATE TABLE statement:

- We can specify a multicolumn PRIMARY KEY, as we did in the example, by specifying PRIMARY KEY followed by the names of the columns that make up the key. We can actually also declare a single column primary key this way. A PRIMARY KEY column is a unique, indexed column that cannot contain nulls.

- INDEX and KEY are synonyms which mean that the specified column(s) will be indexed. Note that these columns do *not* have to contain unique values in MySQL.

- UNIQUE can be used to specify that a particular column must contain unique values. UNIQUE columns will also be indexed.

- FULLTEXT is used to create full-text indexes on a TEXT, CHAR, or VARCHAR column type. You can use full-text indexes only with MyISAM tables. There is an example in Chapter 9.

- The FOREIGN KEY clause allows us to declare foreign keys in the same two ways that we can declare primary keys.

After the closing parenthesis, we can specify some table options for this table. The one we have looked at so far is the table type. We will discuss the table types in detail in Chapter 9. If you do not specify a type, the tables will default to being MyISAM tables. Just briefly, these are the possible values for the table type:

- MyISAM, the default, is very fast and supports full-text indexing. It is a replacement for the previous standard ISAM type.

- ISAM is an older table type. It is similar to MyISAM but with fewer features, so you should always use MyISAM instead.

- InnoDB is the ACID-compliant storage engine that supports transactions, foreign keys, and row-level locking.

- BDB (Berkeley DB) is a storage engine that supports transactions and page-level locking.

- HEAP tables are stored completely in memory and are never written to disk, so they are very fast, but limited in size and are unrecoverable in the event of failure.

- MERGE tables allow you to combine a set of MyISAM tables with the same structure so that they can be queried as if they were one table. This can be used to get around operating-system restrictions on the maximum file—and therefore table—size.

We can also specify some other options for the table. These are not required and are mostly for optimization. We will discuss the use of some of these options in Chapter 18, "Optimizing Your Database." The options are as listed here:

- auto_increment = #   This option allows you to set the initial auto_increment value to something other than 1.

- AVG_ROW_LENGTH = #   This option allows you to estimate what you think will be the average row length in order to aid the storage engine.

- CHECKSUM = 1   This option allows you to turn on checksum calculation for the rows in the table that may help you find the problem if the table becomes corrupt. Set it to 1 to turn it on. Off is the default, and this option works only with MyISAM tables.

- COMMENT = "string"   This option stores a comment about this table.

- **MAX_ROWS = #**   This option sets the maximum number of rows that will be stored in this table.

- **MIN_ROWS = #**   This option sets the minimum number of rows that will be stored in this table.

- **PACK_KEYS = {0 | 1 | DEFAULT}**   By default, MySQL packs (compresses) strings in keys—that is CHARs, VARCHARs, and TEXT. If you set this value to 1, all keys will be packed; if you set this value to 0, then none will be packed.

- **PASSWORD = "string"**   This option does nothing in the standard version of MySQL.

- **DELAY_KEY_WRITE = {0 | 1}**   This option allows you to delay key updates until after the table is closed. This option works only on MyISAM tables.

- **ROW_FORMAT= {default | dynamic | fixed | compressed }**   This option allows you to specify the storage format for rows. This option works only with MyISAM tables.

- **RAID_TYPE= {1 | STRIPED | RAIDO } RAID_CHUNKS=#**
  RAID_CHUNKSIZE=#   This option lets you specify your RAID configuration for optimization purposes.

- **UNION = (table_name,[table_name...])**   This option is only for MERGE tables, and it allows you to specify which tables should be part of the MERGE.

- **INSERT_METHOD= {NO | FIRST | LAST }**   This option is only for MERGE tables and is used to specify which table to insert data into.

- **DATA DIRECTORY="absolute path to directory"**   You can use this option to specify where you would like the data in this table to be stored.

- **INDEX DIRECTORY="absolute path to directory"**   You can use this option to specify where you would like the indexes for this table to be stored.

Finally, if you look back at the CREATE TABLE general form, you can see that you can end a CREATE TABLE with a SELECT statement. SELECT is the SQL statement we use to retrieve rows from one or more tables. (It is covered in Chapters 6 through 8 of this book.) We can use this clause to fill the new table with the data that is returned by the select statement.

Column and Data Types in MySQL

There are three basic column types in MySQL: numerical types, string or text types, and date and time types. We will look at each type in turn.

Numerical Types

Numerical types are used for storing numbers. In our example, we used the types int (integer) and float (floating-point number). These represent the two subtypes of numerical types: the exact numerical types and the approximate numerical types.

Numerical types may be constrained by a display width M and, for floating-point types, a number of decimal places, D. These numbers go after the declaration; for example:

```
salary decimal(10, 2)
```

This has a display width of 10 with two digits after the decimal point.

You may choose to use neither parameter, the display width only, or both the display width and the number of decimal places.

Numerical types may also be followed by the keywords UNSIGNED and/or ZEROFILL.

The UNSIGNED keyword specifies that the column contains only zero or positive numbers. The ZEROFILL keyword means that the number will be displayed with leading zeroes.

The exact types are detailed in the following text.

NUMERIC or DECIMAL

These types are the same, and DECIMAL may also be abbreviated to DEC. These types are used to store exact floating-point values and are typically used to store monetary values. They have the same range as double-precision floating-point numbers.

INTEGER and Variations

This type can be abbreviated as INT. This is a standard integer, stored in 4 bytes, giving a range of 2^{32} possible values. There are also several variations on INT:

- A TINYINT is 1 byte (2^8 possible values). The keywords BIT and BOOL are synonyms for TINYINT.
- A SMALLINT is 2 bytes (2^{16} possible values).
- A MEDIUMINT is 3 bytes (2^{24} possible values).
- A BIGINT is 8 bytes (2^{64} possible values).

The approximate types are detailed in the following text.

FLOAT

This is a single-precision floating-point number. It can represent a positive number between 1.18×10^{-38} to 3.40×10^{38} and a similar range of negative numbers.

DOUBLE

This is a double-precision floating-point number. Synonyms for DOUBLE are REAL and DOUBLE PRECISION. They can represent a positive number between 2.23×10^{-308} to 1.80×10^{308} and a similar range of negative numbers.

String and Text Types

MySQL supports various string and text types. The basic types are CHAR, VARCHAR, TEXT, BLOB, ENUM, and SET. We will discuss each of these in turn.

CHAR

CHAR is used to store fixed-length strings. As in the employee database, CHAR is usually followed by a string length, for example CHAR(20). If you do not specify a length, you will get a CHAR(1). The maximum length of a CHAR is 255 characters. When CHARs are stored, they will always be the exact length you specify. This is achieved by padding the contents of the column with spaces. These spaces are automatically stripped when the contents of a CHAR column are retrieved.

Obviously, storing a CHAR takes up more space on disk than storing an equivalent variable-length string. The trade-off is that it is faster to retrieve rows from a table in which all the columns are of fixed widths (that is, CHAR, numeric, or date). Often, speed is more important than disk space, so you may choose to make text fields that are not going to vary a great deal anyway into CHAR as a small optimization.

Both CHAR and VARCHAR types can be preceded with the keyword NATIONAL, meaning to restrict the contents to the standard character set. This is the default in MySQL, so you need only use it for cross-platform compatibility.

CHAR and VARCHAR can both be followed by the keyword BINARY, meaning that they should be treated as case sensitive when evaluating string comparisons. The default is for strings to be compared in a case insensitive fashion.

VARCHAR

VARCHAR stores variable-length strings. You specify the width in parentheses after the type, for example, VARCHAR(10). The range is 0 to 255.

TEXT, BLOB, and Variations

The TEXT types are used for storing longer pieces of text than you can fit in a CHAR or VARCHAR. BLOB stands for Binary Large OBject. These types are the same except that BLOBs are intended to store binary data rather than text. Comparisons on BLOBs are case sensitive, and on TEXTs, they are not. They are both variable in length, but both come in various sizes:

- TINYTEXT or TINYBLOB can hold up to 255 (that's 2^8-1) characters or bytes.
- TEXT or BLOB can hold up to 65,535 ($2^{16}-1$) characters or bytes (64KB).
- MEDIUMTEXT or MEDIUMBLOB can hold up to 16,777,215 ($2^{24}-1$) characters or bytes (16MB).
- LONGTEXT or LONGBLOB can hold up to 4,294,967,295 ($2^{32}-1$) characters or bytes (4GB).

ENUM

This type allows you to list a set of possible values. Each row can contain one value from the enumerated set. You declare an ENUM as follows:

```
gender enum('m', 'f')
```

Enumerated types can also be NULL, so the possible values of gender are m, f, NULL, or error.

SET

The SET type is similar to ENUM except that rows may contain a set of values from the enumerated set.

Date and Time Types

MySQL supports various date and time types, as discussed next.

DATE

The date type stores a date. MySQL expects the date in ISO year-month-day order, avoiding trans-Atlantic arguments. Dates are displayed as YYYY-MM-DD.

TIME

This type stores a time, displayed as HH:MM:SS.

DATETIME

This is a combination of the previous types. The format is YYYY-MM-DD HH:MM:SS.

TIMESTAMP

This is a useful column type. If you do not set this column in a particular row, or set it to NULL, it will store the time that row was inserted or last changed.

When you retrieve a timestamp, it will be displayed in the DATETIME format. This has changed significantly from MySQL 4.0 to 4.1. You could previously set the display width when declaring a column as of type TIMESTAMP.

YEAR

This type stores a year. When you declare a column of this type, you can declare it as YEAR(2) or YEAR(4) to specify the number of digits. YEAR(4) is the default. YEAR(2) represents the range 1970 to 2069.

Creating Indexes

Usually, you create all the indexes you need when you are creating tables. Any column declared as PRIMARY KEY, KEY, unique, or INDEX will be indexed.

Sometimes you will find that you are running many queries based on an unindexed column, and in this situation, you can add an index using the CREATE INDEX statement.

Interestingly enough, the CREATE INDEX statement is mapped to an ALTER TABLE statement before being executed. The ALTER TABLE statement can be used for this and many other purposes. We will look at its use in the last section of this chapter.

We can, for example, add an index to the employee table as follows:

```
create index name on employee(name);
```

This creates an index called name based on the name field in the employee table.

There are not a great many options on the `create index` statement. We can precede the word `index` with `UNIQUE` to enforce a uniqueness constraint. We can also put the keyword `FULLTEXT` before `index` if we want to create a full-text index on a MyISAM table. (More on this in Chapter 9.)

The one other option is to limit indexes on `char` and `varchar` types to index just the first few characters in each field. You can do this by specifying the number of characters you want to be indexed in parentheses after the name of the index column, for example,

```
create index part_name on employee(name(5));
```

The reason for this is that indexes on text types are not as efficient as indexes on numeric types, and just indexing the first few characters improves performance.

Deleting Databases, Tables, and Indexes

Now that we know how to create databases, tables, and indexes, it is also useful to know how to delete these things. The keyword we need for this purpose is `DROP`.

We can delete an entire database and all its contents with the following statement (and we don't suggest that you type this at this stage!):

```
drop database employee;
```

We can add an optional `IF EXISTS` clause before the name of the database. If you look back at Listing 4.1, you can see that this is the version of the `DROP DATABASE` command we used there.

You can delete a single table with the `DROP TABLE` statement, for example,

```
drop table assignment;
```

The general form of the `DROP TABLE` statement is as follows:

```
DROP [TEMPORARY] TABLE [IF EXISTS] tbl_name [, tbl_name,...]
```

You can specify the `TEMPORARY` keyword for dropping temporary tables. You can also drop multiple tables at once by listing a set of comma-separated names. The optional `IF EXISTS` clause works the same way as it does for `DROP DATABASE`.

You can delete an index with the `DROP INDEX` statement, for example,

```
drop index part_name on employee;
```

As you can see, you need to specify which table the index is on to delete the index.

Altering Existing Table Structures

As well as creating and deleting tables, we often need to be able to change the structure of an existing table. We can do this with the `ALTER TABLE` statement. `ALTER TABLE` has many, many variations we can use to alter table structure.

For example, we could have created the name index on employee as follows:

```
alter table employee
add index name (name);
```

Because the ALTER TABLE statement is very flexible, it has many, many possible clauses. The general form of the statement from the MySQL manual is as follows:

```
ALTER [IGNORE] TABLE tbl_name alter_spec [, alter_spec ...]
```

```
alter_spec:
        ADD [COLUMN] create_definition [FIRST | AFTER col_name ]
   or   ADD [COLUMN] (create_definition, create_definition,...)
   or   ADD INDEX [index_name] (index_col_name,...)
   or   ADD PRIMARY KEY (index_col_name,...)
   or   ADD UNIQUE [index_name] (index_col_name,...)
   or   ADD FULLTEXT [index_name] (index_col_name,...)
   or   ADD [CONSTRAINT symbol] FOREIGN KEY [index_name] (index_col_name,...)
           [reference_definition]
   or   ALTER [COLUMN] col_name {SET DEFAULT literal | DROP DEFAULT}
   or   CHANGE [COLUMN] old_col_name create_definition
              [FIRST | AFTER column_name]
   or   MODIFY [COLUMN] create_definition [FIRST | AFTER col_name]
   or   DROP [COLUMN] col_name
   or   DROP PRIMARY KEY
   or   DROP INDEX index_name
   or   DISABLE KEYS
   or   ENABLE KEYS
   or   RENAME [TO] new_tbl_name
   or   ORDER BY col_name
   or   table_options
```

Most of these options are pretty self-evident or correspond to clauses in the CREATE TABLE statement, such as ADD PRIMARY KEY. We will briefly discuss the ones that may not be obvious.

The CHANGE and MODIFY clauses are the same: They allow you to change the definition of a column or its position in the table.

DROP COLUMN deletes a column from the table, whereas DROP PRIMARY KEY and DROP INDEX delete just the associated index for that column.

The DISABLE KEYS clause tells MySQL to stop updating indexes for a MyISAM table only. ENABLE KEYS turns index updating back on.

The RENAME clause lets you change the name of a table.

The ORDER BY clause will put the rows in the newly altered table in a particular order, like the ORDER BY clause in a SELECT statement, which we will look at in Chapter 6, "Querying MySQL." This order will not be maintained as the data in the table changes over time.

The table_options option lets you specify the same table options as at the end of the CREATE TABLE statement—see earlier in this chapter for details.

Summary

In this chapter, we learned how to create and delete databases, tables, and indexes and how to change the structure of an existing table.

Case Sensitivity and Identifiers

- Database names have the same case sensitivity as directories in your operating system. Table names follow the same rules as filenames. Everything else is case insensitive.

- All identifiers except aliases can be up to 64 characters long. Aliases can be up to 255 characters long.

- Identifiers can contain most characters, but database names may not contain /, \, or . and table names cannot contain . or /.

- You can use reserved words for identifiers as long as you put them in quotes.

Creating a Database

- `create database` *dbname*; creates a database.
- `use database` *dbname*; selects a database for use.

Creating Tables

- Use the `create table` statement, which has this general form:

```
CREATE [TEMPORARY] TABLE [IF NOT EXISTS] tbl_name [(create_definition,...)]
[table_options] [select_statement]
```

or

```
CREATE [TEMPORARY] TABLE [IF NOT EXISTS] tbl_name LIKE old_table_name;
```

```
create_definition:
  col_name type [NOT NULL | NULL] [DEFAULT default_value] [auto_increment]
        [PRIMARY KEY] [reference_definition]
  or    PRIMARY KEY (index_col_name,...)
  or    KEY [index_name] (index_col_name,...)
  or    INDEX [index_name] (index_col_name,...)
  or    UNIQUE [INDEX] [index_name] (index_col_name,...)
  or    FULLTEXT [INDEX] [index_name] (index_col_name,...)
  or    [CONSTRAINT symbol] FOREIGN KEY [index_name] (index_col_name,...)
        [reference_definition]
  or    CHECK (expr)
```

Column Types

- Exact numeric types are TINYINT, SMALLINT, INT, MEDIUMINT, BIGINT, NUMERIC, and DECIMAL.

- Approximate numeric types are FLOAT and DOUBLE.

- String types are CHAR, VARCHAR, TEXT, and BLOB.

- Date and time types are DATE, TIME, DATETIME, TIMESTAMP, and YEAR.

- There are also various aliases to these type names.

Dropping Databases, Tables, and Indexes

- Drop a database with

  ```
  drop database dbname;
  ```

- Drop a table with

  ```
  drop table tablename;
  ```

- Drop an index with

  ```
  drop index indexname on tablename;
  ```

Altering Existing Table Structures

- Change table structure with ALTER TABLE. This is the general structure of the ALTER TABLE command:

  ```
  ALTER [IGNORE] TABLE tbl_name alter_spec [, alter_spec ...]

  alter_spec:
          ADD [COLUMN] create_definition [FIRST | AFTER col_name ]
     or   ADD [COLUMN] (create_definition, create_definition,...)
     or   ADD INDEX [index_name] (index_col_name,...)
     or   ADD PRIMARY KEY (index_col_name,...)
     or   ADD UNIQUE [index_name] (index_col_name,...)
     or   ADD FULLTEXT [index_name] (index_col_name,...)
     or   ADD [CONSTRAINT symbol] FOREIGN KEY [index_name] (index_col_name,...)
             [reference_definition]
     or   ALTER [COLUMN] col_name {SET DEFAULT literal | DROP DEFAULT}
     or   CHANGE [COLUMN] old_col_name create_definition
             [FIRST | AFTER col_name]
     or   MODIFY [COLUMN] create_definition [FIRST | AFTER col_name]
     or   DROP [COLUMN] col_name
     or   DROP PRIMARY KEY
     or   DROP INDEX index_name
     or   DISABLE KEYS
  ```

```
or    ENABLE KEYS
or    RENAME [TO] new_tbl_name
or    ORDER BY col_name
or    table_options
```

Quiz

1. Which of the following is *not* a valid table name in MySQL?

   a) employee

   b) select

   c) employee.skill

   d) employeeSkills

2. Which of the following statements about CHAR and VARCHAR is correct?

   a) A CHAR column always takes up the same amount of disk space, regardless of its contents.

   b) VARCHARs are padded with spaces when they are stored on disk.

   c) A CHAR column, on average, takes up less disk space than an equivalent VARCHAR column.

   d) A VARCHAR column always takes up the same amount of disk space, regardless of its contents.

3. Before we can create tables in a database, we must first

   a) create the indexes for the tables

   b) create the database

   c) create the database and select it for use

   d) create all the table columns

4. Which of the following CREATE TABLE statements is syntactically correct?

   a)

```
create table department
  departmentID int not null auto_increment primary key,
  name varchar(20)
  type=InnoDB;
```

   b)

```
create table department type=InnoDB
(
  departmentID int not null auto_increment primary key,
  name varchar(20)
);
```

c)

```
create department
(
  departmentID int not null auto_increment primary key,
  name varchar(20)
) type=InnoDB;
```

d)

```
create table department
(
  departmentID int not null auto_increment primary key,
  name varchar(20)
) type=InnoDB;
```

5. To delete an entire database (called dbname) and all its contents, you would type

   a) `drop all tables on dbname;`

   b) `drop database dbname;`

   c) `drop dbname;`

   d) `delete database dbname;`

Exercises

1. Write SQL statements to create a database with the following schema:

   customer(<u>customerID</u>, customerName, customerAddress)

   order(<u>orderID</u>, orderDate, <u>customerID</u>)

   orderItem(<u>orderID</u>, <u>itemID</u>, itemQuantity)

   item(<u>itemID</u>, itemName)

   You may make any assumptions you like about data types.

   Test your statements in MySQL and view the resulting tables using SHOW and DESCRIBE.

2. We would now like to add a notes field, which you may assume is of type TEXT, to each order in the orders table. Use an ALTER TABLE statement to achieve this, and check your result with a DESCRIBE statement.

3. Drop the order database.

Answers

Quiz

1. c
2. a
3. c
4. d
5. b

Exercises

```
create database orders;

use orders;

create table customer
(
  customerID int not null auto_increment primary key,
  customerName varchar(20),
  customerAddress varchar(80)
) type = InnoDB;

create table orders
(
  orderID int not null auto_increment primary key,
  orderDate date,
  customerID int not null references customer(customerID)
) type = InnoDB;

create table item
(
  itemID int not null auto_increment primary key,
  itemName varchar(20)
) type = InnoDB;

create table orderItem
(
  orderID int not null references orders(orderID),
  itemID int not null references item(itemID),
  itemQuantity int,
  primary key (orderID, itemID)
) type = InnoDB;
```

```
alter table orders
add column comment text;
```

```
drop database orders;
```

Note that we have changed the name of the table called order to orders because order is a reserved word. You may also choose to put quotes around it to get it to work.

Next

In Chapter 5, "Inserting, Deleting, and Updating Data," we will put some data into the employee database.

III

Using MySQL

5 Inserting, Deleting, and Updating Data

6 Querying MySQL

7 Advanced Queries

8 Using MySQL Built-in Functions with SELECT

Inserting, Deleting, and Updating Data

In this chapter, we will look at how to insert and change data in your MySQL database with the INSERT, DELETE, and UPDATE statements.

We will cover the following:

- Using INSERT
- Using DELETE
- Using UPDATE
- Uploading data with LOAD DATA INFILE
- Extensions: REPLACE and TRUNCATE

We have now moved into the DML (Data Manipulation Language) aspects of SQL. After we have learned how to insert data into a database, we will spend the next few chapters learning the many and varied ways to retrieve data from a database.

Using INSERT

The INSERT SQL statement is used to insert rows into a table. We'll begin by looking at an example. Again, you can type these statements directly into the MySQL monitor or into a file, or you can download this file from the book's Web site.

Some sample insert statements are shown in Listing 5.1.

LISTING 5.1   **employee_data.sql**

```
use employee;

delete from department;
insert into department values
(42, 'Finance'),
```

LISTING 5.1   **Continued**

```
(128, 'Research and Development'),
(NULL, 'Human Resources'),
(NULL, 'Marketing');

delete from employee;
insert into employee values
(7513,'Nora Edwards','Programmer',128),
(9842, 'Ben Smith', 'DBA', 42),
(6651, 'Ajay Patel', 'Programmer', 128),
(9006, 'Candy Burnett', 'Systems Administrator', 128);

delete from employeeSkills;
insert into employeeSkills values
(7513, 'C'),
(7513, 'Perl'),
(7513, 'Java'),
(9842, 'DB2'),
(6651, 'VB'),
(6651, 'Java'),
(9006, 'NT'),
(9006, 'Linux');

delete from client;
insert into client values
(NULL, 'Telco Inc', '1 Collins St Melbourne',   'Fred Smith', '95551234'),
(NULL, 'The Bank', '100 Bourke St Melbourne',   'Jan Tristan', '95559876');

delete from assignment;
insert into assignment values
(1, 7513, '2003-01-20', 8.5);
```

You'll see that before we insert any data into each table, we are running a DELETE statement—again, this isn't necessary, but it will clean out any test data that you may have inserted so far. We'll come back to the DELETE statement in the next section.

Also note that we have inserted the sample data to match the examples in Chapter 3, "Database Design Crash Course." We have added some additional rows as well.

All of these INSERT statements are pretty similar. Let's look at the first one to see how it works:

```
insert into department values
(42, 'Finance'),
(128, 'Research and Development'),
(NULL, 'Human Resources'),
(NULL, 'Marketing');
```

We specify the table that we want to insert data into on the first line—in this case, department. Here, we are inserting four rows into the table. You may recall that the department table has two columns, departmentID and name. (You can check this for yourself by running a describe department command.)

In the first two rows, we have specified the departmentID that we want to use. Let's look back at the definition of departmentID. You may recall that in the last chapter, we declared it as

```
departmentID int not null auto_increment primary key
```

Because this is an auto_increment column, we can specify the value or let MySQL calculate it for us. (Usually, in this case, we would let MySQL allocate a number, but there may be cases like this one in which we have an existing number we want to use.)

In the rows for Human Resources and Marketing, you will see that we have left the departmentID as NULL. This will allow the auto_increment to do its magic and allocate a value. Let's see what we get from this INSERT statement.

If you look through the various INSERT statements, you will see that when we insert data into a string or date type, we enclose it in single quotes, for example, 'Research and Development'. When it is a numerical type, you should not use quotes.

If we are enclosing data in quotes, what do we do when the data contains quotes? The answer is that we need to *escape* the quotes. In simple terms, we need to put a backslash (\) in front of the single quote, for example, 'O\'Leary'.

Obviously, this brings up the question, "What do we do if we want a backslash to be just a backslash, without any special meaning?" In this case, we need to escape the backslash in the same way—replace the backslash with two backslashes (\\).

We retrieve data from the database using the SELECT statement. We will cover SELECT fairly exhaustively in the next few chapters. For the moment, we only need to know that typing

```
select * from tablename;
```

will return all the data currently stored in a table.

If you type

```
select * from department;
```

you should get output similar to the following:

```
+---------------+----------------------+
| departmentID  | name                 |
+---------------+----------------------+
|            42 | Finance              |
|           128 | Research and Develop |
|           129 | Human Resources      |
|           130 | Marketing            |
+---------------+----------------------+
4 rows in set (0.01 sec)
```

You should be able to see that the effect of auto_increment is a value which is one greater than the highest current value in the column.

The general form of the INSERT statement from the MySQL manual is as follows:

```
INSERT [LOW_PRIORITY | DELAYED] [IGNORE]
    [INTO] tbl_name [(col_name,...)]
    VALUES ((expression | DEFAULT),...),(...),...
    [ ON DUPLICATE KEY UPDATE col_name=expression, ... ]
```

```
or  INSERT [LOW_PRIORITY | DELAYED] [IGNORE]
        [INTO] tbl_name [(col_name,...)]
        SELECT ...
```

```
or  INSERT [LOW_PRIORITY | DELAYED] [IGNORE]
        [INTO] tbl_name
        SET col_name=(expression | DEFAULT), ...
        [ ON DUPLICATE KEY UPDATE col_name=expression, ... ]
```

The examples we have looked at all follow the first form of the expression. You will note that the keyword INTO is optional. We could leave it out and begin our query with insert employee values, but we find it a little harder to read.

With this first form, we need to list values for each column value in each row in the same order as the columns are in the table. For example, we had to specify the departmentID first, followed by the name, because that's the way the department table is structured. As demonstrated, this form allows us to insert multiple rows in a table with a single INSERT statement.

The second form ends in a SELECT statement. Rather than inserting values manually, this allows us to retrieve data from another table or tables in the database and store it in this table.

The third form allows us to specify which columns data should be inserted into. An example of using INSERT in this way is

```
insert into department
set name='Asset Management';
```

This form only allows you to insert a single row at a time, but you don't need to specify values for all the columns. In this case, we are setting a value for only the name. All the unspecified values will either take their default value, if one is specified, or be NULL. In this case, departmentID will be set to NULL, which causes the auto_increment to work its magic and generate a new departmentID for us. (You can check this by typing select * from department again.)

There are a couple of optional clauses in the INSERT statement. Let's briefly go through what these do:

- We can specify that an INSERT should be LOW PRIORITY or DELAYED. Both of these clauses will cause the insertion to be delayed until no client is trying to read from the table. The difference between them is that LOW PRIORITY will block the inserting client and DELAYED will not. What this means is that if you run a LOW PRIORITY insert, you may wait for some time before you can continue running queries in your client. With DELAYED, you will be told OK and can continue running queries, but you need to remember that the insert will not be performed until the table is not in use.

- Specifying IGNORE is chiefly useful when you are inserting multiple rows. Normally, if one of the rows you are trying to insert clashes with an existing row's PRIMARY KEY or UNIQUE value, an error will occur and the insert will be aborted. If you specify IGNORE, the error will be ignored and the insert will continue and will attempt to insert the next row.

- We can specify that a column should contain its default value by specifying DEFAULT as the value for that column.

- The ON DUPLICATE KEY UPDATE clause allows us to deal elegantly with clashing primary key or unique values. We follow this clause with an update statement that we can use to change the primary key or unique value in the row already in the table so that it no longer clashes with the new row.

The following short example demonstrates a common style of use for the ON DUPLICATE KEY UPDATE clause:

```
create table warning
(
  employeeID int primary key not null references employee(employeeID),
  count int default 1
) type =InnoDB;

insert into warning (employeeID)
  values (6651)
  on duplicate key update count=count+1;
```

This clause is very useful for situations in which you want to not only record unique events, but also take some action, such as incrementing a counter when non-unique events occur. Any sort of logging would be a good example, but in keeping with the employee database we have been using, we will record employees who have been given a warning in the table warning.

To record somebody's warning, we run this insert statement. Because count has a default value of 1 and we are not specifying a value in the insert, it will be 1 the first time the insert is done for each employeeID. Subsequent inserts with the same employeeID will trigger the ON DUPLICATE KEY UPDATE clause and will increment the counter.

Using REPLACE

The REPLACE statement is exactly like the INSERT statement except that if a key clash occurs, the new row you are inserting will replace the old row.

This is the general form of REPLACE from the MySQL manual:

```
REPLACE [LOW_PRIORITY | DELAYED]
        [INTO] tbl_name [(col_name,...)]
        VALUES (expression,...),(...),...

or  REPLACE [LOW_PRIORITY | DELAYED]
        [INTO] tbl_name [(col_name,...)]
        SELECT ...

or  REPLACE [LOW_PRIORITY | DELAYED]
        [INTO] tbl_name
        SET col_name=expression, col_name=expression,...
```

The similarity to INSERT should be obvious.

Using DELETE

The DELETE SQL statement allows us to delete rows from a table. There are some delete statements in Listing 5.1, for example,

```
delete from department;
```

In this form, the delete statement will delete all the rows from the department table.

We can also limit which rows are deleted using a WHERE clause, for example,

```
delete from department where name='Asset Management';
```

This will only delete the rows matching the criteria in the where clause. In this case, only rows in which the department name is 'Asset Management' will be deleted.

It is unusual to want to delete all the rows from a table. However, because this is the shortest form of the delete statement, you may sometimes type it by accident without a WHERE clause. You can save yourself this anguish by switching on the --safe-updates or --i-am-a-dummy command-line options of the mysql client as discussed in Chapter 2, "Quick Tour." These options prevent you from deleting (or updating) rows without specifying a key constraint in the WHERE clause. That is, you need to specify that you want to delete only rows containing certain key values.

This is the general form of the DELETE statement from the MySQL manual:

```
DELETE [LOW_PRIORITY] [QUICK] FROM table_name
        [WHERE where_definition]
        [ORDER BY ...]
        [LIMIT rows]
```

or

```
DELETE [LOW_PRIORITY] [QUICK] table_name[.*] [, table_name[.*] ...]
      FROM table-references
      [WHERE where_definition]
```

or

```
DELETE [LOW_PRIORITY] [QUICK]
      FROM table_name[.*] [, table_name[.*] ...]
      USING table-references
      [WHERE where_definition]
```

The first form is the one we have seen examples of so far.

The other two forms are designed to allow us to delete rows from one or more tables with references to other tables. For example:

```
delete employee, employeeSkills
from employee, employeeSkills, department
where employee.employeeID = employeeSkills.employeeID
and employee.departmentID = department.departmentID
and department.name='Finance';
```

This example deletes all the employees who work for the Finance department and erases all records of their skills. Note that rows are deleted from employee and employeeSkills (the tables listed in the initial where clause), but not department (because it is listed only in the from clause).

The tables in the initial delete clause will have rows deleted from them, whereas the tables listed in the from clause are used for searching for data and will not have rows deleted unless they are also listed in the delete clause.

Note that this is quite a complex example because it involves three tables! We need three tables to illustrate this example, but we suggest that you come back and review the WHERE clause after reading about joins in Chapter 7, "Advanced Queries."

We have used a couple of new things in this where clause: the AND operator and the table.column notation. We have used AND to join our conditions together. This is a simple Boolean AND. We have also used the notation employee.employeeID. This notation means "the employeeID column of the employee table." We will revisit both of these things in more detail in the next two chapters.

The third form of DELETE is similar to the second form, except that, in this case, we delete only from the tables listed in the FROM clause while referring to the tables in the USING clause. For example:

```
delete from employee, employeeSkills
using employee, employeeSkills, department
where employee.employeeID = employeeSkills.employeeID
and employee.departmentID = department.departmentID
and department.name='Finance';
```

This is equivalent to the preceding example, except that it uses an alternative syntax.

There are a couple of other optional clauses in the general form of the DELETE statement:

- The LOW_PRIORITY clause works in the same way as it does in the INSERT statement.

- Specifying QUICK may speed up the DELETE statement by telling MySQL not to do some of its housekeeping on indexes while deleting from the table.

- The ORDER BY clause specifies the order in which to delete rows. This is most useful in conjunction with the LIMIT clause—we may want to delete the oldest *n* rows from a table, for example.

- The LIMIT clause allows us to set a maximum number of rows that can be deleted by the DELETE statement. This is useful either in conjunction with the ORDER BY clause or to save us from accidentally deleting too many rows.

Using TRUNCATE

The TRUNCATE statement allows us to delete all the rows from a table. For example:

```
TRUNCATE TABLE employee;
```

This query would delete all the employees from the employee table. This is faster than a DELETE statement because it works by dropping the table and re-creating it empty. One thing to bear in mind is that TRUNCATE is not transaction safe.

Using UPDATE

We can use the UPDATE SQL statement to change rows already stored in the database. For example, imagine that one of our employees changes jobs:

```
update employee
set job='DBA'
where employeeID='6651';
```

This statement changes the value of the job column for employee number 6651.

The general form of the UPDATE statement from the MySQL manual is as follows:

```
UPDATE [LOW_PRIORITY] [IGNORE] tbl_name
    SET col_name1=expr1 [, col_name2=expr2 ...]
    [WHERE where_definition]
    [ORDER BY ...]
    [LIMIT rows]


or


UPDATE [LOW_PRIORITY] [IGNORE] tbl_name [, tbl_name ...]
    SET col_name1=expr1 [, col_name2=expr2 ...]
    [WHERE where_definition]
```

The UPDATE statement is similar in many respects to the DELETE statement.

We can use an optional WHERE clause to update particular rows or leave it off to update all rows. Again, you can fall into the trap of forgetting to specify a WHERE clause—I remember one project when a foolish colleague typed something along these lines:

```
update user
set password='test';
```

This again highlights the usefulness of the --i-am-a-dummy mysql option, particularly if you are forced to work with dummies.

The second version of the UPDATE statement listed previously is a multi-table update. This works similarly to the multi-table deletes we looked at before. Note that only the columns you specifically list in the SET clause will be updated.

We have seen all the other clauses of the UPDATE statement before. The LOW_PRIORITY and IGNORE clauses work the same way as they do in INSERT. The ORDER BY and LIMIT clauses work the same way they do in DELETE.

Uploading Data with LOAD DATA INFILE

The LOAD DATA INFILE command allows you to bulk insert data from a text file into a single table without having to write INSERT statements. For example, we could have loaded the data in the department table using this technique as follows. Listing 5.2 shows the contents of a data file containing department information.

LISTING 5.2   department_infile.txt

```
42      Finance
128     Research and Development
NULL    Human Resources
NULL    Marketing
```

This file is in the default LOAD DATA INFILE format, with each row listed on a separate line with tabs between column values. (This is configurable and we will see how in a minute.)

We can load this information into the department table with the following LOAD DATA INFILE statement:

```
load data local infile 'department_infile.txt'
into table department;
```

This facility is particularly useful for converting data from another database format, spreadsheet, or CSV (comma-separated values) file.

The LOAD DATA INFILE statement requires the FILE privilege—see Chapter 11, "Managing User Privileges," for further information, especially if you are having trouble running this command. The privilege to perform this is often restricted for good security reasons—to stop people from loading in /etc/passwd, for example.

The general form of the LOAD DATA INFILE statement is as follows:

```
LOAD DATA [LOW_PRIORITY | CONCURRENT] [LOCAL] INFILE 'fileName.txt'
    [REPLACE | IGNORE]
    INTO TABLE tbl_name
    [FIELDS
        [TERMINATED BY '\t']
        [[OPTIONALLY] ENCLOSED BY '']
        [ESCAPED BY '\\' ]
    ]
    [LINES TERMINATED BY '\n']
    [IGNORE number LINES]
    [(col_name,...)]
```

The optional clauses are as listed here:

- The LOW PRIORITY clause works the same way it does in the INSERT statement by waiting for other clients to stop reading from the table. CONCURRENT, on the other hand, allows other clients to read from the table while the bulk insert is going on.

- In our example, we specified the optional keyword LOCAL, meaning that the data file is on the client machine. If this is not specified, MySQL will look for the infile on the server.

- If you have key clashes while inserting data, REPLACE and IGNORE provide two methods for dealing with this. Specifying REPLACE tells MySQL to replace the old row with the new row, while IGNORE tells MySQL to keep the old row.

- The FIELDS and LINES clauses specify how the data in the infile is laid out. The values in the general form are the defaults—each row on a new line, column values separated by tabs. We can also enclose column values in quotes and use the backslash character to escape any special characters (like single quotes) that might confuse MySQL.

- The IGNORE number LINES clause tells MySQL to ignore the first number lines in the infile.

- The final clause allows you to specify that you only want to read data into some of the table's columns.

A common format to receive data in is CSV or comma-separated values. Many programs can read and write files of this type, but one notable example is Microsoft Excel. Listing 5.3 shows a small CSV file saved from Excel.

LISTING 5.3   **new_programmers.csv**

```
Name,Job,DepartmentID

Julia Lenin,Programmer,128
Douglas Smith,Programmer,128
Tim O'Leary,Programmer,128
```

We can load this data into the employee table with the following query:

```
load data infile 'e:\\new_programmers.csv'
into table employee
fields terminated by ','
lines terminated by '\n'
ignore 2 lines
(name, job, departmentID);
```

You can see that we have used more options to load this data than we did when the data was in the default format. A few points are worth noting:

- Because we have used a Windows/DOS-style path that includes a backslash, we need to escape the backslash. Our path therefore became 'e:\\new_programmers.csv'.

- It possibly goes without saying that the fields in a CSV file are terminated by commas, but we need to specify it.

- We do not need to specify that lines are terminated by a newline character, but we have chosen to.

- This file has a header, so the first two lines do not contain data and should be ignored.

- The data in this file does not contain employeeIDs, so to allocate the three columns of data into the four columns in the database, we need to specify what columns (in order) the data will be mapped to. In this case, we have specified (name, job, departmentID).

Summary

In this chapter, we looked at ways to insert, delete, and update data from the tables in our database.

Inserting Data

- String values should be in quotes. Single quotes or backslashes within a string need to be escaped with a backslash.

- Add data to tables with the INSERT statement:

```
INSERT [LOW_PRIORITY | DELAYED] [IGNORE]
    [INTO] tbl_name [(col_name,...)]
    VALUES ((expression | DEFAULT),...),(...),...
    [ ON DUPLICATE KEY UPDATE col_name=expression, ... ]

or  INSERT [LOW_PRIORITY | DELAYED] [IGNORE]
    [INTO] tbl_name [(col_name,...)]
    SELECT ...
```

```
or  INSERT [LOW_PRIORITY | DELAYED] [IGNORE]
        [INTO] tbl_name
        SET col_name=(expression | DEFAULT), ...
        [ ON DUPLICATE KEY UPDATE col_name=expression, ... ]
```

- The REPLACE statement is just like INSERT, but it overwrites rows where a key clash occurs. INSERT fails or triggers the ON DUPLICATE KEY UPDATE clause when a key clash occurs.

Deleting Data

- Avoid disasters with --i-am-a-dummy.
- Delete data from tables with the DELETE statement:

```
    DELETE [LOW_PRIORITY] [QUICK] FROM table_name
        [WHERE where_definition]
        [ORDER BY ...]
        [LIMIT rows]
or DELETE [LOW_PRIORITY] [QUICK] table_name[.*] [, table_name[.*] ...]
        FROM table-references
        [WHERE where_definition]
or DELETE [LOW_PRIORITY] [QUICK]
        FROM table_name[.*] [, table_name[.*] ...]
        USING table-references
        [WHERE where_definition]
```

- The TRUNCATE TABLE statement deletes all rows from a table.

Updating Data

- Update data in tables with the UPDATE TABLE statement:

```
    UPDATE [LOW_PRIORITY] [IGNORE] tbl_name
        SET col_name1=expr1 [, col_name2=expr2 ...]
        [WHERE where_definition]
        [ORDER BY ...]
        [LIMIT rows]
or UPDATE [LOW_PRIORITY] [IGNORE] tbl_name [, tbl_name ...]
        SET col_name1=expr1 [, col_name2=expr2 ...]
        [WHERE where_definition]
```

LOAD DATA INFILE

- Use LOAD DATA INFILE to load the contents of a text file into a table:

```
LOAD DATA [LOW_PRIORITY | CONCURRENT] [LOCAL] INFILE 'file_name.txt'
    [REPLACE | IGNORE]
    INTO TABLE tbl_name
    [FIELDS
        [TERMINATED BY '\t']
        [[OPTIONALLY] ENCLOSED BY '']
        [ESCAPED BY '\\' ]
    ]
    [LINES TERMINATED BY '\n']
    [IGNORE number LINES]
    [(col_name,...)]
```

Quiz

1. Which of the following statements will successfully insert a row into the employee table?

    a)
    ```
    insert into employee values
    set employeeID=NULL, name='Laura Thomson',
    job='Programmer', departmentID=128;
    ```
    b)
    ```
    insert employee values
    (NULL, 'Laura Thomson', 'Programmer', 128);
    ```
    c)
    ```
    insert into employee values
    (NULL, Laura Thomson, Programmer, 128);
    ```
    d)
    ```
    insert employee values
    (NULL, 'Laura O'Leary', 'Programmer', 128);
    ```

2. The REPLACE statement

    a) is similar to INSERT except that where a key clash occurs, it will replace the old row with the new row

    b) is similar to INSERT except that where a key clash occurs, it will keep the old row and discard the new row

    c) is similar to UPDATE except that where a key clash occurs, it will replace the old row with the new row

    d) is similar to UPDATE except that where a key clash occurs, it will keep the old row and discard the new row

3. The `--i-am-a-dummy` startup option for the mysql client

    a) prevents you from inserting any data

    b) prevents you from updating data without specifying a key constraint

    c) prevents you from deleting data without specifying a key constraint

    d) both b) and c)

4. By default, fields in data files for load data infile are separated by

    a) commas

    b) spaces

    c) tabs

    d) pipes

5. The optional `LOCAL` clause in `LOAD DATA INFILE`

    a) specifies that the client and server are running on the same machine

    b) specifies that the data file is on the server

    c) specifies that the data file is on the client

    d) specifies that the server is running on the local host

Exercises

1. Create a set of `INSERT` statements to place data in each table of your orders table.

2. Delete the data from your tables.

3. Write a data file containing the same data that you inserted in part 1 and load it into your orders database using `LOAD DATA INFILE`.

Answers

Quiz

1. b
2. a
3. d
4. c
5. c

Exercises

There is no single "correct" answer for the exercises in this chapter. Just make sure that you can work through each of the exercises.

Next

In Chapter 6, "Querying MySQL," we will begin looking at the workhorse of SQL: the SELECT statement, in all its many variations.

6

Querying MySQL

So far, we have covered designing, creating, and populating a MySQL database. In this chapter and the two that follow it, we will look at the other end of this process: retrieving data from your database.

In this chapter, we will cover the SQL SELECT statement in some detail. This is probably the most important statement in SQL. It is the statement we use to select rows from one or more database table(s).

In this chapter, we will discuss how to select rows from a single database table. We'll cover the following:

- Overview of SELECT
- Simple queries
- Selecting particular columns
- Column aliases
- Using the WHERE clause to select particular rows
- Using the GROUP BY clause
- Selecting particular groups with HAVING
- Sorting search results with ORDER BY
- Limiting search results with LIMIT

In Chapter 7, "Advanced Queries," we'll cover more advanced queries, specifically queries that span multiple tables and the different types of joins and subqueries.

In Chapter 8, "Using MySQL Built-In Functions with SELECT," we'll look at the range of functions MySQL has built in to help you with your queries.

We'll begin by looking at the general form of the SELECT statement.

Overview of SELECT

The SELECT statement has the following general form:

```
SELECT columns
FROM tables
[WHERE conditions]
[GROUP BY group
[HAVING group_conditions]]
[ORDER BY sort_columns]
[LIMIT limits];
```

This is not a full set of syntax—we'll cover that in the next chapter—but it gives you an idea of the general form of the statement. We will cover all the previously listed clauses in this chapter.

The SELECT statement has many optional clauses. You can use these or not as you choose, but they must appear in the order shown.

Simple Queries

An example of the simplest form of the **SELECT** statement is as follows:

```
select * from department;
```

If you run this query on the data we have in the employee database, you should get a result something like this:

```
+--------------+--------------------------+
| departmentID | name                     |
+--------------+--------------------------+
|           42 | Finance                  |
|          128 | Research and Development |
|          129 | Human Resources          |
|          130 | Marketing                |
+--------------+--------------------------+
4 rows in set (0.00 sec)
```

This query has selected all the data in the chosen table—that is, all the rows and all the columns from the department table.

You can test this out on another table—try selecting all the rows and columns from the employeeSkills table, for example.

Of course, the power of a relational database is not in its capability to give you back *all* the data you put in, but instead in its capability to allow you to search the data for *particular* pieces of information.

Selecting Particular Columns

The next step we can take is to limit the columns that are returned. The * in the previous query (select * from department) means "all the columns in the table." Instead of specifying *, we can list a set of columns we would like returned. This can be a single column, a subset of table columns, or even the complete set of columns in any order that suits us. You should specify the column names as a list of comma-separated values.

For example, the following query selects only the values in the employeeID and name fields of the employee table:

```
select name, employeeID from employee;
```

If you run this query on the employee database, you should get a result that looks similar to the following:

```
+---------------+-------------+
| name          | employeeID  |
+---------------+-------------+
| Ajay Patel    |        6651 |
| Nora Edwards  |        7513 |
| Candy Burnett |        9006 |
| Ben Smith     |        9842 |
+-------------+---------------+
4 rows in set (0.00 sec)
```

You can see that only the two columns we specified have been returned. Note that the columns are displayed in the order in which we requested the columns in the query, rather than the order in which they appear in the database schema.

Specifying Absolute Databases and Tables

An additional piece of notation you should be aware of at this point allows you to absolutely specify which database and table we are talking about. For example, we can refer to the name column in the employee table as employee.name. For example:

```
select employee.name
from employee;
```

This should give something similar to the following result:

```
+---------------+
| name          |
+---------------+
| Ajay Patel    |
| Nora Edwards  |
| Candy Burnett |
| Ben Smith     |
+---------------+
4 rows in set (0.41 sec)
```

Similarly, we can absolutely specify which table in which database we are talking about, for example:

```
select name
from employee.employee;
```

(This should give the same result as the preceding query.)

Here, we are making explicit reference to the employee table within the employee database. The notation here is *database.table*.

If desired, we can specify which database and table a column belongs to. The same example could be written using *database.table.column* syntax like this:

```
select employee.employee.name
from employee;
```

For these simple queries, this syntax is not very useful, but as we move on to more complex queries, this allows us to be unambiguous about what information we are looking for.

Aliases

At this point, we should discuss the concept of column and table aliasing.

We have the ability to rename columns or expressions in a SELECT statement, and the new name will be what is shown in the output. For example, we can use the following query:

```
select name as employeeName
from employee;
```

Here, we have renamed the column name as employeeName just within the context of this query. The results of running this query on the employee database are as shown here:

```
+---------------+
| employeeName  |
+---------------+
| Ajay Patel    |
| Nora Edwards  |
| Candy Burnett |
| Ben Smith     |
+---------------+
4 rows in set (0.01 sec)
```

You can see that in the results, the contents of the name column are now listed under the heading employeeName.

The identifier employeeName is known as an *alias*. There are some rules about what we can and cannot do with aliases, and we will cover these as we come to them.

This specific example of an alias is not particularly useful. As we begin to write more complex queries and queries that involve calculation, you should see its power.

We can also use aliases for tables, like this:

```
select e.name
from employee as e;
```

This will give the same result as if we had written the query not using aliases. This notation will become useful when we begin running queries over multiple tables in the next chapter.

In the last two examples, the keyword AS is optional. We could simply have written

```
select name employeeName
from employee;
```

and

```
select e.name
from employee e;
```

You may choose to write the queries either way. It is simply a matter of style. As you can see here and in many other places in the book, there are many ways to write the same SQL query. Individual programming style in SQL varies as it does in other languages.

Using the WHERE Clause to Select Particular Rows

So far, we have looked at selecting all data from a table and selecting particular columns. Next, we will consider how to select particular rows. This is useful because we frequently want to select records from a table or tables that match particular search criteria. This becomes more important when we need to retrieve a few useful rows from a much larger table.

We can accomplish this using the WHERE clause of the SELECT statement. A simple example follows:

```
select employeeID, name
from employee
where job='Programmer';
```

(Remember, by the way, that we can set queries out on multiple lines. Each query is terminated by a semicolon. We lay out the SELECT statement like this to make it easier to read.)

The results of running this query on the employee database are as shown here:

```
+------------+--------------+
| employeeID | name         |
+------------+--------------+
|       6651 | Ajay Patel   |
|       7513 | Nora Edwards |
+------------+--------------+
2 rows in set (0.42 sec)
```

We used a condition in the WHERE clause to match only the rows in the table that met the specified criteria—in this case, they had to be employed as programmers.

Notice that we have combined this with a specific list of desired columns (employeeID and name) to pull out only the information we are interested in.

In this case, we have used a test of equality in the WHERE clause. Note that SQL uses = for testing equality. This is different from various other languages that use == or eq.

A huge variety of functions are available for use in the WHERE clause, and we will address these in detail in Chapter 8. For the time being, we will mention only the most commonly used operators:

- Equality, or =, which we have seen used previously.

- Inequality, expressed as != or <>.

- All the permutations of > (greater than), < (less than), >= (greater than or equal to), and <= (less than or equal to).

- IS NULL and IS NOT NULL, which are used to test whether a value is or is not NULL. You *cannot* do this by testing whether somevalue=NULL. (We will discuss why in Chapter 8.)

- The arithmetic operators you would expect, typically used in conjunction with comparison operators. For example, we might like to test whether somevalue > someothervalue*10.

- The standard Boolean operators AND, OR, and NOT, which we can use to group tests together. These are lower in precedence than the comparison operators, so, for example, salary > 30000 AND salary < 50000 works as you would expect.

In addition to the operators, we will use one function in some examples. The count() function allows us to count the number of rows returned by a query. For example:

```
select count(*) from employee;
```

This query will tell us how many rows there are in the employee table.

Finally, we can control precedence by grouping expressions with parentheses.

An example of a slightly more complex query using WHERE is as follows:

```
select * from assignment
where employeeID=6651 and hours > 8;
```

This query selects all the work assignments performed by employeeID 6651 (Ajay Patel) in which he performed more than 8 hours of work.

One important point to note is that we are not allowed to use any column aliases in the WHERE clause. We must use the original column name. This is an ANSI SQL limitation. The reason for it is that the value of the aliased column may be unknown at the time the WHERE condition is examined.

Removing Duplicates with DISTINCT

You can use the keyword DISTINCT in your queries to specify that you do not want to see duplicate results. For example, consider the following query:

```
select job
from employee;
```

This will return the following data:

```
+----------------------+
| job                  |
+----------------------+
| Programmer           |
| Programmer           |
| Systems Administrator |
| DBA                  |
+----------------------+
4 rows in set (0.01 sec)
```

Note that the data Programmer appears twice. This is because this value occurs in two rows. This query has simply returned the complete list of values in the job column of this table.

Now, consider this query:

```
select distinct job
from employee;
```

This will return the following rows:

```
+----------------------+
| job                  |
+----------------------+
| Programmer           |
| Systems Administrator |
| DBA                  |
+----------------------+
3 rows in set (0.04 sec)
```

Here, the duplicates have been removed.

In this case, the difference doesn't seem like that big of a deal—sure, the second set of results is a little neater, but it doesn't really improve things much. It would be a little more important for a big table with a lot of repetition, but it would still be presenting accurate information.

On the other hand, consider this:

```
mysql> select count(job) from employee;
+------------+
| count(job) |
+------------+
|          4 |
+------------+
1 row in set (0.01 sec)
```

This query tells us there are four values in the job column. This is kind of misleading. It certainly doesn't tell us that there are four different values in the job column because we can see by inspection of the data that there are only three.

It is relatively easy to type the previous query by mistake when what you actually meant was this:

```
select count(distinct job) from employee;
```

This will give you the following result:

```
+---------------------+
| count(distinct job) |
+---------------------+
|                   3 |
+---------------------+
1 row in set (0.05 sec)
```

This tells us how many *different* values are in the job column, a more useful piece of information.

Using the GROUP BY Clause

The next clause we will look at is the GROUP BY clause. This allows us to consider retrieved rows in groups. This is really useful only when we use it in combination with functions that operate over a group of rows. The only one of these we have mentioned so far is count(), but we will look at many more in Chapter 8.

Consider the following query:

```
select count(*), job
from employee
group by job;
```

This query will count the number of employees in each job grouping—that is, the number of employees who hold each job. If you run this query on the employee database, you should see a result similar to the following:

```
+----------+-----------------------+
| count(*) | job                   |
+----------+-----------------------+
|        1 | DBA                   |
|        2 | Programmer            |
|        1 | Systems Administrator |
+----------+-----------------------+
3 rows in set (0.04 sec)
```

There are two differences between the way GROUP BY works in MySQL and ANSI SQL.

In ANSI SQL, you must group by all the columns you have listed in the initial SELECT clause. MySQL allows you to have additional fields in the SELECT clause that are not in the GROUP BY clause.

MySQL also allows you to sort the group order in which the results are presented. The default order is ascending. If we want to repeat the last query but see the results in descending order, we can use the following query:

```
select count(*), job
from employee
group by job desc;
```

This will produce results similar to the following:

```
+----------+----------------------+
| count(*) | job                  |
+----------+----------------------+
|        1 | Systems Administrator |
|        2 | Programmer           |
|        1 | DBA                  |
+----------+----------------------+
3 rows in set (0.04 sec)
```

As you can see, the names of the jobs are now in reverse alphabetical order. You can also specify ASC (for ascending), but this is the default, so it's redundant to do so.

Selecting Particular Groups with HAVING

The next clause in the SELECT statement is HAVING. A GROUP BY with a HAVING clause is like a SELECT with a WHERE clause. For example:

```
select count(*), job
from employee
group by job
having count(*)=1;
```

This query will select the jobs in the company for which we have only one employee in the role. It should produce results similar to the following:

```
+----------+----------------------+
| count(*) | job                  |
+----------+----------------------+
|        1 | DBA                  |
|        1 | Systems Administrator |
+----------+----------------------+
2 rows in set (0.05 sec)
```

It's been our experience that people who are just beginning to use SQL often get WHERE and HAVING confused. You will use WHERE in just about every query you write to test conditions that relate to individual rows. You will use HAVING when you want to apply a conditional to whole groups.

Sorting Search Results with ORDER BY

The next clause in the SELECT statement is ORDER BY. This clause allows us to sort the result rows on one or more columns. The sort can be either ascending, denoted ASC, or descending, denoted DESC. For example:

```
select *
from employee
order by job asc, name desc;
```

This will select all the rows and columns from the employee table. They will be sorted according to job in alphabetical order, and if two or more people have the same job, they will be sorted in reverse alphabetical order by name. This will give the following results:

```
+-------------+---------------+----------------------+---------------+
| employeeID  | name          | job                  | departmentID  |
+-------------+---------------+----------------------+---------------+
|        9842 | Ben Smith     | DBA                  |            42 |
|        7513 | Nora Edwards  | Programmer           |           128 |
|        6651 | Ajay Patel    | Programmer           |           128 |
|        9006 | Candy Burnett | Systems Administrator|           128 |
+-------------+---------------+----------------------+---------------+
4 rows in set (0.02 sec)
```

If you just specify ORDER BY column with no ASC or DESC, the default is ASC. Note that if ORDER BY is not specified, you can't assume anything about the order in which rows will be returned.

Limiting Search Results with LIMIT

The final clause of the SELECT statement we will look at in this chapter is LIMIT.

The LIMIT clause is used to limit the number and range of rows that are returned from a query. For example, consider the following query:

```
select *
from employeeSkills
limit 5;
```

This query will return only the first five rows that match the selection criteria. In this particular case, we will simply get the first five rows found in the table, as shown here:

```
+-------------+-------+
| employeeID  | skill |
+-------------+-------+
|        6651 | Java  |
|        6651 | VB    |
|        7513 | C     |
|        7513 | Java  |
|        7513 | Perl  |
+-------------+-------+
5 rows in set (0.44 sec)
```

We can also specify that we want a subset of rows other than the first *n*. If we, for example, wanted to retrieve rows 6 through 8 from the preceding query, we would do so like this:

```
select *
from employeeSkills
limit 5, 3;
```

When we pass two parameters to limit, the first parameter is the offset (start point) and the second parameter is the maximum number of rows we would like returned. Contrast this with the previous case: When we pass only a single parameter, it represents the maximum number of rows we would like returned.

Row numbering starts from zero when specifying offsets (as you can see in the preceding example—for the sixth row, we specify offset 5). Our first LIMIT example selected rows 0 to 4, and our second selected rows 5 to 7.

If you specify the second parameter as -1, the query will return the rows from the offset to the end of the table.

The LIMIT clause is normally used with ORDER BY so that the order in which rows are returned makes some sense. Remember that without an ORDER BY clause, the records are not retrieved in any logical order.

This clause is especially useful when building Web or GUI applications using MySQL because it provides an easy mechanism for paging results.

Summary

- The SELECT statement has the following general form:

  ```
  SELECT columns
  FROM tables
  [WHERE conditions]
  [GROUP BY group
  [HAVING group_conditions]]
  [ORDER BY sort_columns]
  [LIMIT limits];
  ```

- The clause select * retrieves all columns; select *columnname* retrieves a particular column.

- We can specify tables as *database.table* and columns as *table.column* or *database.table.column* to avoid ambiguity.

- Aliases are alternative names for tables and columns. Specify them this way:

  ```
  select column as column_alias
  from table as table_alias;
  ```

- The WHERE clause is used to select rows matching search criteria.

- The keyword DISTINCT removes duplicates from the result set.

- The GROUP BY clause treats the rows retrieved group by group. Its chief use is in conjunction with group functions like count().

- The HAVING clause is like a WHERE clause for groups.

- The ORDER BY clause sorts result rows according to the columns you specify.
- The LIMIT clause is used to control which rows are returned from the total possible result set. You can specify the maximum rows returned and an offset from which to start.

Quiz

1. Which of the following queries selects all data stored in the client table?

    a)
    ```
    select *
    from client
    where clientID=2;
    ```

    b)
    ```
    select clientID, name, address, contactPerson, contactNumber
    from client;
    ```

    c)
    ```
    select * from client
    limit 1;
    ```

    d)
    ```
    select all from client;
    ```

2. Which of the following queries selects all the programmers from the employee table?

    a)
    ```
    select *
    from employee
    where job='Programmer';
    ```

    b)
    ```
    select *
    from employee
    having job='Programmer';
    ```

    c)
    ```
    select *
    from employee
    where job='Programmer'
    group by job
    having job='Programmer';
    ```

    d)
    ```
    select job
    from employee;
    ```

3. Which of the following queries will *not* return the total number of employees in the employee table?

   a)

   ```
   select count(employeeID) from employee;
   ```

   b)

   ```
   select count(employeeID) as total from employee;
   ```

   c)

   ```
   select count(distinct employeeID) from employee;
   ```

   d)

   ```
   select count(employeeID) from employee group by employeeID;
   ```

4. Where can we *not* use aliases?

   a) For columns

   b) For tables

   c) In the WHERE clause

   d) In the SELECT clause

5. If we want to return the 15th through 20th rows from a query, the correct LIMIT clause is

   a) LIMIT 15, 20

   b) LIMIT 14, 19

   c) LIMIT 14, 5

   d) LIMIT 15, 5

Exercises

1. Write a query that lists all information about employees who work for department 128.

2. Write a query that lists all the employeeIDs of employees who have worked for client number 1.

3. Write a query that returns the number of employees who know each skill listed in the employeeSkills table.

Answers

Quiz

1. b
2. a
3. d
4. c
5. c

Exercises

1.
```
select *
from employee
where departmentID=128;
```

2.
```
select employeeID
from assignment
where clientID=1;
```

3.
```
select skill, count(skill)
from employeeSkills
group by skill;
```

Next

In the next chapter, "Advanced Queries," we will discuss queries that span multiple tables, as well as further subtleties of the SELECT statement.

7

Advanced Queries

In this chapter, we'll discuss more advanced queries. Principally, we will look at how we can run queries across multiple tables. This will involve learning about the concept of joins—that is, how we join tables together.

We will cover the following:

- Using joins to run queries over multiple tables, including:
  - Natural, inner, and cross joins
  - Straight joins
  - Left and right joins
- Writing subqueries
- Using SELECT statement options

Using Joins to Run Queries over Multiple Tables

All the queries in Chapter 6, "Querying MySQL," retrieved data from only a single table. Given that we've focused on a normalized database design in which information is stored in multiple tables, selecting from a single table is, well, limited. What make well-designed, relational databases interesting are the relationships—that is, the links between the tables. When information is selected from multiple tables, these links are called joins. Let's begin by looking at queries that link two tables.

Joining Two Tables

Consider the following query:

```
select employee.name, department.name
from employee, department
where employee.departmentID = department.departmentID;
```

You will see that we have specified two tables in the FROM clause instead of one. In this case, we want to retrieve employees' names and the names of the departments they work for. The results are as shown here:

```
+---------------+-------------------------+
| name          | name                    |
+---------------+-------------------------+
| Ben Smith     | Finance                 |
| Ajay Patel    | Research and Development |
| Nora Edwards  | Research and Development |
| Candy Burnett | Research and Development |
+---------------+-------------------------+
4 rows in set (0.42 sec)
```

How did we get these results? First of all, we selected columns that appeared in two tables. (You will notice that we used the dot notation to differentiate between the employee name and the department name, as discussed in Chapter 6.) To do this, we needed to include both of these tables in the FROM clause.

The most interesting thing about this query is the WHERE clause. If we run this query without the WHERE clause, as

```
select employee.name, department.name
from employee, department;
```

we get the following result:

```
+---------------+-------------------------+
| name          | name                    |
+---------------+-------------------------+
| Ajay Patel    | Finance                 |
| Nora Edwards  | Finance                 |
| Candy Burnett | Finance                 |
| Ben Smith     | Finance                 |
| Ajay Patel    | Research and Development |
| Nora Edwards  | Research and Development |
| Candy Burnett | Research and Development |
| Ben Smith     | Research and Development |
| Ajay Patel    | Human Resources         |
| Nora Edwards  | Human Resources         |
| Candy Burnett | Human Resources         |
| Ben Smith     | Human Resources         |
| Ajay Patel    | Marketing               |
| Nora Edwards  | Marketing               |
| Candy Burnett | Marketing               |
| Ben Smith     | Marketing               |
+---------------+-------------------------+
16 rows in set (0.01 sec)
```

The first query, with the WHERE clause, shows employees listed with the correct department, whereas the second query shows all possible combinations of employees and departments, with no way of knowing which rows are correct and which are spurious! This result set, containing all possible rows from combining the two tables, is called the *Cartesian product* of the two tables.

The WHERE clause is clearly important in finding the result rows we want. When performing a join, we refer to the condition or set of conditions used to join tables together as the *join condition*. In this case, the condition we used was employee.departmentID = department.departmentID, which is the link between the tables based on the foreign keys in our original schema.

When you need to find information that spans more than one table, you need to use these links between tables to find the information you are seeking. Sometimes this means looking for a path from the information you have to the information you want. We'll come back to this idea in the next section.

One other point to note is that if you look at the previous result sets, both of the columns are headed "name" because this is what each column is called in the context of its own table. We could improve the readability of the results by using aliases, as shown here:

```
select employee.name as employeeName, department.name as departmentName
from employee, department
where employee.departmentID = department.departmentID;
```

This will give the following results:

```
+---------------+-------------------------+
| employeeName  | departmentName          |
+---------------+-------------------------+
| Ben Smith     | Finance                 |
| Ajay Patel    | Research and Development |
| Nora Edwards  | Research and Development |
| Candy Burnett | Research and Development |
+---------------+-------------------------+
4 rows in set (0.55 sec)
```

The presentation of this result set is easier to understand than the previous ones.

Joining Multiple Tables

The principle behind joining more than two tables is the same.

Consider the situation of wanting to find out which department's employees have been assigned to work for the client called Telco Inc. How can we find this information?

We know the client name, and looking this up in the client table gives us the clientID. We can use this to find matching assignments in the assignment table and to see which employees have worked for the client. We get their employeeIDs from the assignment table and can then look these up in the employee table to find out the ids of the departments they work for. From this information, we can then finally go to the department table and look up the department name!

Having worked out this path across four tables, we need to write a query that reflects our logic. This is as follows:

```
select department.name
from client, assignment, employee, department
where client.name='Telco Inc'
and client.clientID = assignment.clientID
and assignment.employeeID = employee.employeeID
and employee.departmentID = department.departmentID;
```

These are the results of running this query:

```
+--------------------------+
| name                     |
+--------------------------+
| Research and Development |
+--------------------------+
1 row in set (0.00 sec)
```

Looking at the query we wrote, you can see that we needed to list all the tables in the path that we followed and then join conditions to make each link from table to table. We have a regular condition—client.name = 'Telco Inc'—and a series of join conditions. Notice that we had three join conditions to join four tables.

You can use this as a guideline to check whether you have all the join conditions you need. If you are joining *n* tables, in most cases, you will have a link between each pair of tables, and therefore have *n-1* join conditions. The joins in this example are shown in Figure 7.1. You can very clearly see why four tables require three (*n*-1) joins.

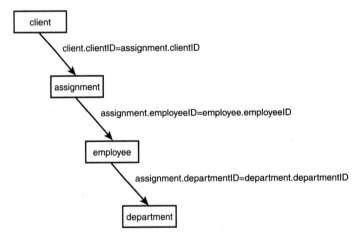

FIGURE 7.1   Joining four tables requires three joins.

Joining a Table to Itself—Self Joins

As well as joining tables to other tables, we can join a table to itself. Why would we want to do this? Sometimes we are looking for relationships between rows in a table. Imagine that we want to know the names of employees who work in the same department as Nora Edwards. To do this, we need to find the departmentID Nora works for from the employee table and then look in the employee table for employees who work for that department.

We can do this as shown here:

```
select e2.name
from employee e1, employee e2
where e1.name = 'Nora Edwards'
and e1.departmentID = e2.departmentID;
```

You can see that, in this query, we have actually declared two different aliases for the employee table. Effectively, we are telling MySQL that we want to pretend we have two separate tables, e1 and e2, which just happen to contain the same data. Then, we can simply join them as we would any two other tables. We begin by finding Nora's row in e1 (where e1.name='Nora Edwards'). We can then look for rows in e2 that have the same departmentID as Nora (e1.departmentID = e2.departmentID).

This can take a little getting used to, but as long as you can pretend you are dealing with two different tables, you shouldn't have too much trouble.

These are the results of the preceding query:

```
+---------------+
| name          |
+---------------+
| Ajay Patel    |
| Nora Edwards  |
| Candy Burnett |
+---------------+
3 rows in set (0.00 sec)
```

These are all the employees who work in the same department as Nora. You can see that Nora herself is included in the list. We can easily add a further condition to exclude her from the result set:

```
select e2.name
from employee e1, employee e2
where e1.name = 'Nora Edwards'
and e1.departmentID = e2.departmentID
and e2.name != 'Nora Edwards';
```

Understanding the Different Join Types

There are various types of joins and various kinds we can use in MySQL.

Understanding the Basic Join

In the preceding section, we mentioned the concept of a *Cartesian product*. This is sometimes called a *full join* or *cross join*, but regardless of nomenclature, it returns a complete set of combinations. When we add a conditional statement to the join (like `employee.departmentID = department.departmentID`), we make it into something called an *equijoin*, which limits the number of rows in the result set.

So far, we have used a set of tables listed in the FROM clause separated by the comma operator. This gives us a cross join, as described previously, converted to an equijoin with the WHERE clause. MySQL has various forms of syntax we can use for this type of join.

Consider our original query:

```
select employee.name, department.name
from employee, department
where employee.departmentID = department.departmentID;
```

Optionally, we could have used the keyword JOIN, instead of a comma:

```
select employee.name, department.name
from employee join department
where employee.departmentID = department.departmentID;
```

Instead of JOIN, we could just as well have written CROSS JOIN or INNER JOIN.

When we perform this type of join, MySQL looks at the tables we are joining and tries to work out the most efficient way to join them together, rather than necessarily joining the tables in the order we have listed. Sometimes the query optimization can go slightly wrong. We will discuss this in more detail in Chapter 19, "Optimizing Your Queries." If you want to override the optimizer and force MySQL to join tables in the order in which you list them, replace the word JOIN with STRAIGHT JOIN.

Understanding LEFT and RIGHT Joins

When we used equijoins in the preceding section, we were using a JOIN, CROSS JOIN, INNER JOIN, or perhaps STRAIGHT JOIN and were looking for rows that matched in two or more tables. What about cases in which we want to find rows in one table that don't have a corresponding row in the other table?

Consider, for example, a situation in which we want to find employees who have not yet worked on any outside assignments—that is, employees whose employeeIDs are not listed in the assignment table. We can do this using LEFT JOIN, as follows:

```
select employee.name
from employee left join assignment
on employee.employeeID = assignment.employeeID
where clientID is null;
```

This will give the following results:

```
+---------------+
| name          |
+---------------+
| Ajay Patel    |
| Candy Burnett |
| Ben Smith     |
+---------------+
3 rows in set (0.49 sec)
```

You can easily confirm by visual inspection of the tables that this is the right answer, but why and how does it work?

The left join works by taking the left-hand table in the join (in this case, employee) and trying to match it to rows in the right-hand table. These matching rows are placed alongside the left table. For each row in the left table that has no matching rows in the right table, the LEFT JOIN substitutes a row of NULL values. We can find rows from the left table that have no matching row in the right table by searching for a NULL key value.

Look back at the example. In this join, for each employee who has worked on an assignment, we will get a row showing the employee and the assignment details. When an employee has no matching row in the assignment table, the left join will make up a "dummy row" consisting of all NULLs. We can find these dummy rows by looking for employees who have worked on an assignment for which the clientID is NULL. (The clientID is a key field, so this should never occur in the assignment table.)

In versions of MySQL prior to 4.1, this technique was often used to work around the absence of subqueries. Subqueries are covered later in this chapter.

In this example, we have used LEFT JOIN, but we could as easily have used RIGHT JOIN, which does the same thing but uses the right table as a base and fills any missing rows from the left table with NULLs.

Writing Subqueries

A subquery is a query within a query—that is, a query in which we reuse the result in another query. They are sometimes called nested queries or subselects. Subqueries are new in MySQL 4.1. They are a feature that users have been requesting for a long time. Subqueries do not add new functionality, but queries are often more readable using subqueries, rather than a complex set of joins.

We have already looked at one kind of subquery without realizing it. The multi-table deletes and updates that we looked at in Chapter 5, "Inserting, Deleting, and Updating Data," are a type of specialized subquery.

In this chapter, we will look at subqueries in SELECT statements.

Two basic kinds of subqueries have been added to MySQL:

- Derived table subqueries
- Expression subqueries

Expression subqueries appear in the WHERE clause of a SELECT statement. These come in two further types:

- Subqueries that return a single value or row
- Subqueries that are used to test a Boolean expression

We'll look at an example of each of these in turn.

Using Derived Table Subqueries

Derived table subqueries allow us to list a query in the FROM clause of another query. This effectively allows us to create a temporary table and add it to the query. For example, consider the following simple query:

```
select employeeID, name from employee where job='Programmer';
```

It should be obvious that this will retrieve the names and ids of all the programmers. We can use this query within another for another useful result:

```
select programmer.name
from (select employeeID, name from employee where job='Programmer')
        as programmer,
        assignment
where programmer.employeeID = assignment.employeeID;
```

In this case, we have used the subquery (select employeeID, name from employee where job='Programmer') to make a derived table that contains only the rows employeeID and name, and we have aliased this table to call it 'programmer'. We can then query it as we would any other table. In this case, we use it to find out which programmers have worked on outside assignments to garner the following results:

```
+--------------+
| name         |
+--------------+
| Nora Edwards |
+--------------+
1 row in set (0.01 sec)
```

Using Single-Value Subqueries

As in the preceding section, we will start with a simple query:

```
select max(hours) from assignment;
```

This will retrieve a single value, representing the maximum number of hours an employee has worked on an assignment. We are using a MySQL function we have not yet mentioned: max(), which finds the greatest value in a particular column. We will revisit max() in Chapter 8, "Using MySQL Built-In Functions with SELECT." Using the result returned by this type of function is a common application of single-value subqueries.

As before, we can go on and use this query within another query.

Single-value subqueries return a single column value and are then typically used for comparison. For example, consider the following query:

```
select e.employeeID, e.name
from employee e, assignment a
where e.employeeID = a.employeeID
and a.hours = (select max(hours) from assignment);
```

Here, we are looking for what might be termed the company's hardest working employee: Who is the employee who has put in the greatest number of hours on a particular day on an assignment?

Here are the results of running this query:

```
+-------------+--------------+
| employeeID  | name         |
+-------------+--------------+
|        7513 | Nora Edwards |
+-------------+--------------+
1 row in set (0.42 sec)
```

We can also write subqueries that return a row, rather than a single value, although this is often of limited usefulness. We will not look at an example of this here.

Using Boolean Expression Subqueries

Boolean expression subqueries are used to check our query against some special functions that return a Boolean expression. These special functions are IN, EXISTS, and (grouped together) ALL, ANY, and SOME.

We can use the keyword IN to check against a set of values. Consider the following query:

```
select name
from employee
where employeeID not in
      (select employeeID
        from assignment);
```

This query has the same effect as the one we looked at using LEFT JOIN. It allows us to look for employees who are not in the set of employees who have worked on an outside assignment. The keyword IN lets us look for values in a set of values. We get the same result here as we did from our LEFT JOIN query:

```
+---------------+
| name          |
+---------------+
| Ajay Patel    |
| Candy Burnett |
| Ben Smith     |
+---------------+
3 rows in set (0.45 sec)
```

Interestingly enough, another use of IN is to just test against a listed a set of values, as shown here:

```
select name
from employee
where employeeID not in (6651, 1234);
```

The EXISTS keyword works in a slightly different fashion than the IN keyword. In queries using EXISTS, we actually use data from the outer query in the subquery. This is sometimes called a *correlated* subquery.

For example, consider the following query:

```
select e.name, e.employeeID
from employee e
where not exists
        (select *
         from assignment
         where employeeID = e.employeeID);
```

Here, we are looking for employees who have never worked on an outside assignment.

In the subquery, we are looking at rows in the assignment table and we are checking for rows where the assignment employeeID is the same as the employee.employeeID. The e.employeeID comes from the outer query. Here's what MySQL is actually doing: For each row in the employee table, we check the results of the subquery, and if there is no matching row (WHERE NOT EXISTS), we add the employee's details to the result set.

Although some users find this an easier syntax to understand, we can get the same result using a LEFT JOIN as we did before. It will also be more efficient and, therefore, faster to execute if written as a left join. This query yields exactly the same results:

```
+---------------+------------+
| name          | employeeID |
+---------------+------------+
| Ajay Patel    |       6651 |
| Candy Burnett |       9006 |
| Ben Smith     |       9842 |
+---------------+------------+
3 rows in set (0.00 sec)
```

The ALL, ANY, and SOME keywords are used to compare against a set of values returned from a subquery.

Suppose that Nora Edwards, who you may remember is our hardest working programmer, wants to establish that nobody works longer hours than the programmers. She comes up with the following query to establish this fact:

```
select e.name
from employee e, assignment a
where e.employeeID = a.employeeID
```

```
and a.hours > all
        (select a.hours
        from assignment a, employee e
        where e.employeeID = a.employeeID
        and e.job='Programmer');
```

The subquery finds the list of hours worked on assignments by programmers in the company. It then looks for any other employees who have worked on an assignment for longer than these programmers, using the check a.hours > ALL (the programmers' hours).

You will not be surprised to know that this query returns no rows, establishing that, in fact, nobody in this company works harder than the programmers.

Using SELECT Statement Options

When we first looked at the select statement, we looked at an abbreviated form of the general syntax for the statement. Let's come back and look at the complete syntax and see what we don't know.

According to the MySQL manual, this is the form of a SELECT statement:

```
SELECT [STRAIGHT_JOIN]
       [SQL_SMALL_RESULT] [SQL_BIG_RESULT] [SQL_BUFFER_RESULT]
       [SQL_CACHE | SQL_NO_CACHE] [SQL_CALC_FOUND_ROWS] [HIGH_PRIORITY]
       [DISTINCT | DISTINCTROW | ALL]
    select_expression,...
    [INTO {OUTFILE | DUMPFILE} 'file_name' export_options]
    [FROM table_references
      [WHERE where_definition]
      [GROUP BY {unsigned_integer | col_name | formula} [ASC | DESC], ...]
      [HAVING where_definition]
      [ORDER BY {unsigned_integer | col_name | formula} [ASC | DESC] ,...]
      [LIMIT [offset,] rows | rows OFFSET offset]
      [PROCEDURE procedure_name(argument_list)]
      [FOR UPDATE | LOCK IN SHARE MODE]]
```

Most of these clauses are now familiar to us. Let's briefly go through the ones we have not yet covered:

- The STRAIGHT JOIN clause at the beginning can be used to force the query optimizer to join the tables in the order you specify. This has the same effect as specifying STRAIGHT JOIN in the WHERE clause, as discussed earlier in this chapter. This is an extension to ANSI SQL.

- The SQL_SMALL_RESULT, SQL_BIG_RESULT, and SQL_BUFFER_RESULT options are designed to help with optimization. You can use SQL_SMALL_RESULT and SQL_BIG_RESULT to tell MySQL that you expect the result set to have either few rows or a large number of them. SQL_BUFFER_RESULT tells MySQL that it must put the result set into a temporary table. You can use this when it takes significant time to send the results to the client to avoid having the queried tables locked for that time. These options are MySQL extensions to ANSI SQL.

- `SQL_CACHE` and `SQL_NOCACHE` tell MySQL whether to cache the results. (Another extension to ANSI SQL.)

- `SQL_CALC_FOUND_ROWS` is for use with the `LIMIT` clause; it tells MySQL to work out how many rows would have been returned if there had been no `LIMIT` clause. We can then retrieve this number with `select found_rows();` (another extension to ANSI SQL). This is intended to reduce duplicated effort. In versions without it, a common task is to run a `COUNT(*)` query and then a `SELECT` with a `LIMIT`.

- `HIGH PRIORITY` tells MySQL that this query should be given priority over any `UPDATE` statements that are waiting to use the involved tables.

- We have already talked about `DISTINCT`, but `DISTINCTROW` is a synonym for it. `ALL` is the opposite (return all duplicates) and is the default option.

- The `SELECT INTO OUTFILE` is the opposite of the `LOAD DATA INFILE` command we looked at in Chapter 5, "Inserting, Deleting, and Updating Data." This puts the result of the `SELECT` statement into the specified file. The *export_options* clause is the same as the options in `LOAD DATA INFILE` (see Chapter 5 for details).

- The `PROCEDURE` clause allows you to specify a procedure that can be applied to the result set before it is sent to the client. This procedure must be written in C++ and, as such, is beyond the scope of this book, but see the MySQL manual if you need more information.

- The `FOR UPDATE` and `LOCK IN SHARE MODE` clauses affect you only if your storage engine uses page- or row-level locking—in practice, this is InnoDB and BDB. If you specify `FOR UPDATE`, you will set an exclusive lock, and if you use `LOCK IN SHARE MODE`, you will set a shared lock. We will discuss locking in Chapter 10, "Using Transactions with InnoDB Tables."

Summary

Joins

- A join is the process of linking two tables together. We specify the tables to join in the `FROM` clause, along with the type of join. We should also specify a join condition to describe how the tables should be joined together.

- The comma operator, `JOIN`, `INNER JOIN`, and `CROSS JOIN` all work the same way: They combine tables so that we can search for data across them.

- `LEFT` and `RIGHT` joins allow us to look for rows in one table that have no corresponding row in another table.

Subqueries

- A subquery is a query nested inside another query.

- Subqueries can return a single value, a row, or a set of values. They can also be used to evaluate the Boolean conditions SOME, ALL, or ANY.

- Using EXISTS, we can check whether a row exists in the subquery that correlates to a row in the outer query.

SELECT Statement Options

- The SELECT statement allows us to specify various optimization options.

- We can dump data to an external file with SELECT INTO OUTFILE in the same way that we performed LOAD DATA INFILE in Chapter 5.

- We can add procedures (written in C++) for result processing to MySQL.

Quiz

1. A Cartesian product
   a) represents all possible combinations of rows in two or more tables
   b) represents the combinations of matching rows from two or more tables
   c) represents the rows from one table matched with rows from a second table; where this is not possible, the result row is filled with NULLs where the data from the second table would have been
   d) none of the above

2. A left join
   a) represents all possible combinations of rows in two or more tables
   b) represents the combinations of matching rows from two or more tables
   c) represents the rows from one table matched with rows from a second table; where this is not possible, the result row is filled with NULLs where the data from the second table would have been
   d) none of the above

3. An equijoin:
   a) represents all possible combinations of rows in two or more tables
   b) represents the combinations of matching rows from two or more tables
   c) represents the rows from one table matched with rows from a second table; where this is not possible, the result row is filled with NULLs where the data from the second table would have been
   d) none of the above

4. A correlated subquery is called this because

   a) it correlates rows between tables

   b) it correlates rows in a single table

   c) it correlates two joins

   d) it correlates the rows in an outer query with rows in an inner query

5. The difference between the two queries marked 5.1 and 5.2 in the following text is that

   a) there is no difference

   b) they return different data

   c) they return the same data but the left join (Query 5.1) is likely to execute faster

   d) they return the same data but the subquery (Query 5.2) is likely to execute faster

   Query 5.1:

```
select employee.name
from employee left join assignment
on employee.employeeID = assignment.employeeID
where clientID is null;
```

   Query 5.2:

```
select e.name, e.employeeID
from employee e
where not exists
        (select *
         from assignment
         where employeeID = e.employeeID);
```

Exercises

1. Write a query that lists an employee's name and all her skills.

2. Write a query using a LEFT JOIN that lists clients who have not had any employees working for them on assignment.

3. Rewrite your query from exercise #2 to use EXISTS.

Answers

Quiz

1. a
2. c
3. b
4. d
5. c

Exercises

1.

```
select name, skill
from employee, employeeSkills
where employee.employeeID = employeeSkills.employeeID;
```

2.

```
select client.clientID, name
from client left join assignment
on client.clientID = assignment.clientID
where employeeID is NULL;
```

3.

```
select clientID, name
from client
where not exists
        (select *
         from assignment
         where assignment.clientID = client.clientID);
```

Next

In Chapter 8, "Using MySQL Built-In Functions with SELECT," we will take a tour of the functions MySQL makes available for use in SELECT queries.

## 8

Using MySQL Built-In Functions with SELECT

MySQL has a wide variety of built-in operators and functions that can be useful for writing queries. Most of these are for use in the SELECT and WHERE clauses. There are also some special grouping functions for use in the GROUP BY clause. We have already used the basic comparison operators and the count() and max() functions. A vast number of functions are available. In this chapter, we take a tour of the most useful ones. This book is not trying to be a function reference by any means—we are just trying to give you a feel for the types of functionality available.

We will cover the following:

- Operators
- Control flow functions
- String functions
- Numeric functions
- Date and time functions
- Cast functions
- Other functions
- Functions for use with GROUP BY clauses

One important point to note is that, in MySQL, any expression containing NULL will evaluate to NULL, with a few exceptions we will note as we go along. We will discuss this further in the section on comparison operators.

In this chapter, we will make some use of the SELECT statement without any tables. We can use SELECT as a basic calculator. For example, if we type

```
select 2+2;
```

we will get the result

```
+-----+
| 2+2 |
+-----+
|   4 |
+-----+
1 row in set (0.42 sec)
```

We can execute any expression without tables and have access to a full range of math and other operators and functions. Although the capability to execute 2+2 is trivial, the capability to do math at the SELECT level is not always so. For example, this lets you perform financial analysis of values in tables and display the results in a report.

In all MySQL expressions, you can use parentheses to control the order in which subexpressions are evaluated, as you would in any programming language.

We will begin by looking at the operators.

Operators

There are three main sets of operators in MySQL: arithmetic, comparison, and logical. We briefly talked about these operators back in Chapter 6, "Querying MySQL." Let's look at them in more detail now.

Arithmetic Operators

MySQL has the arithmetic operators you would expect: addition (+), subtraction (-), multiplication (*), and division (/). Division by zero produces a safe NULL result.

Comparison Operators

The main trick to remember with comparison operators is that, with the exception of a few special cases, comparing anything to NULL gives a NULL result. This includes comparing NULL to NULL:

```
select NULL=NULL;
```

```
+-----------+
| NULL=NULL |
+-----------+
|      NULL |
+-----------+
1 row in set (0.00 sec)
```

Compare this to the following query:

```
select NULL IS NULL;
```

```
+--------------+
| NULL IS NULL |
+--------------+
|            1 |
+--------------+
1 row in set (0.00 sec)
```

This reinforces the point that we made in Chapter 6, that you must be careful when using comparison operators when a NULL may be involved.

A second point to remember is that string comparisons in MySQL are case insensitive for the most part. If you want strings to be compared in a case-sensitive fashion, prefix one of them with the keyword BINARY. For example,

```
select * from department where name='marketing';
```

This query will match the word 'marketing' regardless of case, and we will get the following results:

```
+--------------+----------+
| departmentID | name     |
+--------------+----------+
|          130 | Marketing |
+--------------+----------+
1 row in set (0.41 sec)
```

If case is important, we can add the keyword binary as follows:

```
select * from department where name = binary 'marketing';
```

This will give us no matching rows in the employee database:

```
Empty set (0.18 sec)
```

Having said all that, let's look at the comparison operators. The most commonly used ones are shown in Table 8.1.

TABLE 8.1 **Comparison Operators**

Operator	Meaning
=	Equality
!= or <>	Inequality
<	Less than
<=	Less than or equal to
>	Greater than
>=	Greater than or equal to

TABLE 8.1   Continued

Operator	Meaning
n BETWEEN *min* AND *max*	Range testing
n IN (*set*)	Set membership. Can be used with a list of literal values or expressions or with a subquery as the set. An example of a set is (apple, orange, pear)
<=>	NULL safe equal. This will return 1 (true) if we compare two NULL values
n IS NULL	Use to test for a NULL value in *n*
ISNULL(*n*)	Use to test for a NULL value in *n*

Logical Operators

MySQL supports all the usual logical operators that can be used to join expressions. Logical expressions in MySQL can evaluate to 1 (true), 0 (false), or NULL. In addition, MySQL interprets any nonzero, non-null value as true.

Some of the truth tables are a little different from what you might expect when NULLs are involved. The logical operators are shown in Table 8.2.

TABLE 8.2   Logical Operators

Operator	Example	Meaning
AND or &&	*n* && *m*	Logical AND. Here is the truth table: true&&true = true false&&anything = false All other expressions evaluate to NULL.
OR or ||	*n* || *m*	Logical OR. Here is the truth table: true||anything = true NULL||false = NULL NULL||NULL = NULL false||false = false
NOT or !	NOT *n*	Logical NOT. Here is the truth table: !true = false !false = true !NULL = NULL
XOR	*n* XOR *m*	Logical exclusive OR. Here is the truth table: true XOR true = false true XOR false = true false XOR true = true NULL XOR *n* = NULL *n* XOR NULL = NULL

Control Flow Functions

The first set of functions we will consider are the control flow functions. The most useful of these are IF and CASE. These work similarly to an `if` statement and a `switch` or `case` statement (respectively) in most programming languages.

The IF function has the prototype

```
IF (e1, e2, e3)
```

If the expression *e1* is true, IF returns *e2*; otherwise, it returns *e3*. For example, using the employee database, we can run the following query:

```
select name, if(job='Programmer', "nerd", "not a nerd")
from employee;
```

This will produce the following result:

```
+---------------+----------------------------------------+
| name          | if(job='Programmer', "nerd", "not a nerd") |
+---------------+----------------------------------------+
| Ajay Patel    | nerd                                   |
| Nora Edwards  | nerd                                   |
| Candy Burnett | not a nerd                             |
| Ben Smith     | not a nerd                             |
+---------------+----------------------------------------+
4 rows in set (0.00 sec)
```

The CASE function has the following two possible prototypes (from the MySQL manual):

```
CASE value
WHEN [compare-value] THEN result
[WHEN [compare-value] THEN result ...]
[ELSE result]
END
```

or

```
CASE
WHEN [condition] THEN result
[WHEN [condition] THEN result ...]
[ELSE result]
END
```

We can use this function to return one of a number of values. For example, consider the following query:

```
select workdate, case
        when workdate < 2000-01-01 then "archived"
        when workdate < 2003-01-01 then "old"
        else "current"
        end
from assignment;
```

This query evaluates the workdate for each assignment in the assignment table. Assignments from the last century are categorized as "archived", ones prior to this year are categorized as "old", and everything else is "current".

String Functions

MySQL's string functions fall into two categories: the string processing functions and the string comparison functions. You will find the latter more useful than the former.

String Processing Functions

A list of the more useful string functions is shown in Table 8.3. There are many more in the manual.

TABLE 8.3   String Processing Functions

Function	Purpose
concat(s1, s2, ...)	Concatenate the strings in s1, s2, ...
conv (n, original_base, new_base)	Convert the number n from original_base to new_base. (It may surprise you to see this as a string function, but some bases use letters in their notations, such as hexadecimal.)
length(s)	Returns the length in characters of the string s.
load_file(filename)	Returns the contents of the file stored at filename as a string.
locate(needle, haystack, position)	Returns the starting position of the needle string in the haystack string. The search will start from position.
lower(s) and upper(s)	Convert the string s to lowercase or uppercase.
quote(s)	Escapes a string s so that it is suitable for insertion into the database. This involves putting the string between single quotes and inserting a backslash.
replace(target, find, replace)	Returns a string based on target with all incidences of find replaced with replace.
soundex(s)	Returns a soundex string corresponding to s. A soundex string represents how the string sounds when pronounced. It can be easier to match soundex strings of names than names themselves, for example.
substring (s, position, length)	Returns length characters from s starting at position.
trim(s)	Removes leading and trailing whitespace from s. (You can also use ltrim() to just remove whitespace from the left or rtrim() for the right.)

String Comparison Functions

In addition to offering the equality operator for comparing two strings, MySQL provides various comparison functions we can also use:

- LIKE: Performs string wildcard matching.
- RLIKE: Performs regular expression matching.
- STRCMP: String comparison, just like the strcmp() function in C.
- MATCH: Performs full-text searching.

We will discuss LIKE, RLIKE, and STRCMP in this section. Full-text searching is a feature specific to MyISAM tables. It is discussed in Chapter 9, "Understanding MySQL's Table Types."

Using LIKE for Wildcard Matching

Let's consider an example using LIKE:

```
select *
from department
where name like '%research%';
```

Rather than looking for names that are equal to 'research', we are looking for names containing 'research'. This produces the following results:

```
+--------------+-------------------------+
| departmentID | name                    |
+--------------+-------------------------+
|          128 | Research and Development |
+--------------+-------------------------+
1 row in set (0.04 sec)
```

The LIKE function supports two kinds of wildcard matching. The percentage sign (%), as used in the preceding example, matches any number of characters (including zero). Hence, the expression '%research%' matches all strings that have the word research in them somewhere. Note that string matching is generally case insensitive, as discussed earlier in this chapter.

The other wildcard character is the underscore (_). This matches any single character. For example '_at' matches the strings 'cat', 'mat', 'bat', and so on.

Using RLIKE for Regular Expression Matching

The RLIKE function can be used to match on the basis of regular expressions.

A regular expression is a pattern that describes the general shape of a string. There is a special notation for describing the features we would like to see in matching strings. We will take a brief look at this notation.

First, a literal string matches that string. So, the pattern 'cat' matches 'cat'. However, it also matches 'catacomb' and 'the cat sat on the mat'. The pattern 'cat' matches 'cat' anywhere inside the target string.

If we want to match only the word 'cat', then the pattern would need to be '^cat$'. The caret (^) means "anchor to the start of the string;" in other words, the first thing at the start of a matching string is the word 'cat'. The dollar sign ($) means "anchor to the end of the string;" in other words, the last thing in the string must be the word 'cat'. So, the pattern '^cat$' can match only the string 'cat' and nothing else.

Regular expressions also support wildcards, just as LIKE does. However, the wildcard is different. We have only one, the dot (.), that will match any single character. So, '.at' matches 'cat', 'bat', 'mat' and so on.

We only need a single wildcard character because we can also specify how often characters (including wildcards) can appear in a string.

For example, the special * character after a character means that character may appear zero or more times. So, the pattern 'n*' matches '', 'n', 'nn', 'nnn', and so on. We can group characters with parentheses, so '(cat)*' matches '', 'cat', 'catcat', 'catcatcat', and so on. We can also use a wildcard, so '.*' matches any number of any characters—basically anything.

Similarly, the plus sign (+) means that the character or string before it should be repeated one or more times, and the question mark (?) means to match zero times or one time. You can also list a specific range, so, for example, '(cat){2,4}' matches 'catcat', 'catcatcat', and 'catcatcatcat'.

As well as listing specific characters and strings, we can list sets of characters. These appear in square brackets. For example, the pattern '[a-z]' matches any single letter, and '[a-z]*' matches any number of letters.

Finally, there are a number of character classes, which are predefined sets. For example, [[:alnum:]] matches any alphanumeric character.

If you are a Perl programmer, it is worth noting that MySQL uses POSIX-style regular expressions, which have a different syntax from Perl regular expressions.

Now, let's look at an example of how to use these patterns with RLIKE. Consider the following query:

```
select * from department where name rlike 'an';
```

This will find all the department names that contain the string 'an' somewhere inside them:

```
+--------------+--------------------------+
| departmentID | name                     |
+--------------+--------------------------+
|           42 | Finance                  |
|          128 | Research and Development |
|          129 | Human Resources          |
+--------------+--------------------------+
3 rows in set (0.00 sec)
```

Regular expressions can be very powerful and can get quite complex. If you would like more examples and syntax detail, there are many good tutorials on the Web.

Using STRCMP() for String Comparison

The STRCMP() function in MySQL uses the same conventions as it does in other programming languages, such as C or PHP. It has the prototype

STRCMP(*s1*, *s2*)

and returns the following values:

- 0 if the strings are equal
- -1 if *s1* is less than *s2*—that is, if it comes before *s2* in the sort order
- 1 if *s1* is greater than *s2*—that is, if it comes after *s2* in the sort order

For example, the following queries return the following results:

```
mysql> select strcmp('cat', 'cat');
+----------------------+
| strcmp('cat', 'cat') |
+----------------------+
|                    0 |
+----------------------+
1 row in set (0.42 sec)

mysql> select strcmp('cat', 'dog');
+----------------------+
| strcmp('cat', 'dog') |
+----------------------+
|                   -1 |
+----------------------+
1 row in set (0.00 sec)

mysql> select strcmp('cat', 'ant');
+----------------------+
| strcmp('cat', 'ant') |
+----------------------+
|                    1 |
+----------------------+
1 row in set (0.00 sec)
```

Note that sort order changes with the character set. If you are using a non-English language such as German, strings will still sort in the order you expect them to, as long as you have set the character encoding when creating the table.

Numeric Functions

A list of the more useful numeric functions is shown in Table 8.4. There are many more in the manual.

TABLE 8.4   **Numeric Functions**

Function	Purpose
abs(*n*)	Returns the absolute value of *n*—that is, the value without a sign in front of it.
ceiling(*n*)	Returns the value of *n* rounded up to the nearest integer.
floor(*n*)	Returns the value of *n* rounded down to the nearest integer.
mod(*n*,*m*) and div	These two functions divide *n* by *m*. div returns the integral quotient, and mod() returns the integral remainder.
power(*n*,*m*)	Returns *n* to the power of *m*.
rand(*n*)	Returns a random number between 0 and 1. The parameter *n* is optional, but if supplied, it is used as a seed for the pseudorandom number generation. (Giving the same *n* to rand will produce the same pseudorandom number.)
round(*n*[,*d*])	Returns *n* rounded to the nearest integer. If you supply *d*, *n* will be rounded to *d* decimal places.
sqrt(*n*)	Returns the square root of *n*.

Let's look at an example using mod() and div. One confusing thing about these functions is that whereas mod can be expressed as

mod(9,2)

or

9 mod 2

or even

9 % 2

the div function can be expressed only as

9 div 2

So, for example,

div(9, 2)

will not work and will give a syntax error.

Running mod and div in MySQL gives the following results:

```
mysql> select 9 mod 2;
+---------+
| 9 mod 2 |
+---------+
|       1 |
+---------+
1 row in set (0.00 sec)

mysql> select 9 div 2;
+---------+
| 9 div 2 |
+---------+
|       4 |
+---------+
1 row in set (0.00 sec)
```

Date and Time Functions

A list of the more useful date and time functions is shown in Table 8.5. Because of MySQL's data warehousing heritage, it has a very extensive set of time and date functions. The list here is far from complete.

TABLE 8.5 **Date and Time Functions**

Function	Purpose
adddate(*date*, INTERVAL *n type*) and subdate(*date*, INTERVAL *n type*)	These functions are used to add and subtract dates. Both start from the date supplied in *date* and add or subtract the period specified after the keyword INTERVAL. You need to specify both a quantity *n* and the type of that quantity.
	The type can be SECOND, MINUTE, HOUR, DAY, MONTH, YEAR, MINUTE:SECOND (the format of n should be 'm:s'), HOUR:MINUTE ('h:m'), DAY_HOUR ('d h'), YEAR_MONTH ('y-m'), HOUR_SECOND ('h:m:s'), DAY_MINUTE ('d h:m'), DAY_SECOND ('d h:m:s').
	These functions are really useful, but remembering the data formats is virtually impossible (because they are all different), so you will usually have to look them up.

TABLE 8.5   **Continued**

Function	Purpose
curdate(), curtime(), now()	These return the current date, the current time, and the current date and time, respectively.
date_format(*date*, *format*) and time_format(*time*, *format*)	These are used to reformat dates and times to pretty much any format you like. You do this by supplying a format string, such as date_format(workdate, '%W %D of %M, %Y'). (This gives, for example, 'Monday 16th of June, 2003'). There is a massive list of formats, so consult the manual for details.
dayname(*date*)	This returns the name of the day in *date* (for example, 'Monday').
extract(*type* FROM *date*)	This returns the value of *type* in *date*. For example, if you specify YEAR, it will return the year from *date*. The types are the same as in adddate() and subdate().
unix_timestamp(*[date]*)	This returns the current Unix timestamp. (That's the number of seconds since the first of January 1970.) If called with a *date*, this returns the timestamp corresponding to that *date*.

Let's look at an example using adddate(). We will start from the 1st of January 1999 and add 1 year and 6 months to it:

```
select adddate("1999-01-01", INTERVAL "1-6" YEAR_MONTH);
```

We get the following result:

```
+-------------------------------------------------+
| adddate("1999-01-01", INTERVAL "1-6" YEAR_MONTH) |
+-------------------------------------------------+
| 2000-07-01                                      |
+-------------------------------------------------+
1 row in set (0.41 sec)
```

For many applications in which you are formatting output with an external program, this may not be the most useful way to receive the date. Unix timestamps are not humanly readable, but they are very compatible with the APIs that come with other programming languages.

The same query with the unix_timestamp() function

```
select unix_timestamp(adddate("1999-01-01", INTERVAL "1-6" YEAR_MONTH));
```

generates output useless to humans but directly usable by other code that is such as the date() function built into PHP:

```
+-----------------------------------------------------------------+
| unix_timestamp(adddate("1999-01-01", INTERVAL "1-6" YEAR_MONTH)) |
+-----------------------------------------------------------------+
|                                                       962373600 |
+-----------------------------------------------------------------+
1 row in set (0.01 sec)
```

Cast Functions

There are only two cast functions, cast() and convert(). They do the same thing with slightly different syntaxes. Cast functions perform typecasting—that is, they convert results from one type (for example, signed integer) to another (for example, char).

The prototypes are as shown here:

```
cast(expression AS type)
convert(expression, type)
```

The cast() function is ANSI compliant, and convert() is ODBC compliant.

Valid types are BINARY, CHAR, DATE, DATETIME, SIGNED (INTEGER), and UNSIGNED (INTEGER).

Most casting in MySQL happens automatically when needed; for example, if feeding numbers into a string function, they will automatically be cast as strings.

Other Functions

MySQL also has a set of miscellaneous functions. Many of these have to do with hashing or encryption, but there are also some other very useful functions in this set. A list of the more useful ones is shown in Table 8.6.

TABLE 8.6   Miscellaneous Functions

Function	Purpose
benchmark(count, expression)	Evaluates *expression* *count* times. Always returns zero—the point of this function is to time execution and look at the execution time at the bottom of the result set.
encrypt(s[,salt])	Encrypts *s* using a Unix crypt system call. The *salt* string is an optional two-character string. If crypt is not available on your system (for example, Windows), this function will return NULL.

TABLE 8.6   **Continued**

Function	Purpose
found_rows()	Returns the number of rows that would have been returned by the last query if no limit clause was used. Works only if SQL_CALC_FOUND_ROWS was specified in the SELECT statement, as discussed in Chapter 7.
last_insert_id()	Returns the last automatically generated AUTO_INCREMENT value. This is useful if we have inserted a row into one table and now need that row's id to insert as a foreign key into another table.
md5(s)	Returns the 128-bit MD5 hash of string s. If you are writing an application to store usernames and passwords, this is the recommended method for storing passwords in your database.
	Encryption algorithms have a limited useful lifetime. As the power of computers increases, stronger algorithms are required. MD5 is currently regarded as fairly secure.
password(s)	Calculates a password string for the string s. This is the scheme that is used to represent MySQL user passwords, as we will discuss in Chapter 11, "Managing User Privileges." It is *not* recommended that you use password() to store passwords in your own applications.

Functions for Use with GROUP BY Clauses

Some functions are designed specifically for use with GROUP BY. These are sometimes called grouping functions or aggregate functions. You can also choose to run these functions over the entire result set of a query, treating all the rows as a single group. We saw this used in queries like this:

```
select count(*)
from employee;
```

This query will count the number of rows in the employee table.

We typically use these functions over groups, as shown here:

```
select job, count(job)
from employee
group by job;
```

This will tell us how many employees are in each job grouping.

A list of the more useful grouping functions is shown in Table 8.7.

TABLE 8.7 **Grouping Functions**

Function	Purpose
avg(*column*)	Returns the average value in *column*.
count(*column*)	Returns the number of values in *column*.
min(*column*)	Returns the smallest value in *column*.
max(*column*)	Returns the largest value in *column*.
std(*column*)	Returns the standard deviation of the values in *column*.
sum(*column*)	Returns the sum of values in *column*.

Summary

- MySQL has a full set of arithmetic, comparison, and logical operators. You need to be careful when using operators with NULL because this does not always produce the expected results.
- MySQL provides a set of functions that can be used to perform string, numeric, date, casting, and miscellaneous functions.
- The grouping functions are performed over a set of column values. These sets are groups if a GROUP BY clause is specified, or they provide the complete set of returned values in a column if no GROUP BY clause is specified.

Quiz

1. Which one of the following operators *cannot* be used to test whether a value is NULL?

    a) ISNULL()

    b) <=>

    c) IS NULL

    d) =

2. The call strcmp('fred', 'Fred') returns

    a) -1

    b) 0

    c) 1

    d) 2

3. Which of the following functions would you use to retrieve the name of a month from a date?

   a) dayname()

   b) extract()

   c) subdate()

   d) now()

4. Which of the following functions does MySQL use to encrypt its own internal user passwords?

   a) password()

   b) encrypt()

   c) md5()

   d) sha()

5. If we use a grouping function in a SELECT statement with no GROUP BY clause,

   a) we will get a syntax error

   b) the entire table will be treated as one group

   c) the entire result set will be treated as one group

   d) each row will be treated as one group

Exercises

1. Write a query that returns employee names and jobs, but, if an employee's job is 'Programmer', rewrites this as 'Analyst / Programmer'.

2. Write a query to insert a new department called Property Services. Then, write a query to insert a new employee called Fred Smith, job DBA, who works for that department. Use last_insert_id() to insert the department number.

3. Write a query that selects the most recent assignment from the assignment table. (Hint: use the max() grouping function.)

Answers

Quiz

1. d
2. b
3. b
4. a
5. c

Exercises

1.

```
select name, replace(job, 'Programmer', 'Analyst/Programmer')
from employee;
```

2.

```
insert into department values
(NULL, 'Property Services');
```

```
insert into employee values
(NULL, 'Fred Smith', 'DBA', last_insert_id());
```

3.)

```
select max(workdate) from assignment;
```

Next

This completes Part III, "Using MySQL." In the next part of the book, "MySQL Table Types and Transactions," we will look at the different storage engines MySQL supports and their special features.

IV

MySQL Table Types and Transactions

9   Understanding MySQL's Table Types

10   Using Transactions with InnoDB Tables

9

Understanding MySQL's Table Types

In this chapter, we'll review the different table types available to the MySQL database designer. We have generally used InnoDB or MyISAM tables in the examples in this book, but there are others.

Designing a database management system, like many other design tasks, involves many compromises. For example, many database tasks should be done in a transaction-safe way, but providing for this increases time, disk, and memory requirements. The creators of MySQL have deferred some of the compromises to you, the database designer, by offering you a choice of table types. You can choose one of the transaction-safe types, if needed, for your application, or you can choose a higher performance non–transaction-safe type. In any case, you need to know what compromises you are making.

You might hear table types referred to as storage engines. This reflects the fact that some of the table types rely on large amounts of separate source code that manage their own caching, indexing, locking, and disk access. It also reflects the core of a database's purpose: It stores things.

The term *transaction* or *transaction safe* will come up a lot in this chapter. It is an important criterion to understand when selecting a table type. Examples so far in the book have involved SQL queries being executed in isolation, but for many applications, this is not what really happens.

Imagine for a moment that you had a database that contained bank account details. If you wanted to transfer $1,000 from one account to another, you would need at least two SQL queries—one to deduct $1,000 from one account, and one to add $1,000 to the other. It would be a disaster if something (such as a power failure) caused one query to complete, but the other to fail. It would be far preferable in a case like this for the two related queries to either both happen or both fail because the database must be left in a consistent state.

Transaction-safe tables allow you to specify that a set of queries is one indivisible unit of work—a transaction. The whole transaction should complete, or the database must *roll back* or return to the same state it was in before the transaction started.

We will cover transactions and the MySQL syntax to use them in Chapter 10, "Using Transactions with InnoDB Tables."

The table types available in MySQL are

- ISAM
- MyISAM
- InnoDB
- BerkeleyDB (BDB)
- MERGE
- HEAP

We will look at each table type in turn, but will devote most space to the most commonly used types: MyISAM and InnoDB. InnoDB and BerkeleyDB are transaction safe. The others (ISAM, MyISAM, MERGE, and HEAP) are not.

We will also cover the special features of MyISAM tables in this chapter, specifically compressed tables and full-text searching. We will spend the whole of Chapter 10 on the special features of the InnoDB storage engine.

ISAM Tables

ISAM tables are included in MySQL purely for legacy support. Their functionality has been entirely replaced by MyISAM tables, so they will not be examined in any detail here. They are scheduled to be removed from MySQL in version 5.0.

The following code will create an ISAM table, should you want to for some reason:

```
create table asset
(
  assetID int not null,
  description varchar(255)
) type=ISAM;
```

ISAM tables offer fast but not transaction-safe storage. Most of what we will say about MyISAM tables holds true for ISAM tables, but the older ISAM tables have several limitations.

Improvements offered by MyISAM include the following:

- *Table portability.* Tables stored on disk or backup media can be loaded onto another system running MySQL, regardless of the platform. This is not true for ISAM tables.
- *Support for very large tables.* ISAM tables have a hard limit of 4GB. MyISAM allows tables to be as large as the underlying operating system will allow. This will be important only to some users, and it means choosing your operating system (and file system) carefully. Many file systems limit files to being 2GB in size. (Note that we can actually get around this limitation using MERGE tables.)

- *More efficient use of disk space.* Spaces and fragmentation are reduced.
- *Less restricted keys.* ISAM tables allow 16 keys per table and a default maximum key length of 256 bytes. MyISAM tables allow 64 keys per table and a default maximum key length of 1024 bytes.

ISAM tables should be regarded as being deprecated. They still exist, but they should not be used for new development. If you have any existing ISAM tables, you should strongly consider converting them to MyISAM. It takes very little effort and offers significant advantages.

MyISAM Tables

Many people use MySQL for years without discovering that it offers different table types. These people are using MyISAM tables because this has been the default in all recent versions.

MyISAM tables offer very fast but not transaction-safe storage. They provide high performance in most situations, even if the designer makes mistakes, and in the hands of a skilled administrator, they can handle massive and/or busy databases.

The following code will create a MyISAM table:

```
create table article (
  articleID int not null auto_increment primary key,
  title varchar(255),
  body text
);
```

The final line could optionally have been

```
) type=MyISAM;
```

but would produce the same result.

MyISAM tables can be one of three types: dynamic, static, or compressed. A table automatically becomes dynamic or static depending on the definition of its columns. Compressed tables must be deliberately created with the myisampack tool.

Tables with fixed-length rows will be created as static tables, and tables with variable-length rows will be created as dynamic tables. How can we tell whether a table has fixed- or variable-length rows?

The char and numeric types all have a fixed size. The size of varchar, text, and blob columns can vary with the size of their contents. A table with only char and numeric columns will be created as a static table, but a table containing any varchar, text, or blob columns will be dynamic.

In the section "Full-Text Searching on MyISAM Tables," we will create an example table called article. This will be created as a dynamic table because it contains a varchar column and a text column. The storage requirement for each row in the table will therefore vary depending on the amount of data in each of these fields.

There are a number of advantages to a static table. It is faster to search than a dynamic table or a compressed table. It is very easy for the database to retrieve a particular record based on an index when each record is at a particular offset from the start of the file. It is very easy to cache. It is less likely to suffer serious corruption in the event of a crash—the repair facility can usually recover all rows except the damaged one.

The disadvantage to static tables is that forcing real data to fit into fixed-size columns nearly always wastes disk space. This may be a price you are willing to pay for data that varies only a little in size, such as people's names, but are unwilling to pay for data that varies a great deal in size. If you decide that nearly all employee surnames will be less than 80 characters, you may or may not be willing to waste 75 bytes each time you store a Smith.

Dynamic tables need more complex management within MySQL. It is not as straight-forward a task for the engine to cache, find, or repair records. This is partly just because they vary in size, but it is also because they can become fragmented. If a row is modified and becomes larger, part of its data will remain at the original location, and part will be stored as a new fragment elsewhere in the file. This means that a segment of a file that has been cached by the operating system cannot be guaranteed to contain all parts of a row. Corruption may also be harder to fix because if fragments or links become lost, it will not be obvious which parts belong to which rows.

To repair or defragment a MyISAM table, you can use the command-line tool myisamchk or the MySQL command REPAIR TABLE. (This is covered in more detail in Chapter 13, "Administering Your Database.") To defragment but not repair, you can use the MySQL command OPTIMIZE TABLE. (This is covered in more detail in Chapter 18, "Optimizing Your Database.")

Compressing MyISAM Tables

Although tables become static or dynamic without your specific request (but in response to your design decisions), tables are not automatically compressed. To compress a table, you need to use the command-line program myisampack. (There is a version of this for pure ISAM tables, should you be using them, which is called pack_isam.)

Compression sounds like a positive thing, but it makes sense only for some applications because compressed tables become read-only. If you need to alter, update, or insert data in the table, you need to uncompress the entire table, make your changes, and then recompress the table.

The compression performed by myisampack includes a mixture of true compression (Huffman coding) and a set of optimizations aimed at shrinking columns, such as converting types to smaller types and converting columns to enums. Because each record is compressed separately, there is only a small overhead to be paid when decompressing a record. This may even be counterbalanced on slow devices by the reduction in data that needs to be read from disk.

Full–Text Searching on MyISAM Tables

One feature that currently comes only with MyISAM tables is full-text searching and indexing. Normal indexes are very good at finding rows where a value in the table matches a given value, but it is common to want to search for words or strings within a block of text. This is where full-text searching comes in handy.

The following SQL will create a MyISAM table with a full-text index:

```
create table article (
  articleID int not null auto_increment primary key,
  title varchar(255),
  body text,
  fulltext (title,body)
);
```

The following query will retrieve any records containing the word 'merger':

```
select title
from article
where match (title,body) against ('merger');
```

More complicated searches are supported. The following query will retrieve records containing any of the words 'merge', 'acquisition', 'acquire', or 'takeover'.

```
select title from article
where match (title,body) against ('merge acquisition acquire takeover');
```

Note that we are matching any record that contains at least one of the words. We are not searching for the string or for a record containing every word listed. We can do both of these types of searches using the IN BOOLEAN MODE modifier, which we will come to later.

We needed to search for 'acquire' and 'acquisitions' separately because MySQL does not currently support stemming. Stemming is a technique implemented in many other full-text search systems that recognizes sets of words as having a common stem word. For example, 'acquire' is the stem of many words such as 'acquires', 'acquired', and 'acquisition'.

Each match found is assigned a relevance value, and the results are automatically sorted into relevance order. You may want to see the relevance scores for records. The following query will retrieve an unsorted list of scores for all records. Any records with a score of zero have no similarity and will not be retrieved.

```
select title, match (title,body)
against ('merge acquisition acquire takeover')
as relevance
from article;
```

Note that relevance is not a keyword. It is just an alias for match(title,body) against ('merge acquisition acquire takeover'). We have included it so that the output will be tidier.

More usefully, the following query will retrieve article titles and scores for matched documents. Because we have the MATCH condition in the WHERE clause, the results will be sorted, and unrelated rows will be ignored.

```
select title, match (title,body)
against ('merge acquisition acquire takeover')
as relevance
from article
where match (title,body) against ('merge acquisition acquire takeover');
```

There are certain words you cannot search for. To improve performance, some words are excluded from indexes or are ignored when searching.

Short words are not indexed. By default, words with fewer than four characters are ignored. For some installations, most famously Slashdot.org, this is a problem because three-letter acronyms are often an important part of the content in technical material. You can change this limit by altering the variable ft_min_word_len, but you will need to regenerate your indexes.

Stop words are used by full-text indexes. A stop word is a word with no semantic value. Generally, these are common words that are important for sentence construction, but are unlikely to be important parts of the content. Words like 'the', 'and', 'then', and 'soon' are necessary, but are not usually useful to search for. As well as providing standard lists, MySQL allows you to specify your own list of stop words for each human language you are indexing.

One thing to note about full-text indexing is that because it is a complex task, it has some very real performance limits. When your MySQL tables get large (say more than 1,000,000 rows), full-text search performance slows down. For small applications this should not be a problem, but for larger applications you should keep this fact in mind.

Words that are common in your data are not used when searching. If your table contains company newsletter articles for Acme PTY Ltd., it is likely that many articles would contain the word 'Acme'. Searching for this would generate many results, which is not usually a good thing. If 50% or more of your records contain a word, that word is taken to have no value when calculating relevance.

Boolean Full-Text Search

You can exert greater control over the search by using the IN BOOLEAN MODE modifier.

The following query will match only records than contain the word 'linux' and the string "Open Source", but not the word 'desktop'. The words 'Java' and 'Oracle' are optional, but when deciding on relevance, finding 'Java' in a record will improve its ranking, whereas finding 'Oracle' will degrade the ranking. The order of words in the search string or the record is not important.

```
select title
from article
where match (title,body)
       against ('+linux +"Open Source" -desktop Java ~Oracle' IN BOOLEAN MODE);
```

The full set of operators is shown in Table 9.1.

TABLE 9.1   **Boolean Mode Search Operators**

Operator	Meaning
+	This word is compulsory.
-	This word must not appear.
<	This word is less important.
>	This word is more important.
( )	Group words together as a subexpression.
~	This word may appear, but it has a negative effect on ranking.
*	Wildcard suffix. For example, `merge` will not match `merger`, but `merge*` will match both `merge` and `merger`. May be used only at the end of a word.
" "	This is a phrase. Matches only exactly the same content in the same order.

It is not required that you have full-text indexes to do Boolean mode searches. You can search unindexed tables this way, but it will be very slow.

Another small difference between full-text searches and Boolean searches is that when the search is done in Boolean mode, words that are common in your data are not ignored. The 50% rule does not apply. If we were searching Acme PTY Ltd. newsletter articles, the next query would probably return nearly all rows, whereas the one following that would result in an empty result set.

```
select title from article
where match (title,body) against ('Acme' IN BOOLEAN MODE);

select title from article
where match (title,body) against ('Acme');
```

InnoDB Tables

The next table type we will discuss is InnoDB. InnoDB is a fast, transaction-safe storage engine. Its transaction capabilities are so important that we will spend the entire next chapter discussing how to use them.

InnoDB tables offer

- *Transactions.* See Chapter 10.

- *Row-level locking.* This means that only the row we are using in a particular query is unavailable to other users. Most of the other storage engines (with the exception of BDB) use table-level locking—that is, while one process is updating a table, it is not available to other processes.

- *Support for foreign keys.* The examples in earlier chapters that include foreign keys would not work with other table types.

- *Consistent nonlocking reads in* SELECTs. (The idea for this is borrowed from Oracle.)

InnoDB has its own configuration options, its own directory, and its own way of storing data. Whereas MyISAM stores one table per file, InnoDB stores all its tables and indexes in a tablespace, which means that they may be stored over multiple files. This allows InnoDB to have very large tables that will be unaffected by any operating-system file size restrictions. Note, though, that in comparison to MyISAM, an InnoDB table uses a lot more disk space to store the same records.

We will spend the next chapter, Chapter 10, discussing how to use the special features in InnoDB.

InnoDB requires a certain amount of configuration effort. We supplied a basic configuration in Chapter 1, "Installing MySQL," and we will discuss these options in more depth in Chapter 12, "Configuring MySQL."

InnoDB, though developed separately from most of MySQL, is available under the same dual-licensing agreement.

Many of the large, high-profile Web sites that use MySQL, such as Slashdot (www.slashdot.org), Google (www.google.com), and Yahoo! Finance (http://finance.yahoo.com), use the InnoDB engine. It is especially good for dealing with large volumes of data at high speeds in a transaction-safe environment.

InnoDB is one of the fastest transaction-safe systems in the world, but providing this safety involves sacrifices. For most usage patterns, MyISAM will be faster, but the difference will not generally be huge.

InnoDB is made by a separate company, InnoBase Oy, and it has its own Web site. For the most up-to-date information on InnoDB, go to www.innodb.com.

BerkeleyDB (BDB) Tables

The other option you have for a transaction-safe storage engine for MySQL is BerkeleyDB (usually abbreviated to BDB). BDB is provided by Sleepycat software (www.sleepycat.com). It is not as widely used for transaction work in MySQL as InnoDB. The BDB engine has been around for a long time, but the MySQL integration is still relatively new, and the manual tells us the interface with MySQL is of "gamma" quality. That is, it's more reliable than a beta, but with the odd bug. Mind you, MySQL's idea of beta tends to be more reliable than many companies' gold releases.

BDB uses page-level locking and, as such, will give you slightly worse performance than InnoDB. It is also slow if you open a large number of tables at the same time.

All BDB tables must have a primary key (not that this is much of a problem because we would recommend this anyway). In fact, one will be created silently for you if you do not create one for yourself.

BDB tables are stored as b-trees. Compare this to most other table types that store their indexes as b-trees. This slows down table scanning (such as when you are retrieving all rows from the table or performing unindexed queries). BDB tables also take up more space on disk.

One important limitation of BDB tables is that you cannot move the stored data around on disk. This is because the data stored for a table includes the path to the data. You must also be careful when backing up BDB tables to remember to back up the log files because you will be unable to restart without them.

MERGE Tables

MERGE tables are a clever way to get around operating-system restrictions on maximum file sizes. Because each MyISAM table is stored in a single file, tables are limited in size by the maximum file size of the operating system. We get around this by creating a MERGE table, a construct that allows you to treat multiple MyISAM tables as a single table for the purpose of queries.

Let's look at an example. Code to create a MERGE table consisting of three log tables is shown in Listing 9.1.

LISTING 9.1   **A MERGE Table Example**

```
create database logs;
use logs;

create table log2003Jan
(logid int auto_increment primary key,
logts datetime,
entry char(255));
insert into log2003Jan values
(NULL, '2003-01-01', 'first jan entry');

create table log2003Feb
(logid int auto_increment primary key,
logts datetime,
entry char(255));
insert into log2003Feb values
(NULL, '2003-02-01', 'first feb entry');

create table log2003Mar
(logid int auto_increment primary key,
logts datetime,
entry char(255));
insert into log2003Mar values
(NULL, '2003-03-01', 'first mar entry');

create table logs
(logid int auto_increment primary key,
logts datetime,
entry char(255))
type = merge
union = (log2003Jan, log2003Feb, log2003Mar)
insert_method = last;
```

What we have done in this listing is to create three tables that are identical in structure, log2003Jan, log2003Feb, and log2003Mar. Logging is a common application of MERGE tables, as you will see in a moment.

After inserting some test data into these three tables, we have created a MERGE table of the three. We have done this by creating a table called logs that has the same structure as the three tables to be merged and by specifying that it is of type MERGE and that it is the UNION of the three tables. We also specify the INSERT_METHOD as last. This means that if we insert data into the MERGE table, it will be added to the last table in the merge, in this case log2003Mar. The other options are FIRST (insert into the first table in the list) or NO (don't allow inserts into the MERGE table).

This gives us a table we can interact with that appears to contain all the data in the merged tables. If we run the query

```
select * from logs;
```

we will obtain the following output:

```
+-------+---------------------+-----------------+
| logid | logts               | entry           |
+-------+---------------------+-----------------+
|     1 | 2003-01-01 00:00:00 | first jan entry |
|     1 | 2003-02-01 00:00:00 | first feb entry |
|     1 | 2003-03-01 00:00:00 | first mar entry |
+-------+---------------------+-----------------+
3 rows in set (0.01 sec)
```

As you can see, all the data from the three tables is represented. One really important thing to note is that although we specified logid as the primary key in the MERGE table, it is a bit different from the way primary keys normally work. Usually, they must be unique, but because the MERGE table manages three sets of primary keys, there may well be more than one row with the same primary key, as in the preceding output.

Even with the MERGE table, we can still query the component tables as usual. We cannot DROP, ALTER, DELETE FROM TABLE, REPAIR, TRUNCATE, OPTIMIZE, or ANALYZE any of the component tables. You will be able to do some of these things (DELETE FROM TABLE) if the MERGE table is not currently open. You can close it with FLUSH TABLES. The manual says that you should be able to do any of these things after a FLUSH, but we have found that this is sometimes not the case. For example, at the time of writing, dropping one of the component tables leads to the MERGE table also being silently dropped. If you need to make these sorts of changes, you may be better off dropping the MERGE table and re-creating it. Dropping the MERGE table does not affect the component tables or their data.

You can compress individual tables in the MERGE with myisampack. This is particularly useful for examples like ours, in which we are storing logfiles—we can compress the earlier months' log files because we are writing to only the most recent log.

HEAP Tables

HEAP tables are extremely fast tables that are stored wholly in memory. They use a hashed indexing scheme that is responsible for their speed.

The downside to having tables stored completely in memory is, of course, that if you have any power issues, your HEAP data is gone forever. They are, however, great for storing temporary tables.

You can create a HEAP table like this:

```
create table testHeap
(id int not null primary key,
data char(100))
type=heap
max_rows = 100;
```

As you can see, we have specified the table type as HEAP. We have also followed a good practice guideline here by limiting the maximum number of rows in the table. If your HEAP tables grow large, you can easily run out of memory. The number of rows can also be limited by the configuration directive max_heap_table_size.

HEAP tables have a few limitations:

- They don't support AUTO_INCREMENT.
- They don't support BLOB or TEXT types.
- HEAP tables cannot use the leftmost prefix of an index to find rows. (If you would like more information about what this means, you can read more about indexing in Chapter 19.)
- Indexes will be used only to find rows with queries that use the = or <=> operators in the search clause.

Summary

- MySQL has six table types: ISAM, MyISAM, InnoDB, BDB, MERGE, and HEAP.
- Only InnoDB and BDB tables are transaction safe.
- Only MyISAM tables support full-text indexing and searching.

ISAM

- ISAM had been deprecated and superceded by MyISAM.
- ISAM tables have a hard size limit of 4GB.
- ISAM tables are not portable.
- You can have a maximum of 16 keys per table and a maximum key length of 256 bytes (characters).

MyISAM

- MyISAM is the default table type. It is very fast, but not transaction safe.
- MyISAM tables support table compression.
- The size of MyISAM tables is limited only by the operating system, and this can be worked around with MERGE tables.
- The data files that store MyISAM tables are portable from system to system.
- You can have a maximum of 64 keys per table and a maximum key length of 1024 bytes.

InnoDB

- InnoDB tables are transaction safe.
- InnoDB supports row-level locking.
- There is no theoretical maximum table size because tables may be stored in more than one file.
- InnoDB provides consistent nonlocking reads in SELECT.
- InnoDB tables are portable from system to system.
- InnoDB tables take more disk space than MyISAM tables.
- Foreign keys are supported between InnoDB tables.

BDB

- Like InnoDB tables, BDB tables are transaction safe. BDB tables are not as widely used with MySQL as InnoDB.
- BDB supports page-level locking.
- BDB tables are not portable.

MERGE

- MERGE tables are used to treat multiple MyISAM tables as a single table, and therefore, the maximum file size limitation is removed from MyISAM tables.

HEAP

- HEAP tables are stored only in memory and need to be limited in size to avoid running out of memory.
- Data stored in a HEAP table is volatile and will be lost in the event of a power failure.
- HEAP tables are super fast, as long as you have enough physical memory to keep them.
- HEAP tables do not support AUTO_INCREMENT, TEXT, or BLOB.

Quiz

1. We need transactions and tables that can easily be ported to another system. We should use
   a) ISAM
   b) MyISAM
   c) InnoDB
   d) BDB

2. We need to create a temporary table for fast lookups. We should use
   a) ISAM
   b) MyISAM
   c) MERGE
   d) HEAP

3. We need to have extremely large tables. We should *not* use
   a) ISAM
   b) MERGE
   c) InnoDB
   d) any of the above

4. We need to perform a full-text search. We should use
   a) MyISAM
   b) InnoDB
   c) BDB
   d) HEAP

5. Consider the following full-text search query:

```
select title
from article
where match (title,body)
        against ('+php +pdf pdflib >tutorial ~reference' IN BOOLEAN MODE);
```

Which of the following statements about this query is *false*?

a) The importance of the search term `'tutorial'` is increased.

b) The ranking of results containing `'reference'` will be increased.

c) Search results must contain `'php'`.

d) Search results that contain `'pdflib'` will be ranked more highly than those that do not.

Exercises

For this chapter, there are no formal exercises, but you might like to experiment with creating and using tables of the different types.

Answers

Quiz

1. c
2. d
3. a
4. a
5. b

Next

In the next chapter, "Using Transactions with InnoDB Tables," we will discuss exactly what is meant by a transaction, why transactions are so important, and how to implement them with InnoDB tables.

## 10

Using Transactions with InnoDB Tables

In this chapter, we will cover transactions in MySQL. When dealing with practical examples, we will primarily look at the InnoDB table type, but nearly everything said here applies equally well to BerkeleyDB tables.

Specifically, we will look at the following:

- What transactions are
- Using transactions in MySQL
- The InnoDB transaction model and ACID compliance

What Are Transactions?

The first thing to address in this chapter is what exactly is a transaction? In the context of a database management system, a transaction is a sequence of related instructions that must be treated as one indivisible unit. That is, all the work in the transaction must be done, or all of it must be left undone. This concept is known as atomicity. A transaction is atomic because it cannot be broken down into parts—it all gets processed or it all gets ignored.

This has particular implications when considering concurrent access by multiple users, processes, or threads and also for recovery. Modern computers are often accessed by more than one person at a time. They usually have more than one program running at one time, and they often run programs such as Web server software that create many processes or threads that run at the same time. Each of these users, programs, processes, or threads may need access to the database server.

Multiple threads must not interfere with each other when running concurrently. If an error occurs, the database must honor transactions when recovering. This means returning the database to the state it was in before the error occurred or finishing the whole transaction. It is generally better to lose an entire transaction of related changes than to recover to a state partway through a sequence of updates that might result in the database being in an inconsistent state.

This concept can be expressed more formally, but an example is probably the easiest way to come to grips with it. Consider a very simple (but potentially very important) database that records bank account details. Each account has, at minimum, a unique identifier and a balance.

We can create this table as follows:

```
create table account
(
  number int not null auto_increment primary key,
  balance float
) type = InnoDB;
```

It probably is not a shock that we can create two new accounts with these queries:

```
insert into account (balance) values (0.0);
insert into account (balance) values (1000.0);
insert into account (balance) values (2000.0);
```

There is not very much that can go wrong here, and the result should be this data:

```
+--------+---------+
| number | balance |
+--------+---------+
|      1 |       0 |
|      2 |    1000 |
|      3 |    2000 |
+--------+---------+
```

As long as we are not making assumptions about the account numbers generated by the auto-increment column, it does not matter in what order these queries are eventually run. It does not matter if we are running them from three different interactive clients simultaneously and cannot be sure which will be processed first.

This is often not true for more complex queries or sets of queries. Consider the following pair of statements intended to deposit $500 into account 2:

```
# first check balance
select balance from account where number = 2;
# query gives us a result of $1000
# now store updated balance
update account set balance = 1500 where number = 2;
```

These queries are related. They need to be run together. If other clients can update the balance of this account between our balance check and our balance update, we may not get the result we expected.

If two clients were running pairs of queries like this at the same time, our final result would depend on timing. If we were attempting to deposit $500 with these queries and another client was attempting to deposit $100 with the following pair, the end result could be a balance of $1100 or $1500—neither of which is the right result.

```
# first check balance
select balance from account where number = 2;
# query gives us a result of $1000
# now store updated balance
update account set balance = 1100 where number = 2;
```

This is obviously not desirable, but in this case the problem is easily solved. Making our updates relative rather than absolute will make them into single, indivisible units and will solve the problem. The following query will run correctly, regardless of what other queries are running at the same time:

```
update account set balance = balance + 500 where number = 2;
```

A single update statement in MySQL is always atomic. It cannot be interrupted by another query or half succeed. It will complete or will completely fail on an error.

More complex scenarios are harder to address. Consider the following pair of queries intended to transfer $1000 from account 2 to account 1:

```
update account set balance = balance - 1000 where number = 2;
update account set balance = balance + 1000 where number = 1;
```

Our updates are both relative, but it is important that these two queries be run together for sensible results. The total amount of money in the system should be the same after the queries as before. Money should be moved from account to account, not created or destroyed. If a power failure happened between running the first query and running the second query, our data would no longer be consistent.

In simple cases, a workaround is to collapse the queries into one SQL statement. In this case we could write this:

```
update account as source, account as dest
  set source.balance = source.balance - 1000,
    dest.balance = dest.balance + 1000
  where source.number = 2 and dest.number = 1;
```

By using two aliases to the account table (source and dest), we have ensured that this is one atomic update that will either succeed or fail. We do not need to worry about the server stopping between parts of our operation.

In this case the only casualty is readability. The combined query is harder to read and debug than our first attempt.

In many cases, it may not be possible to collapse all the related queries into one like this. The solution in those cases, and anytime you want more readable code, is to use MySQL's transaction syntax. By marking a set of statements as a transaction, you inform the database that they are a related, indivisible set. They should be treated as an atomic unit and either all succeed or all have no effect. You can run these two queries as a single transaction using the following SQL statements:

```
start transaction;
update account set balance = balance - 1000 where number = 2;
update account set balance = balance + 1000 where number = 1;
commit;
```

An important property of transactions is that they are not visible to other sessions until they are complete and committed. No other thread can read inconsistent data from the table(s) while you are in the process of updating it.

Another benefit of transactions is that partially performed transactions can be undone. As long as we attempt to roll back the transaction before we have committed it, then any changes made by queries that are part of the transaction will be undone.

In the case of our transfer example, if we added a SELECT statement to check that we were not removing more money from the source account than it contained, we could use the keyword ROLLBACK if we wanted to cancel the whole transaction. The syntax would look like this:

```
start transaction;
update account set balance = balance - 1000 where number = 2;
update account set balance = balance + 1000 where number = 1;
select balance from account where number = 2;
# select tells us that account #2 has a negative balance!
# we'd better abort
rollback;
```

Calling ROLLBACK aborts the transaction and undoes any changes it would have made. A transaction that was rolled back instead of committed leaves no trace in the data. Because partial results were never visible to other sessions, it is exactly as though it never happened.

Using Transactions in MySQL

To use transactions as demonstrated in the preceding section, you must be using a transaction-safe table type—either InnoDB or BDB. There are various pieces of syntax that will get the same effect.

The syntax START TRANSACTION is synonymous with BEGIN or BEGIN WORK. You may like to use one of these forms to make your code more compatible with another database you use, but because START TRANSACTION is the SQL-99 syntax, it is generally recommended.

Setting the Autocommit Mode

Normally, MySQL runs in autocommit mode. Each query you run is effectively isolated in a transaction. You can think of it as adding START TRANSACTION and COMMIT to each of your queries for you. A couple of simple queries like these

```
update account set balance = balance - 1000 where number = 2;
update account set balance = balance + 1000 where number = 1;
```

will be run as though they were written like this:

```
start transaction;
update account set balance = balance - 1000 where number = 2;
commit;
start transaction;
update account set balance = balance + 1000 where number = 1;
commit;
```

Note that if you manually type

```
start transaction;
```

normally nothing will be committed until you manually type

```
commit;
```

You can disable the autocommit behavior using the SET command as follows:

```
set autocommit=0;
```

As you would probably guess, the following command will put MySQL back into autocommit mode:

```
set autocommit=1;
```

The autocommit variable is local to a single session, so changing the mode will affect only queries run from your session and only for as long as your session is connected.

If you turn autocommit off, you will not need to call START TRANSACTION to start a transaction. It is very important, though, that you remember to call COMMIT periodically to commit any changes you have made to the database.

Regardless of whether autocommit is on or off, there are times when your changes will automatically be committed. If you are using a non-transaction-safe table type, such as MyISAM, all of your changes will be committed immediately, regardless of the autocommit setting. You can happily group your statements with START TRANSACTION and COMMIT; it is just that this will have no effect on the non-transaction-safe tables. You can even call ROLLBACK. It will not give an error—it will just have no effect on anything you have altered in a non-transaction-safe table. This might be useful if you are testing code or reloading a dump file on servers with different table types.

For transaction-safe tables, there are actions (other than typing COMMIT) that will automatically trigger a COMMIT. Requesting a lock will implicitly commit any outstanding queries.

Using Locks

An alternative way of obtaining some of the benefits of a transaction is to manually lock and unlock tables.

If we really wanted to write our bank account deposit code as two separate transactions, we could implement it as follows:

```
lock tables account write;
select balance from account where number = 2;
update account set balance = 1500 where number = 2;
unlock tables;
```

A call to LOCK TABLES tries to lock any tables you list so that the current thread can work with it without interference. A call to UNLOCK TABLES releases any locks that this thread holds. Unlocking is straightforward. The only thing to note about it is that if you have locked a table, you should unlock it as soon as possible to limit the impact on other threads. Locking is a more complicated issue.

You need to request all the locks you need at once. The preceding example requested only one, but if we intended to access multiple tables or even multiple aliases to the one table, we would need to add them to the same call, for example:

```
lock tables account write, account as a read, othertable low_priority write;
```

Calling LOCK TABLES releases all locks you currently hold, so if you attempt to collect the locks you need over multiple statements, you will release all the early ones and will only actually hold the locks requested in the final statement.

There are two main types of locks: read and write. If you need access to a table to write, and you cannot allow other threads to use the table at the same time, a write lock will stop any other thread from reading or writing to the table until you release it. A read lock is less extreme. If you only intend to read from a table, there is no harm in allowing other threads to read at the same time. A read lock bars other threads only from writing to the table during the period that your thread holds the lock.

A write lock can also be marked as low_priority. Any system that distributes locks, including MySQL, needs a policy to decide who gets locks first when there are conflicting demands. MySQL generally gives write lock requests priority over read lock requests to ensure that updates to the stored data are made as soon as possible. If you do not want this behavior, you can request a low-priority write lock, as we did for the table named othertable in the preceding example. There is a catch, though. Whenever you request a lock, you may have to wait before it is granted. A low-priority lock will be granted only if there are no other threads requesting read or write locks on that table. It is possible on a busy server that this might never happen.

You will probably not often manually control locking in this way, but there are some reasons to do it. If you have an application that requires very high performance but needs transaction-like behavior only occasionally, it might be worth using a fast non-transaction-safe table type and using locks to solve your transaction issue.

Another common instance in which you would call LOCK TABLES is while manipulating MySQL's data files directly. For instance, if you wanted to ensure that the disk files stayed consistent and unmodified while you backed them up, you would need to lock them.

The most important thing to bear in mind about locking is that you should release your locks as soon as possible because other systems and users will be kept waiting. Some tasks you may lock while performing, such as reindexing or backing up large files, can take significant amounts of time.

The InnoDB Transaction Model

Transactional database management systems are generally striving for the same goals, using differing approaches. To isolate transactions, InnoDB uses a fine-grained, row-level locking mechanism. This means that different transactions can run on the same table at the same time as long as they are all only reading or do not use the same rows if they are writing.

Uncommitted changes lock other threads out of only affected rows, not a whole table. This is one of the features that gives InnoDB high performance while delivering the kinds of features you expect from a modern RDBMS. One of these features, or sets of features, is ACID compliance.

ACID Compliance

An important database term that we have not yet defined is the acronym ACID. ACID stands for Atomicity, Consistency, Isolation, and Durability. Much used to be made of the fact that MySQL using MyISAM tables did not pass the "ACID Test." Using InnoDB tables, MySQL is ACID compliant.

Atomicity means that transactions are atomic and indivisible. Either all of a transaction's changes are stored in the database, or none of them are stored. In the event of an external error, it is obviously ideal if the recovery process can complete any transactions that were in progress at the time; however, it is also acceptable for those transactions to be completely rolled back.

Consistency means that operations transform the database from one valid state to another. There are no intermediate stages where the data is inconsistent. The database should also disallow operations that violate consistency constraints. If you are storing bank accounts that relate to bank customers, it should not be possible to create an account for a customer who does not exist, and it should not be possible to delete a customer from the customers table if there are still accounts referring to them in the accounts table.

Isolation means that transactions do not affect each other while they are running. Each transaction should be able to view the world as though it is the only one reading and altering things. In practice this is not usually the case, but locks are used to achieve the illusion. Depending on the database and option settings, you will have different levels of isolation in practice. (See the "Transaction Isolation" section in this chapter for more detail.)

Durability means that after a transaction has been committed to the database, its effects are permanent. This would be a fairly simple requirement to satisfy in a simple program, but in a complex RDBMS that uses locking and multiversioning to allow concurrent multiuser access and caching to improve performance, it is a minefield. In addition, durability implies that we should be able to recover the current state of the database in the event of a failure. If a power failure, hard-disk crash, or other catastrophe occurs between a client sending a transaction to the database and that transaction being recorded on disk, then we should be able to combine a backup and a log to bring the database back to its precrash state and perhaps process transactions that had been logged but not yet executed or committed.

If you are using InnoDB tables (or BerkeleyDB tables), MySQL is ACID compliant. Using the transaction syntax gives you atomicity. Transactions and foreign key constraints give you consistency. You can choose the level of isolation that transactions have from one another. The binary log and repair tools provide durability. (Using replication, you can have a highly durable system without any single point of failure.)

Transaction Isolation

InnoDB tables can run in four different transaction isolation levels. In order from strongest to weakest, they are

- Serializable
- Repeatable read
- Read committed
- Read uncommitted

As with many options, you have a trade-off between robustness and performance.

Serializable isolation is the ideal from a purity and robustness angle. With serializable isolation, reads and writes on the database should appear to be happening in a sequence, with changes from a write being completely recorded before the next read starts. Transactions will not always have to be performed in a noninterleaved sequence to achieve this appearance because many do not interfere with each other, but in cases in which there are clashes, they will. This locking and waiting, combined with the overhead of predicting which combinations of transactions will interfere, makes serializable isolation the slowest isolation mode. If you want to use this mode, this is the command to run:

```
set transaction isolation level serializable;
```

The default level for InnoDB is *repeatable read*. In this isolation mode, each transaction gets to work in an isolated version of the table where each row remains as it was when the transaction started. Reading a row is guaranteed to be repeatable. If you call

```
select * from account where number=1;
```

at the start of the transaction and perform the same query later in the transaction, you will get the same results both times. You can, however, get what are called *phantom reads*. It is possible that another transaction which commits before yours is adding new rows to the table. If you perform the same query with a condition twice, such as

```
select * from account where balance>1000;
```

it is possible that you will get new rows—phantom rows—the second time.

In practice you should very rarely see phantom reads from MySQL. InnoDB uses an algorithm called *next key locking* to solve the problem, as long as the column that your condition applies to is indexed. You probably already know that InnoDB has row-level locking. When a transaction uses a row, it locks that row so that the transaction can be isolated from others. As well as locking the rows used, next key locking also locks the gaps between rows found in the index. Because phantom reads are addressed in this way, few systems really need to be put in serialized isolation mode.

If you set the server to *read committed*, your transactions are no longer very isolated. If you perform a query and repeat it later in the same transaction, you will get different results the second time if another transaction has modified the data in the meantime and committed. Should you want to do this, the command is

```
set transaction isolation level read committed;
```

At the weakest isolation level, *read uncommitted*, it is distinctly arguable not only that your transactions are no longer isolated, consistent, and therefore ACID compliant, but that you no longer really have transactions. In this mode, it is possible for transactions to read changes that other transactions have made before the changes have been committed. This is called a *dirty read*. You would tolerate this only in fairly unusual circumstances, such as at a time when you know all active threads will be reading or writing, but not both. To enable read uncommitted mode, use this:

```
set transaction isolation level read uncommitted;
```

Table 10.1 summarizes the characteristics of each mode.

TABLE 10.1   Transaction Isolation Level Characteristics

	Dirty Read	Nonrepeatable Read	Phantom Read
Read Uncommitted	Possible	Possible	Possible
Read Committed	Not possible	Possible	Possible
Repeatable Read	Not possible	Not possible	Possible (but unlikely)
Serializable	Not possible	Not possible	Not possible

Summary

- A transaction is a related set of SQL queries treated as a single atomic unit. It can be either entirely committed or entirely rolled back.

- The standard SQL way to express a transaction is

```
start transaction;
# do work
commit;
```

  but there are many equivalent ways to get the same effect.

- ACID stands for Atomicity, Consistency, Isolation, and Durability. You should understand what these terms mean or other geeks will refuse to talk to you.

- In order from strongest to weakest, the transaction isolation levels are serializable, repeatable read, read committed, and read uncommitted. The InnoDB default is repeatable read.

Quiz

1. With autocommit off, a transaction will be committed
   a) when you call COMMIT
   b) when you request a lock
   c) both a) and b)
   d) none of the above

2. Atomicity means
   a) either all of a transaction is performed or none of it is performed
   b) operations transform the database from one consistent state to another
   c) transactions do not interfere with each other
   d) committed transactions should be permanent

3. Isolation means
   a) either all of a transaction is performed or none of it is performed
   b) operations transform the database from one consistent state to another
   c) transactions do not interfere with each other
   d) committed transactions should be permanent

4. Durability means

    a) either all of a transaction is performed or none of it is performed

    b) operations transform the database from one consistent state to another

    c) transactions do not interfere with each other

    d) committed transactions should be permanent

5. In repeatable read mode

    a) you may experience a dirty read

    b) you may experience a nonrepeatable read

    c) you may experience a phantom read

    d) none of the above

Exercises

The MySQL/InnoDB manual contains many hints for improving the performance of your system when using InnoDB tables. Apply as many of these as appropriate to your system.

    You can start by looking here:

```
www.innodb.com/ibman.html#InnoDBTuning
```

On a noncritical server, cause MySQL to stop while you are halfway through a transaction. You should not need to drop your hard drives from a great height or kick the power plug out of the wall. Killing the process should be sufficient. Examine the binary log and see what happens when you restart the server.

Answers

Quiz

1. c
2. a
3. c
4. d
5. c

Next

In Chapter 11, "Managing User Privileges," we will examine MySQL's advanced user privilege system. You have a great deal of choice about what power you give to users of the database. In this chapter you'll learn about these options and how to control them.

V

Administering MySQL

11 Managing User Privileges

12 Configuring MySQL

13 Administering Your Database

14 Backup and Disaster Recovery

15 Securing Your MySQL Installation

16 Replicating Your Database

Managing User Privileges

One of MySQL's strengths is its advanced user privilege system. In this chapter, we'll discuss user account creation, the different privileges available, and how these privileges are represented within MySQL tables. We'll cover the following:

- Creating user accounts with GRANT and REVOKE
- Privilege levels
- Understanding the privilege tables

Creating User Accounts with GRANT and REVOKE

User privileges are given with the GRANT statement and are taken away with the REVOKE statement. These are standard SQL statements that you can execute like any other statement in this book. All MySQL user information and user privileges are eventually stored in a MySQL database, just like your own applications.

To run the statements in this section, you will yourself need to have a certain level of privilege. If you installed MySQL, you will have access to the root account and, therefore, will have the appropriate level of privilege. If you are using MySQL on a machine controlled by somebody else (such as at work or at an ISP), you may not have the appropriate privilege level to run these queries. If you do not, you will receive an error message along these lines:

```
ERROR 1045: Access denied for user: 'laura@127.0.0.1' (Using password: YES)
```

Granting Privileges

We'll begin by looking at the GRANT statement. This statement is used to create user accounts and give users access to databases, tables, and functions. Let's look at a simple example first, as follows:

```
grant usage
on *
to luke@localhost identified by 'password';
```

This statement creates an account for the user called luke when he is trying to log in from localhost. It sets up a password for him (the highly secure password password—obviously, you should use something better!). The word usage indicates the privilege we are giving to luke. It means that he can log in, but not do anything else. The ON clause is used to specify what things we are granting privileges on. Because we are only granting the ability to log in in this case, the ON clause is not really relevant here.

The general form of the GRANT statement from the MySQL manual is

```
GRANT priv_type [(column_list)] [, priv_type [(column_list)] ...]
ON {tbl_name | * | *.* | db_name.*}
TO user_name [IDENTIFIED BY [PASSWORD] 'password']
    [, user_name [IDENTIFIED BY 'password'] ...]
[REQUIRE
    NONE |
    [{SSL| X509}]
    [CIPHER cipher [AND]]
    [ISSUER issuer [AND]]
    [SUBJECT subject]]
[WITH [GRANT OPTION | MAX_QUERIES_PER_HOUR # |
                      MAX_UPDATES_PER_HOUR # |
                      MAX_CONNECTIONS_PER_HOUR #]]
```

The GRANT clause lists the privileges we are granting. We will look at what these are in the next section. Some privileges are global (that is, they apply across all databases), and some apply only to certain items (databases, tables, or columns).

The ON clause specifies the items we are granting privileges on. This can be a named table or a named database with all its tables (dbname.*). We can also specify *.*, which means all databases and all tables. If we specify *, the privileges are granted on the currently selected database. If no database is selected, the privileges are granted as if we had specified *.* in this clause.

The TO clause is used to specify the user we are granting privileges to. If this user already has an account, the new privileges will be added to it. If not, an account will be created for the user. We can specify more than one user in this clause. We can also specify the hosts they can log in from, for example, fred@localhost. If you are having trouble logging in as a newly created user, try adding the hostname you are logging in from to the GRANT statement. The MySQL username need not be the same as a user's operating system username. Usernames can be up to 16 characters long.

The IDENTIFIED BY clause sets the password for a new user or resets it for an existing user.

Users can change their passwords by typing

```
set password = password('newpassword');
```

You can change a user's password by typing, for example,

```
set password for fred@localhost = password('newpassword');
```

You need to have access to the database called mysql to do this.

The clause WITH GRANT OPTION is a special privilege that allows the user to grant privileges. If you found that you could not grant any privileges to users, this is the privilege you yourself were missing. Also, you may not grant a privilege to other users that you do not have yourself.

The WITH clause can also be used to limit the number of queries, updates, or connections that a user can make in an hour. The default value for these is zero, meaning no limitation.

The REQUIRE clause allows you specify that a user must connect using a secure connection. To use this, you will need to configure MySQL appropriately. We will discuss this further in Chapter 15, "Securing Your MySQL Installation."

Privilege Levels

The privileges we can grant using the GRANT statement can be divided into two basic categories: user-level privileges and administrator-level privileges.

User-Level Privileges

The user-level privileges are shown in Table 11.1.

TABLE 11.1   User-Level Privileges

Privilege	Meaning
CREATE	User can create tables.
CREATE TEMPORARY TABLES	User can create temporary tables.
DELETE	User can delete rows.
EXECUTE	User can execute procedures.
INDEX	User can create indexes.
INSERT	User can insert rows.
LOCK TABLES	User can lock tables.
SELECT	User can select rows.
SHOW DATABASES	User can execute a SHOW DATABASES command to retrieve the list of available databases.
UPDATE	User can update rows.
USAGE	User can log in, but cannot do anything else.

Administrator-Level Privileges

Privileges that should be granted only to administrators are shown in Table 11.2. Some of these can be granted to users with caution at your discretion, but they should not be granted to users by default.

TABLE 11.2   Administrator-Level Privileges

Privilege	Meaning
ALL	User has all the privileges except WITH GRANT OPTION.
ALTER	User can alter tables. You may give this to some power users, but proceed with caution because it may be used to change the privilege tables.
DROP	User can drop tables. You may give this to trusted users.
FILE	User can load data from a file. Again, you may give this to trusted users. Beware of users trying to load arbitrary files, such as /etc/passwd or similar files!
PROCESS	User can show full process list—that is, see all the processes that MySQL is executing.
RELOAD	User can use the FLUSH statement. This has various purposes. We will look at FLUSH PRIVILEGES later in this chapter and will revisit FLUSH in Chapter 13.
REPLICATION CLIENT	User can check where the masters and slaves are.
REPLICATION SLAVE	Special privilege designed for the special replication user on the slave. See Chapter 16 for more details.
SHUTDOWN	User can run mysqladmin shutdown. For more information see Chapter 13.
SUPER	User can connect even if MySQL has its maximum number of connections and can execute the commands CHANGE MASTER, KILL (thread), mysqladmin debug, PURGE MASTER LOGS, and SET GLOBAL.
WITH GRANT OPTION	User can pass on any privileges he has.

There is one other privilege called REFERENCES. This is reserved for future use, and although you can grant it, at present, it doesn't do anything.

Evaluating Privileges

Four sets of privileges are granted with the GRANT statement:

- Global privileges apply across all databases. These are specified with *.* in a GRANT statement. For example:

```
grant all on *.* to fred;
```

- Database privileges apply to one particular database. These are granted with *database*.* in a GRANT statement:

```
grant all on employee.* to fred;
```

- Table privileges apply to a single table. These are granted by naming a specific table in the GRANT statement:

```
grant select on department to fred;
```

- Column privileges apply to a single column. These are specified in the GRANT clause of the GRANT statement. For example:

```
grant select (employeeID) on employee to fred;
```

When trying to work out whether a user has a privilege to do a particular task, MySQL will look at the combination of that user's global privileges plus his database privileges plus his table privileges plus his column privileges ORed together.

Using the REVOKE Statement

The REVOKE statement is the opposite of GRANT. It is used to take privileges away from a user. For example:

```
revoke all on employee.* from fred;
```

The general form of the revoke statement is as follows:

```
REVOKE priv_type [(column_list)] [, priv_type [(column_list)] ...]
ON {tbl_name | * | *.* | db_name.*}
FROM user_name [, user_name ...]
```

As you can see, it has basically the same clauses as the GRANT statement and can be used to revoke the corresponding privileges.

Understanding the Privilege Tables

The underlying data that is changed by the GRANT and REVOKE statements is stored in the database called mysql. Rather than using GRANT and REVOKE, you can modify the tables in this database directly if you know what you are doing. You can also read the data in them to help you resolve any privilege problems that may crop up.

If you modify these tables directly, you will need to execute the statement

```
flush privileges;
```

before the changes will take effect.

There are six tables in the mysql database:

- user
- db
- host

- tables_priv
- columns_priv
- func

Only the first five have to do with user privileges. (The func table stores user-defined function information that is beyond the scope of this book.)

The first three tables—user, db, and host—are used to determine whether you are allowed to connect to the database. All five of the privilege tables are used to determine whether you have the right to execute any given command.

Understanding the user Table

The user table contains information about a user's global privilege set.

The user table contains the following columns:

- *Scope columns*   These are used to determine when a row is relevant. These are the scope columns:

    Host: Where the user is connecting from

    User: The username

    Password: The user's password, as encoded by the PASSWORD() function

- *Privilege columns*   Each one corresponds to one of the global privileges. They can have the value Y (if the user has the global privilege) or N (if the user does not). These are the privilege columns:

Select_priv	Shutdown_priv
Insert_priv	Process_priv
Update_priv	File_priv
Delete_priv	Show_db_priv
Index_priv	Super_priv
Alter_priv	Create_tmp_table_priv
Create_priv	Lock_tables_priv
Drop_priv	Execute_priv
Grant_priv	Repl_slave_priv
References_priv	Repl_client_priv
Reload_priv	

- *Secure connection columns*   These represent the information from the REQUIRE clause of the grant statement. These are the secure connection columns:

    ssl_type

    ssl_cypher

    x509_issuer

    x509_subject

- *Resource limitation columns*   These represent any limitations on user resource use you may have specified at the end of a GRANT statement. These are the resource limitation columns:

    max_questions

    max_updates

    max_connections

Understanding the db Table

The database table stores a user's privileges for particular databases. It contains the following columns:

- *Scope columns*   MySQL uses these to determine when a row of privileges is relevant. If you have different rules for different hosts, leave the host field blank and then create a corresponding set of rows in the host table to give more information. These are the scope columns:

    Host

    Db

    User

- *Privilege columns*   These specify whether the combination of Host, Db, and User have each of the listed privileges. Again these columns can contain the values Y or N. These are the privilege columns:

Select_priv	Create_priv
Insert_priv	Drop_priv
Update_priv	Grant_priv
Delete_priv	Create_tmp_table_priv
Index_priv	Lock_tables_priv
Alter_priv	

Understanding the host Table

MySQL consults the host table when it finds a blank host entry in the db table. You will not get this effect from a GRANT statement, but you can set it up manually. This table contains the following columns:

- *Scope columns*   MySQL uses these to determine when a row of privileges is relevant. Each row here gives information for a single database accessed from a single host. These are the scope columns:

    Host

    Db

- *Privilege columns*   These specify whether the combination of Host and Db have each of the listed privileges. Again, these columns can contain the values Y or N. These are the privilege columns:

Select_priv	Create_priv
Insert_priv	Drop_priv
Update_priv	Grant_priv
Delete_priv	Create_tmp_table_priv
Index_priv	Lock_tables_priv
Alter_priv	

Understanding the tables_priv Table

The tables_priv table expresses user privileges that relate to individual tables. It contains the following columns:

- *Scope columns*   These work as they do in the previous three tables. Here we also have the Table_name privilege, which lists the specific table that a grant applies to. These are the scope columns:

  Host

  Db

  User

  Table_name

- *Grant columns*   These store information about who granted this privilege and when. These are the grant columns:

  Grantor

  Timestamp

- *The* Table_priv *column*   This is a set that determines what privileges the Host/Db/User has on the table listed in Table_name. It can contain the following values: Select, Insert, Update, Delete, Create, Drop, Grant, References, Index, and Alter.

- *The* Column_priv *column*   This is a set that tells us what privileges the user has over all the columns in this table. It can contain the following values: Select, Insert, Update, and References. If a privilege is missing here, MySQL can look in the columns_priv table for more detailed information about what is and what is not allowed with this table's columns.

Understanding the columns_priv Table

The columns_priv table expresses user privileges relating to individual columns. It contains the following columns:

- *Scope columns*   These determine when a row in this table is relevant. These are the scope columns:

  Host

  Db

  User

  Table_name

  Column_name

- *The* Column_priv *column*   This is a set that determines which privileges have been granted to the combination outlined by the scope column. It can contain the following values: Select, Insert, Update, and References.

- *The* Timestamp *column*   This column tells us when this privilege was granted.

Summary

GRANT and REVOKE

- The GRANT statement is used to grant privileges to a user or to create a user account. It has the following format:

```
GRANT priv_type [(column_list)] [, priv_type [(column_list)] ...]
ON {tbl_name | * | *.* | db_name.*}
TO user_name [IDENTIFIED BY [PASSWORD] 'password']
    [, user_name [IDENTIFIED BY 'password'] ...]
[REQUIRE
    NONE |
    [{SSL| X509}]
    [CIPHER cipher [AND]]
    [ISSUER issuer [AND]]
    [SUBJECT subject]]
[WITH [GRANT OPTION | MAX_QUERIES_PER_HOUR # |
                      MAX_UPDATES_PER_HOUR # |
                      MAX_CONNECTIONS_PER_HOUR #]]
```

- The REVOKE statement is used to take privileges away from a user. It has the following format:

```
REVOKE priv_type [(column_list)] [, priv_type [(column_list)] ...]
ON {tbl_name | * | *.* | db_name.*}
FROM user_name [, user_name ...]
```

Privileges

- Individual privileges can be granted to users.
- These are the user privileges:

CREATE	LOCK TABLES
CREATE TEMPORARY TABLES	SELECT
DELETE	SHOW DATABASES
EXECUTE	UPDATE
INDEX	USAGE
INSERT	

- These are the administrator privileges:

ALL	REPLICATION CLIENT
ALTER	REPLICATION SLAVE
DROP	SHUTDOWN
FILE	SUPER
PROCESS	WITH GRANT OPTION
RELOAD	

Privilege Tables

- MySQL's account and privilege information is stored in the database called mysql.
- There are five privilege tables.
- The user table stores usernames, passwords, and global privilege information.
- The db table stores information about privileges for specific databases.
- The host table stores information about which databases can be accessed from which hosts.
- The tables_priv table stores information about table-level privileges.
- The columns_priv table stores information about column-level privileges.

Quiz

1. The GRANT OPTION privilege
   a) allows a user to load data from a file
   b) allows a user to pass on his privileges
   c) allows a user to log in, but nothing else
   d) allows a user to flush privileges

2. The USAGE privilege

    a) allows a user to load data from a file

    b) allows a user to pass on his privileges

    c) allows a user to log in, but nothing else

    d) allows a user to flush privileges

3. The RELOAD privilege

    a) allows a user to load data from a file

    b) allows a user to pass on his privileges

    c) allows a user to log in, but nothing else

    d) allows a user to flush privileges

4. The FILE privilege

    a) allows a user to load data from a file

    b) allows a user to pass on his privileges

    c) allows a user to log in, but nothing else

    d) allows a user to flush privileges

5. An entry in the tables_priv.table_priv column

    a) lists the privileges a user has on this table as a set

    b) records with Y or N whether a user has access to this table

    c) records a single privilege a user has on this table

    d) records whether there is an entry in the columns_priv table for this table

Exercises

1. Write a GRANT statement to create a user called bill, with password secret, who has access to select, update, insert, and delete from the department table.

2. Write a REVOKE statement to remove this user's privileges.

Answers

Quiz

1. b
2. c
3. d
4. a
5. a

Exercises

1.

```
grant select, update, insert, delete
on employee.department
to bill@localhost
identified by 'secret';
```

2.

```
revoke select, update, insert, delete
on employee.department
from bill;
```

Next

In the next chapter, "Configuring MySQL," we will discuss MySQL's plethora of configuration options.

Configuring MySQL

In this chapter, we'll follow up on the brief introduction to configuration you received in Chapter 1, "Installing MySQL." We'll cover the various configuration options, with a special section on internationalization.

We will cover the following:

- Setting MySQL configuration options
- Multi-install configuration options
- Configuring for internationalization

Setting MySQL Configuration Options

As you will have seen throughout this book, many of the MySQL programs have configuration options. These can be specified on the command line, but in many cases they can also be specified via an options file. A single options file can be used to specify default command-line options for several of the MySQL programs, specifically mysql, mysqladmin, mysqld, mysqld_safe, mysql.server, mysqldump, mysqlimport, mysqlshow, mysqlcheck, myisamchk, and myisampack.

The advantage of using an options file is that it allows you to set all your standard options in one place. Under Unix, MySQL also supports the use of separate options files for the whole server and for individual users.

The options file approach is particularly useful if you are managing multiple servers. If the servers have the same configuration, as is often the case when replication is involved, you can simply use the same configuration file across machines.

We first looked at options files in Chapter 1. Let's recap with more detail this time. You can find the options file(s) in the locations detailed next.

Under Windows, you have a choice of putting the options file in your Windows directory and calling it my.ini or putting it in the root directory of the drive that the server is on (for example, C:\) and calling it my.cnf. This is a global options file—that is, these options will be applied to all users on the server.

Under Unix, you can have a global options file, an options file for each MySQL server on the machine, and an options file for each user. (You can run more than one MySQL server per physical machine, as we will discuss later in this chapter.)

The global options file is located in /etc/my.cnf. Per-server files are in the data directory for each server, and per-user files are in the home directory of each user. Note that per-user files are prefixed with a dot—that is, .my.cnf instead of my.cnf.

Let's look back at the options file we began with in Chapter 1 as an example of the syntax of these files. It is repeated here for your reference in Listing 12.1.

LISTING 12.1   **Sample my.cnf File**

```
[mysqld]
# turn on binary logging and slow query logging
log-bin
log-slow-queries

# InnoDB config
# This is the basic config as suggested in the manual
# Datafile(s) must be able to
# hold your data and indexes.
# Make sure you have enough
# free disk space.
innodb_data_file_path = ibdata1:10M:autoextend
# Set buffer pool size to
# 50 - 80 % of your computer's
# memory
set-variable = innodb_buffer_pool_size=70M
set-variable = innodb_additional_mem_pool_size=10M
# Set the log file size to about
# 25 % of the buffer pool size
set-variable = innodb_log_file_size=20M
set-variable = innodb_log_buffer_size=8M
# Set ..flush_log_at_trx_commit
# to 0 if you can afford losing
# some last transactions
innodb_flush_log_at_trx_commit=1
```

Let's discuss the format of this file.

The first line in this file is

```
[mysqld]
```

This means that the options specified following this line are options for mysqld. If we want to specify options for other programs, we must specify the program at the start of the options. You just need to list the name of the program in square brackets.

As well as specifying options for individual programs, you can specify options for [client], which sets options for all client programs.

Lines beginning with # are comments.

There are three forms of syntax for setting individual options:

- Specifying the option you want switched on; for example:

```
log-bin
```

  This is equivalent to specifying `mysqld --log-bin`.

- Specifying the option you want with a value; for example:

```
innodb_flush_log_at_trx_commit=1
```

- Specifying the option you want with a value using the `set-variable` syntax; for example:

```
set-variable = innodb_log_buffer_size=8M
```

  This third syntax is deprecated, but we include it for completeness. You will also note that some sample files use this syntax, so it's important to understand what it means. For instance, the examples in the sample `my.cnf` file that use it are taken from the simple InnoDB configuration given in the MySQL manual.

Certain options that have to do with how options files are used will work for all these programs:

- `--no-defaults` means that no options files are to be read.
- `--print-defaults` will tell you what the values of all the options are being set to for this program.
- `--defaults-file=/path/to/file` will tell the program to use the specified file instead of any other options files it has. This is useful for testing configuration changes.
- `--defaults-extra-file=/path/to/file` will read the specified file after reading the global options file but before reading any individual user options files.

Most of the programs you can configure using an options file have their options discussed elsewhere in this book. The exception is mysqld. We will now take an overview of the more important and useful command-line options for the MySQL server.

Setting Options for mysqld

This list of options is not comprehensive, but it aims to give you a guide to the more frequently used options for mysqld. Each of these options can be set via the command line when starting mysqld or, as we have been discussing, through an options file.

You can obtain a complete list (warning: it's long) by opening a command prompt and typing

```
mysqld --help
```

Here are some useful options:

- `ansi`: Run the server in ANSI compatibility mode. This makes MySQL use ANSI-99 SQL.
- `basedir`: Set the base directory of your installation if you want to put it in a nonstandard location.
- `datadir`: The same thing as `basedir`, but for the data directory.
- `log-bin`: Turn on binary logging. You can specify a filename for the location of the log.
- `log-error`: Turn on error logging. Again, you can specify the location of the log.
- `log-slow-queries`: Turn on slow query logging.
- `port`: Specify the port that the server should listen on. The default is 3306.
- `user`: Specify the user that the MySQL server should run as.

We will look at a few other options through the course of this chapter and some others in Chapter 17, "Optimizing Your MySQL Server Configuration."

Setting InnoDB Configuration Options

In the sample options file we looked at, we set some options relating to InnoDB. You can use InnoDB without setting any of these options, but you should set them for better performance. These are the options we set previously:

- `innodb_data_file_path = ibdata1:10M:autoextend`

  This option tells MySQL where to store InnoDB data. Unlike MyISAM tables, in which each table gets its own file, InnoDB tables are stored in a shared tablespace, which may consist of one or more files. This particular example tells MySQL to store all the InnoDB data in a single file called `ibdata1`, to set the initial file size to 10MB, and to automatically make it bigger (8MB at a time) if the tablespace becomes full.

  The general format of this option is

  `filename:filesize[;filename:filesize;...][:autoextend[:max:size]]`

  The `autoextend` option allows the tablespace to grow. The `max` option allows you to set a maximum size to which it can grow.

- `innodb_buffer_pool_size=70M`

  This option sets the size of the buffer used to cache InnoDB table data and indexes. As with any cache, the bigger it is, the less disk I/O you will have. How much you put into the buffer pool will depend on whether there are other applications and users on the server and how much memory you have.

- `innodb_additional_mem_pool_size=10M`

  This option sets aside memory to store internal MySQL data structures. If MySQL is running out of room here, it will begin writing warnings to the error log.

- `innodb_log_file_size=20M`

  This option sets the size of each log file. InnoDB rotates between *n* log files—where *n* is the value set in the `innodb_log_files_in_group` option, which defaults to 2, the recommended value.

- `innodb_log_buffer_size=8M`

  This option sets the size of the buffer in which logs are stored before they are written to disk.

- `innodb_flush_log_at_trx_commit=1`

  Setting this option to 1 means that every time a transaction is committed the log will be flushed to disk. This is the normal behavior. If it is set to zero, the log will be written to and flushed to disk only roughly once per second. If it is set to 2, the log will be written to with each commit, but flushed only once per second. Values of 0 or 2 will improve performance, but are obviously a fairly risky proposition.

There are various other InnoDB configuration options. See the MySQL manual for details.

Multi-Install Configuration Options

It is often useful to be able to run multiple MySQL servers on the same machine. For example, different ISP users may have their own installation. We use this feature to allow students learning about MySQL to each set up and configure their own server.

For each server you start, you must set different values for each of the following options to mysqld:

- `port`: Each server must listen on a different port.
- `socket`: Under Unix, each server must use a different socket file. Under Windows, the `socket` option sets the name of the named pipe used by the server. In both cases, this value for `socket` must be different for each server.
- `shared-memory-base-name` (Windows only): Each server must use a different piece of shared memory.
- `pid-file` (Unix only): Each server needs a different file in which to write its process id (pid).
- Logging options: If you set any of the log file options, such as `log-bin`, you will need to set up different log file locations for each server.

An easy way to get some of these is to set the `basedir` option differently for each server. This will force the data directories and log files to be different. We strongly recommend that each server has its own separate data directory to avoid all sorts of unpleasantness.

The `--defaults-file` option is really useful for starting each server instance with a different set of defaults (or for installing each server as a Windows service with a separate set of defaults).

One point to note is that if you are running multiple servers, you will need to specify to client programs and other programs that connect to a server, such as mysqladmin, which server you want to connect to. You can use the `--port` command switch to these programs to do this. In this situation, it can be very useful to set up `my.conf` files on a per-user basis with the client port set appropriately so that users automatically connect to their own servers.

Configuring for Internationalization

Two options to mysqld allow you to set the default character set and collation. The character set is the set of symbols used by default on the server. The collation is the set of rules for performing comparisons—that is, the sort order—on the character set, which varies from country to country.

You can set the default character set with the `--default-character-set` option. Each character set has an associated default collation, but you can specify another one with the `--default-collation` option. If the combination of default character set and default collation is not valid, mysqld will give you an error message.

The default character set, if these options are not specified, is latin1, and the default collation is `latin1_swedish_ci`. This character set can also be described as ISO-8859-1 West European, which is the one used in this book. The collation represents the sort order for latin1 used by the Swedes and Finns. (If you are a monolinugal English speaker, you may not know that different groups who use the same character set you use sort vowels into different orders.) There are also collations for latin1 that represent the ways that Germans, Danes, and Norwegians sort strings.

For more information on the character sets supported by MySQL, especially if you are looking for one in particular, consult the MySQL manual.

Summary

- The MySQL programs mysql, mysqladmin, mysqld, mysqld_safe, mysql.server, mysqldump, mysqlimport, mysqlshow, mysqlcheck, myisamchk, and myisampack all support the use of a common options file.

- You can set options on a global basis, on a server basis, on a user-by-user basis, or all by of these.

- The syntax of the file begins with the name of the program in square brackets, followed by options for that program. Comments start with #. Each option may be expressed as *option*, *option=value*, or set-variable *option=value*.

- You can obtain a complete list of options to mysqld with `mysqld --help`.

- You can run multiple MySQL servers on the same physical machine as long as options are set to avoid clashes. You must set up different ports, sockets, and log files for each server.

- You can use the options file to set the default character set and collation for the server. The character set is the set of symbols used. The collation is the sort order.

Quiz

1. The option --no-defaults to mysqld means
   a) don't use any default values; use only values from the options file
   b) don't read any options files
   c) read only the global options files
   d) none of the above

2. The InnoDB option used to set the tablespace filesize is
   a) `innodb_buffer_pool_size`
   b) `innodb_data_file_path`
   c) `innodb_log_buffer_size`
   d) none of the above

3. The InnoDB option used to set the size of the table data buffer is
   a) `innodb_buffer_pool_size`
   b) `innodb_data_file_path`
   c) `innodb_log_buffer_size`
   d) none of the above

4. Multiple servers on the same physical machine do *not* need the following items to be separate:
   a) log files
   b) ports
   c) sockets
   d) clients

5. Which of the following is true?
   a) A collation is valid only for a single character set.
   b) A collation is valid for all character sets.
   c) A character set can have only a single collation.
   d) None of the above.

Exercises

Install an older version of MySQL (for example, 3.23) on your machine. Set it up so that you have both a current version server and an older version server running on the same physical machine. Make sure that you can connect to each one.

Answers

Quiz

1. b
2. b
3. a
4. d
5. a

Next

In the next chapter, "Administering Your Database," we will discuss the day-to-day maintenance tasks you will need to perform on your MySQL database.

13

Administering Your Database

In this chapter we will cover the day-to-day administration activities associated with running a MySQL database, including the following:

- Starting up and shutting down
- Getting information about the server and databases
- Setting variables
- Killing threads
- Clearing caches
- Analyzing tables
- Understanding the log files

Although this chapter is structured in a task-oriented fashion, we will make use of one important script, `mysqladmin`, for several of these tasks.

The `mysqladmin` script is used with appropriate parameters to perform a wide variety of administrative tasks. A summary of these appears at the end of this chapter.

We will also cover the use of the `mysqlshow` and `mysqlcheck` scripts and the KILL, RESET, CHECK, REPAIR, and ANALYZE TABLE SQL commands in this chapter.

Starting Up and Shutting Down the MySQL Server

As we discussed in Chapter 1, "Installing MySQL," you will typically configure your system to start the MySQL server automatically. However, there will be situations in which you need to shut down or restart the server in the event of a problem.

We have already discussed how to start the MySQL server. The way you do this varies depending on your operating system, path settings, and install choices. Under Linux, you can start the server with

```
/etc/init.d/mysqld start
```

but only if you have a copy of the `mysqld` executable in the standard Red Hat location. If you have it somewhere else, you will need to use the correct path. See Chapter 1 for more information. You can also start the server by running

```
safe_mysqld
```

This script attempts to determine the correct startup options automatically and then starts MySQL with those options. Again, if the script is not in your path, you will need to enter the full path to find it.

To shut down your MySQL server under Linux, you have a couple of options. You can use

```
/etc/init.d/mysqld stop
```

or

```
mysqladmin -u root -p shutdown
```

You can, of course, use a different administrator account, but `root` will work. Normal user accounts should not be given this privilege.

Under Windows, if you have installed mysqld as a service, the easiest way to start the service is to open the Control Panel and go to Administrative Tools, Services. If you select the MySQL service, Windows will give you options to Stop, Pause, or Restart the service, as shown in Figure 13.1. (This screenshot is from Windows XP Professional, so your display may vary a little depending on the version.)

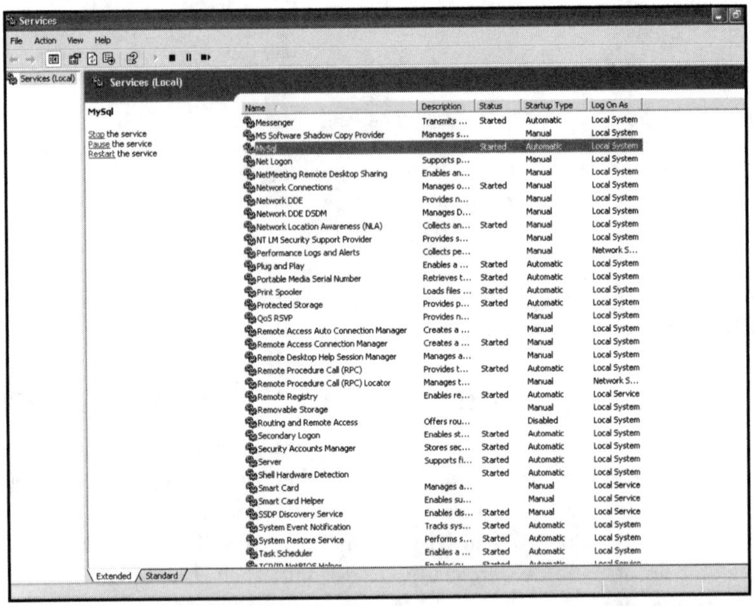

FIGURE 13.1.   The Services window in Windows Administrative Tools

You can also shut down the server using the `mysqladmin` script for Linux, as stated previously.

Getting Information About the Server and Databases

The mysqlshow script and SHOW SQL command allow you, as an administrator, to get a lot of information about what is going on with your databases and server.

Retrieving Database Information

The mysqlshow script gives information about databases. If you run it without any parameters, as

```
mysqlshow
```

it will give you a list of databases accessible to you as a user. This gives the same result as running

```
show databases;
```

from within the mysql monitor or other user interface.

As with most of the command-line scripts, you can supply mysqlshow with -u and a username and -p to supply that user's password. It also has various useful options. Running

```
mysqlshow --help
```

will supply you with a full list of these options.

One option is to provide a database name to get more information about a particular database. For example, if you specify a database as follows, you will get a list of the tables in that database:

```
mysqlshow -u username -p database
```

You can get more information about the tables by adding --status to the end of this line. Try it for yourself with the employee database, as shown here:

```
mysqlshow -u username --status employee
```

The output is a little hard to read because it's so wide, but it includes information about the storage engine used in each table, how much data is in each table, the current value of any auto-increment column in a table, and the character set used in each table.

You can also use the SQL command SHOW inside your MySQL client to get information about a database and the status of the server. By this stage in this book, you should be familiar with using

```
show databases;
```

and

```
show tables;
```

to get information about databases and tables. However, the SHOW statement has a huge number of other options you can use.

You can use

```
show columns from tablename;
```

to give you the same information you would get from a DESC statement. Similarly, you can use

```
show table status
```

to get the same information we got from `mysqlshow --status`.

Viewing Server Status and Variables

To get information about the server and how it's running, we can look at the server status and the values of variables.

To see the status of your MySQL server, you can use either

```
SHOW STATUS
```

inside MySQL, or

```
mysqladmin -u username -p -extended-status
```

from the command line.

What this mostly gives you is a lot of statistics about what the server has been doing since it was started. You may be interested to look at the values named com_*—for example, com_select tells you how many select statements have been executed by the server.

Some other particularly interesting values to look at are listed here:

- threads_connected: This is the current number of connections to the server.

- slow_queries: This is the number of queries this server has run that have taken more time than the value of the server variable long_query_time. These queries are logged in the Slow Query Log. We will return to slow queries in Chapter 19, "Optimizing Your Queries."

- uptime: This is how long this server instance has been running in seconds.

To see the values of server variables, you can use

```
show variables;
```

from inside MySQL or

```
mysqladmin -u username -p variables
```

from the command line.

The values of most of these variables can be set in your configuration file, from the command line when you start the server, or dynamically inside MySQL using the SET command. Configuration is covered in Chapter 12, "Configuring MySQL," and the use of SET is covered later in this chapter.

Viewing Process Information

You can see what processes are currently running on your server by running the following command inside MySQL:

```
show processlist;
```

At a minimum you will see information about the query you just typed (`show processlist`).
   You can get the same information from the command line using

```
mysqladmin -u username -p showprocesslist
```

Viewing Grant and Privilege Information

You can see what privileges an individual user has been granted by typing

```
show grants for username@host;
```

This is expressed in terms of a GRANT statement that could be used to reproduce the privileges the user has. For example,

```
mysql> show grants for root@localhost;
```

on my system will produce the following results:

```
+----------------------------------------------------------------------+
| Grants for root@localhost                                            |
+----------------------------------------------------------------------+
| GRANT ALL PRIVILEGES ON *.* TO 'root'@'localhost' WITH GRANT OPTION |
+----------------------------------------------------------------------+
1 row in set (0.40 sec)
```

You can also remind yourself what the various privileges are by typing

```
show privileges;
```

This will give you a reference list of the privileges available on the system.

Viewing Reference Information About Tables

You can see what table types are installed and available by typing

```
show table types;
```

You can see the `create` statement that would be needed to create any particular table in a database by typing

```
show create table tablename;
```

For example, in our sample employee database, typing

```
show create table department;
```

will give us back this:

```
CREATE TABLE 'department' (
  'departmentID' int(11) NOT NULL auto_increment,
  'name' varchar(30) default NULL,
  PRIMARY KEY ('departmentID')
) TYPE=InnoDB CHARSET=latin1
```

(Note that the column names are quoted to be safe, and the default character set—which we didn't specify—is specified here.)

Setting Variables

The SET statement is used to set the value of server variables—the same variables we could see via the show variables statement in the preceding section. This statement uses the syntax

```
set variable=value;
```

For example, we might use:

```
set sql_safe_updates=1;
```

This turns on safe updates (as we can at the command line with --i-am-a-dummy).

We will make good use of this statement when we come to server optimization in Chapter 17, "Optimizing Your MySQL Server Configuration."

Killing Threads

The show processlist statement we looked at earlier in this chapter allows us to see what threads are running on a server. This command also tells you the id or unique identifier for each thread. If we have a problematic thread (for example, a query that is taking forever, or a problem user), we can terminate the thread using

```
kill process_id;
```

Clearing Caches

MySQL has a set of internal caches. These can be cleared using the FLUSH and RESET commands. For example, if we have updated user privileges by manually altering the grant tables, we can make sure that these changes roll through the system by executing a

```
flush privileges;
```

statement.

Another common use of FLUSH is to clear the query cache:

```
flush query cache;
```

This will defragment the query cache, improving performance.

The RESET statement is used in a similar way to FLUSH. For example, we can use

```
reset query cache;
```

Rather than defragmenting the query cache, this will actually clear it altogether.

A complete list of flushable and resettable variables can be found in the MySQL manual.

Understanding the Log Files

MySQL keeps various log files that may be useful to you. Most of these logs are not enabled by default, so if you want logging, you will have to switch it on. Each of these logs can be turned on with a command-line option on server startup or via the set command.

These are the logs you can keep:

- *Error log:* Tracks all the errors that have occurred. This one is logged by default and will appear in your data directory. The file is called `hostname.err` on Linux and `mysql.err` on Windows. You can set the location to something else with the option `log-error=filename` in your `my.ini` or `my.cnf` file.

- *Query log:* Logs all the queries run on the system. You can turn on this log and specify the location with the option `log=filename`.

- *Binary log:* Logs all the queries that change data. This replaces the update log, which will still be around until MySQL version 5.0, but is deprecated. You can turn on this log and specify the location with the option `log-bin=filename`.

- *Slow query log:* Logs all queries that took longer to execute than the value stored in the variable `long_query_time`. You can turn on this log and specify the location with the option `log-slow-queries=filename`

All of these except the binary log are simply text files. The binary log can be viewed using

```
mysqlbinlog logfile
```

We will look at the use of the slow query log in Chapter 19.

Log files will continue to grow larger so you should regularly rotate your log files. If you are using Linux, MySQL comes with a script called `mysql-log-rotate` to do this for you.

If you are using another operating system, you can move the old log files to a safe location manually and then tell MySQL to start using a new log file with the command

```
mysqladmin flush-logs
```

mysqladmin Option Summary

There are many options, with varying degrees of usefulness, that control `mysqladmin`.

Certain tasks can be done in SQL or using `mysqladmin`, such as creating and dropping databases:

```
mysqladmin create databasename
```

```
mysqladmin drop databasename
```

A common use for `mysqladmin` is to get information about the server and current status. The information can be as simple as "Is the server up?" (`ping`) or much more detailed, giving a list of available variables or processes. Many of the uses for `mysqladmin` follow.

To find out whether the server is up, use this:

```
mysqladmin ping
```

To find out what version of the MySQL server software is on this machine, use this:

```
mysqladmin version
```

To retrieve a short or long status message from the server, use this:

```
mysqladmin status
mysqladmin extended-status
```

To get a list of current active threads within the server, use this:

```
mysqladmin processlist
```

If you do get a list of processes (threads), you can selectively kill them like so:

```
mysqladmin kill id1,id2,id3...
```

To print the value of MySQL variables, use this:

```
mysqladmin variables
```

Summary

- Start the server with `mysqladmin`, by running the `mysqld` executable, or by using the Windows Services manager.
- Shut down the server with `mysql.server stop` or `mysqladmin shutdown`.
- Use `mysqlshow` or `SHOW` to get information about the current database or MySQL server.
- Set variables with `set variable=value;`.
- See threads with `show processlist` and kill them with `kill processid`.
- Clear caches with `FLUSH` and `RESET`.

- Improve the speed of joins with `analyze table tablename;`.
- MySQL stores log information in the error log, the query log (all queries), the binary log (queries that change data), and the slow query log (queries that take longer than `long_query_time`).

Quiz

1. Which of the following logs are enabled by default?

    a) query log

    b) slow query log

    c) error log

    d) binary log

    e) all of the above

2. The SQL command SHOW can be used to show

    a) the list of databases available

    b) the list of tables in a database

    c) the list of columns in a table

    d) all of the above

3. The script mysqladmin can be used to

    a) reload privileges to make sure that any changes take effect

    b) check on the current status of the server

    c) stop and start the server

    d) close and reopen log files

    e) all of the above

Exercises

Turn on all four log file options. After running various queries, examine their contents. If you do not have access to a large database, it may be hard to get an entry in the slow query log. The minimum definition of slow is one second.

Answers

Quiz

1. c
2. d
3. e

Next

In Chapter 14, "Backup and Disaster Recovery," we will look at how to make backup copies of your databases and what to do when things go wrong.

14

Backup and Disaster Recovery

In this chapter we will look at how to back up or make copies of your databases, how to move them to another machine, and how to recover when things go wrong.

We will cover the following:

- Backing up your databases
- Restoring from backups
- Checking and repairing tables

Backing Up and Restoring Your Database

Obviously, as with any electronic file, you should back up your database files. You may also want to make a copy of your database for replication purposes or to move to a new machine.

There are four ways you can make a backup in MySQL:

- Use the `mysqldump` script to create a dump file, that is, a file containing the SQL statements necessary to re-create the database.
- Use the `mysqlhotcopy` script to create a data file. This copies the data files for a particular database directly.
- Directly back up the data files yourself. This is really doing what `mysqlhotcopy` does, but manually. If you choose to use this option, you will need to either shut down the database or flush and lock all tables before copying to make sure that they are internally consistent. Both `mysqldump` and `mysqlhotcopy` will flush and lock for you, so they are easier, safer options.
- Use the `BACKUP TABLE` and `RESTORE TABLE` commands to back up or restore a specified table or set of tables.

We'll look at each of these options in turn.

Bear in mind that although backups are vitally important, all backups involve restricting access to the user while backups are being made. Why? To take a consistent snapshot of a database, tables need to be flushed and held constant while the backup is performed. This can be done by locking tables (in most cases) or by taking down the server (not recommended), but either way you are going to reduce database responsiveness while you are backing up.

One solution to this issue is replication. You can take down one slave and back it up while users continue blissfully about their business. We will discuss replication in detail in Chapter 16, "Replicating Your Database."

Backing Up and Restoring with mysqldump

The most common way to run a backup is using the `mysqldump` script from the command prompt on your system. This script connects to the MySQL server and creates an SQL dump file. The dump file contains the SQL statements necessary to re-create the database.

For example, typical usage of this script would be

```
mysqldump --opt -u username -p password employee > backup.sql
```

In this case we are using the --opt option, which encapsulates a few other options—we'll look at these in a minute. We have listed the database name and are redirecting the output to the backup file we want to use.

Using this script on the simple employee database will give you an output file similar to the one shown in Listing 14.1.

LISTING 14.1   **Sample Output from mysqldump**

```
-- MySQL dump 10.2
--
-- Host: localhost     Database: employee
----------------------------------------------------------
-- Server version     4.1.0-alpha-max-debug


--
-- Table structure for table 'assignment'
--

DROP TABLE IF EXISTS assignment;
CREATE TABLE assignment (
  clientID int(11) NOT NULL default '0',
  employeeID int(11) NOT NULL default '0',
  workdate date NOT NULL default '0000-00-00',
  hours float default NULL,
  PRIMARY KEY  (clientID,employeeID,workdate)
) TYPE=InnoDB CHARSET=latin1;
```

LISTING 14.1   **Continued**

```
--
-- Dumping data for table 'assignment'
--

/*!40000 ALTER TABLE assignment DISABLE KEYS */;
LOCK TABLES assignment WRITE;
INSERT INTO assignment VALUES (1,7513,'0000-00-00',5),(1,7513,'2003-01-20',8.5);
UNLOCK TABLES;
/*!40000 ALTER TABLE assignment ENABLE KEYS */;


--
-- Table structure for table 'client'
--

DROP TABLE IF EXISTS client;
CREATE TABLE client (
  clientID int(11) NOT NULL auto_increment,
  name varchar(40) default NULL,
  address varchar(100) default NULL,
  contactPerson varchar(80) default NULL,
  contactNumber varchar(12) default NULL,
  PRIMARY KEY  (clientID)
) TYPE=InnoDB CHARSET=latin1;


--
-- Dumping data for table 'client'
--

/*!40000 ALTER TABLE client DISABLE KEYS */;
LOCK TABLES client WRITE;
INSERT INTO client
VALUES
  (1,'Telco Inc','1 Collins St Melbourne','Fred Smith','95551234'),
  (2,'The Bank','100 Bourke St Melbourne','Jan Tristan','95559876');
UNLOCK TABLES;
/*!40000 ALTER TABLE client ENABLE KEYS */;


--
-- Table structure for table 'department'
--

DROP TABLE IF EXISTS department;
CREATE TABLE department (
  departmentID int(11) NOT NULL auto_increment,
  name varchar(30) default NULL,
  PRIMARY KEY  (departmentID)
) TYPE=InnoDB CHARSET=latin1;
```

LISTING 14.1 **Continued**

```
--
-- Dumping data for table 'department'
--

/*!40000 ALTER TABLE department DISABLE KEYS */;
LOCK TABLES department WRITE;
INSERT INTO department
VALUES
  (42,'Finance'),
  (128,'Research and Development'),
  (129,'Human Resources'),
  (130,'Marketing'),
  (131,'Property Services');
UNLOCK TABLES;
/*!40000 ALTER TABLE department ENABLE KEYS */;


--
-- Table structure for table 'employee'
--

DROP TABLE IF EXISTS employee;
CREATE TABLE employee (
  employeeID int(11) NOT NULL auto_increment,
  name varchar(80) default NULL,
  job varchar(30) default NULL,
  departmentID int(11) NOT NULL default '0',
  PRIMARY KEY  (employeeID)
) TYPE=InnoDB CHARSET=latin1;


--
-- Dumping data for table 'employee'
--

/*!40000 ALTER TABLE employee DISABLE KEYS */;
LOCK TABLES employee WRITE;
INSERT INTO employee
VALUES
  (6651,'Ajay Patel','Programmer',128),
  (7513,'Nora Edwards','Programmer',128),
  (9006,'Candy Burnett','Systems Administrator',128),
  (9842,'Ben Smith','DBA',42),
  (9843,'Fred Smith','DBA',131);
UNLOCK TABLES;
/*!40000 ALTER TABLE employee ENABLE KEYS */;
```

LISTING 14.1   **Continued**

```
--
-- Table structure for table 'employeeSkills'
--

DROP TABLE IF EXISTS employeeSkills;
CREATE TABLE employeeSkills (
  employeeID int(11) NOT NULL default '0',
  skill varchar(15) NOT NULL default '',
  PRIMARY KEY  (employeeID,skill)
) TYPE=InnoDB CHARSET=latin1;


--
-- Dumping data for table 'employeeSkills'
--

/*!40000 ALTER TABLE employeeSkills DISABLE KEYS */;
LOCK TABLES employeeSkills WRITE;
INSERT INTO employeeSkills
VALUES
  (6651,'Java'),
  (6651,'VB'),
  (7513,'C'),
  (7513,'Java'),
  (7513,'Perl'),
  (9006,'Linux'),
  (9006,'NT'),
  (9842,'DB2');
UNLOCK TABLES;
/*!40000 ALTER TABLE employeeSkills ENABLE KEYS */;
```

We could reload or re-create the employee database elsewhere by doing the following:

1. Creating an appropriately named database on the target machine.

2. Loading this file using

   ```
   mysql -u username -p < backup.sql
   ```

The mysqldump script has many options for use. In this case we have used --opt, which encompasses the following options:

- --quick: This tells MySQL to dump the data directly to the file, rather than buffering it in memory first (the default). This will speed things up.

- --add-drop-table: Tells MySQL to add a DROP TABLE statement before each CREATE TABLE in the dump. (You can see these in Listing 14.1.)

- --add-locks: Adds the LOCK TABLES and UNLOCK TABLES statements you can see in the dump file.

- **--extended-insert:** Tells MySQL to use the multiline insert syntax to insert multiple rows with a single INSERT. For example, in the listing, these look like the following:

```
INSERT INTO employeeSkills
VALUES
   (6651,'Java'),
   (6651,'VB'),
   (7513,'C'),
```

  If we have to use our backup to re-create the database, this will be faster to execute than a series of single INSERT statements.

- **--lock-tables:** Tells MySQL to lock all the tables before starting to dump.

Note that the --opt (meaning optimized) will optimize the length of time it takes to *reload the dump file*, rather than the length of time it takes to *create the dump file*. Creating the dump file can be slow.

Here are a couple of other useful options:

- **--databases:** Allows you to list more than one database for dumping.

- **--all-databases:** Tells MySQL to dump all the databases it has in storage.

- **--allow-keywords:** If you ever use field names that are MySQL keywords (or might become keywords in the future), this option tells MySQL to fully qualify every column name with its table name.

- **-d or --no-data:** Dumps only the database structure, not the contents. This is very useful if you are testing and deploying databases on different machines.

The advantages of using mysqldump are that it is simple to use and it takes care of table locking issues for you.

There are a couple of disadvantages. The first is that this script locks tables: Running this script on your server will lock out users for seconds or minutes, depending on the size of the tables. If you are planning on doing a dump on a single, nonreplicated server, you should try to do this in a nonpeak period or your users will tend to get a little irritated. If you have a lot of data and users at all times of the day, you should choose another backup option.

The other disadvantage is that, because mysqldump works through the MySQL server, it will be slower to run than mysqlhotcopy. The script mysqlhotcopy does not make much use of the MySQL server. It does most of its work directly through the file system.

Backing Up and Restoring with mysqlhotcopy

The mysqlhotcopy script differs from mysqldump in that it copies the actual database data files, rather than retrieving data through a connection to the server. It does make a connection in order to flush and lock the database tables, but because it is mostly engaged in file-system operations rather than database queries, it should run a little faster than mysqldump.

You can use it as shown here:

```
mysqlhotcopy -u username -p database_name backup_location
```

This script is a Perl script. If you are using a Unix or Unix-like machine, you will almost certainly have a `perl` executable somewhere. If you are using Windows, you will need to install Perl to use it. You can download Perl for Windows from ActiveState if you don't have it already:

```
www.activestate.com/Products/ActivePerl
```

The files produced by `mysqlhotcopy` are replicas of the database data files. To use these backups, you should stop the MySQL server and replace the data files in the MySQL data directory with the backed-up files.

Backing Up and Restoring Manually

Instead of using `mysqlhotcopy`, you can replicate what it does manually. This means flushing and locking the tables and copying the data files to a backup location while the tables are still locked.

This means you will need an open MySQL session. You can begin by issuing a LOCK TABLES command to lock all the tables you plan to back up:

```
lock tables
employee read,
department read,
client read,
assignment read,
employeeSkills read;
```

The LOCK TABLES statement takes as parameters a list of table names and the type of lock we would like to acquire, READ or WRITE. For a backup, a read lock is generally sufficient. This means that other threads (connections) can continue to read from the tables but will be unable to write to them while we are performing a backup.

Locking is important in situations like this because backups can take a significant amount of time. Using our example, it would be unfortunate if after the employee table had been backed up, but before the department table had been backed up, somebody deleted all employees in one department and then deleted the department. We would be left with an inconsistent backup, showing employees working for a nonexistent department.

Next, you should issue a FLUSH TABLES command:

```
flush tables;
```

If you are backing up all of your databases, you can do these two steps in one with the following command:

```
flush tables with read lock;
```

Now you can copy the data files. It is very important that you leave your session (where you locked and flushed the tables) open while you do this. This makes sure that the locks are maintained. When you close that session, the tables will be unlocked.

After copying your files, you should of course unlock the tables:

```
unlock tables;
```

This procedure is the same as that in the mysqlhotcopy script, and you can restore in the same way.

Backing Up and Restoring with BACKUP TABLE and RESTORE TABLE

As an alternative to the approaches we have just discussed, there are two SQL statements we can use to achieve the same effects. These are BACKUP TABLE and RESTORE TABLE. These commands work only on the MyISAM table type.

You can back up a MyISAM table like this:

```
backup table t1 to 'path/to/backup';
```

Note that if you are using Windows, you will need to specify the drive letter, for example,

```
backup table t1 to 'c:/path/to/backup';
```

This copies the files that represent the specified MyISAM table to the specified path. The table will be read locked before it is backed up.

You can also specify a comma-separated list of tables; however, each one will be locked and backed up in turn. If you want a consistent set of tables, you should issue a LOCK TABLES statement first (see the preceding section, "Backing Up and Restoring Manually," for details on how to do this).

To restore from the backup, use this:

```
restore table t1 from 'c:/tmp';
```

This will work only if the tables you restore do not exist in the current database. If you have a table with this name, you will need to issue a DROP TABLE before you use RESTORE.

Again, RESTORE works only on MyISAM tables.

Restoring from the Binary Log

In most cases when you restore from a backup, some inserts and updates will have been made since the backup was taken. The database can be regenerated by restoring from the backup as described in each of the previous sections and then re-executing any changes made since the backup was taken.

These changes are stored in your binary log or your update log. This is why the binary log is so important. You can extract a list of operations from the binary log using

```
mysqlbinlog logfile > updates.sql
```

It's a good idea to look at this file before re-executing the queries, in case you want to not re-execute any of them. It is possible that a poorly-thought-through SQL query caused you to need to resort to a backup.

For example, we once had a programmer type something along the lines of

```
update user set password='password';
```

Obviously, when restoring the table, we did not want to re-execute this particular query and again set the password for *every user* in our system to be password!

Testing Your Backup

Whichever backup method you choose, it is *very important* to test your backup or, more precisely, your recovery. It is not unusual to find administrators who dutifully create a backup on a regular basis but have never checked whether they can recover from a backup if needed.

A backup procedure should be something you give serious consideration when analyzing your risks and deciding how to do it. Where can you put the backup so that it is on a different physical disk? How can you ensure that a copy of the backup is stored securely offsite? Having made these decisions and scheduled the backup for regular processing, you should not be worrying about whether it works. If you have tried to recover as a test, you can find any problems before they are crucial.

One important part of your MySQL installation and recovery process to check is the binary log. It is not enabled by default, but it is needed to bring a restored database back up to date.

Checking and Repairing Tables

Checking tables for corruption is part of routine table maintenance and is also part of your disaster recovery routine, for example, in the event of a power failure.

MySQL allows us to check tables in three ways: using CHECK TABLE, using myisamchk (or isamchk), and using mysqlcheck. We can then repair any problem tables using REPAIR TABLE or again with myisamchk (or isamchk) or mysqlcheck.

There are a few factors you should take into account when determining which of these options to use. The CHECK and REPAIR commands can be used from inside MySQL, whereas the other techniques are used from the command line. CHECK and REPAIR can be used on both MyISAM and InnoDB tables. The isamchk script can be used on ISAM tables, whereas myisamchk and mysqlcheck can be used on MyISAM tables.

You should not use myisamchk or isamchk on tables that are currently in use. It is better if you take the server down before using these scripts, but you can resort to locking if needed. If you use these scripts on tables while they are being used by other MySQL threads, your data may become corrupted. CHECK, REPAIR, and mysqlcheck are all safe to use when the server is up and tables are in use.

We will look at the use of each of these tools.

Checking and Repairing Tables with CHECK and REPAIR

You can check a table with CHECK TABLE as in this example:

```
check table department;
```

CHECK TABLE works on MyISAM and InnoDB tables.

This should (all being well) give you a response like this:

```
+--------------------+-------+----------+----------+
| Table              | Op    | Msg_type | Msg_text |
+--------------------+-------+----------+----------+
| employee.department | check | status   | OK       |
+--------------------+-------+----------+----------+
1 row in set (0.00 sec)
```

You may also get Table is already up to date, which also means everything is fine.

If you get any other message, you have a problem and should try to repair the table. You can do this with REPAIR TABLE (as long as it's a MyISAM table) as shown here:

```
repair table t1;
```

If the repair works (or if no repair was actually needed), you should get a result similar to this:

```
+---------+--------+----------+----------+
| Table   | Op     | Msg_type | Msg_text |
+---------+--------+----------+----------+
| test.t1 | repair | status   | OK       |
+---------+--------+----------+----------+
1 row in set (0.03 sec)
```

If you get any message other than OK, the REPAIR hasn't worked and you will need to resort to the more powerful myisamchk.

Checking and Repairing Tables with myisamchk

In this chapter we consider only myisamchk and ignore isamchk. If you have any ISAM tables, we suggest that you convert them to MyISAM (see Chapter 9, "Understanding MySQL's Table Types").

The myisamchk program is incredibly useful and will get you out of some unpleasant spots you might find yourself in. Again, remember that you should not use myisamchk when the server is in use. It is safest to stop the server.

The simplest way to invoke myisamchk is by typing

```
myisamchk table
```

at the command prompt.

The table should be the path to a .MYI file that represents a MyISAM table.

This will report virtually all errors. If it doesn't seem to be finding your problem, you can try running it with the -m switch. The default behavior looks for corruption in the indexes; with this switch, the rows are scanned as well.

You can also repair errors with myisamchk. The vast majority of table errors you will encounter with MyISAM tables can be fixed in this way. You can invoke myisamchk with the -q -r options for quick recovery, as shown here:

```
myisamchk -q -r table
```

If this doesn't work, you can back up the data file and then try a full recovery:

```
myisamchk -r table
```

If that doesn't work, you can try the --safe-recover option, which will fix some errors not fixed by the -r option:

```
myisamchk --safe-recover table
```

The myisamchk program has a large number of options, which you can review by typing myisamchk at the command prompt with no parameters.

Checking and Repairing Tables with mysqlcheck

The mysqlcheck program can be used to check MyISAM and InnoDB tables and to repair MyISAM tables safely while the server is up and running.

To check database tables with mysqlcheck, you can invoke it as in the following example:

```
mysqlcheck -u username -p employee
```

You can follow this with a list of tables you would like checked, but by default it will check all the tables in the specified database (a nice feature). If all is well, you should see output similar to the following:

```
employee.assignment                      OK
employee.client                          OK
employee.department                      OK
employee.employee                        OK
employee.employeeSkills                  OK
```

You can also use the --databases switch to specify a list of databases to check or the --all-databases option to check all the databases on the server.

You can use mysqlcheck with the -r option to repair any corrupted MyISAM tables that it encounters.

Summary

Backup

- `mysqldump` creates a dump file of SQL statements.
- `mysqlhotcopy` copies the data files to a backup location.
- `BACKUP TABLE` copies the data file for a table to a backup location.
- You can manually back up by locking and flushing the tables and then copying the files.

Restoration

- Reload dump files from `mysqldump`.
- Copy back data files from `mysqlhotcopy` or a manual backup.
- Restore from `BACKUP TABLE` with `RESTORE TABLE`.
- Re-execute operations since the backup from the binary log.

Checking and Repairing Tables

- Check tables with `CHECK TABLE`, `myisamchk`, `isamchk`, or `mysqlcheck`.
- Repair tables with `REPAIR TABLE`, `myisamchk`, `isamchk`, or `mysqlcheck`.
- Don't use `myisamchk` while the server is being used.

Quiz

1. If you want to back up your database, it is necessary to
   a) take down the server
   b) lock and flush the tables
   c) both a) and b)
   d) none of the above

2. You should lock tables manually before executing
   a) a manual backup
   b) `mysqldump`
   c) `mysqlhotcopy`
   d) none of the above

3. Which table types can you check with CHECK TABLE?

   a) InnoDB and MyISAM

   b) MyISAM only

   c) MyISAM and BDB

   d) InnoDB and BDB

4. Which table types can you repair with REPAIR TABLE?

   a) InnoDB and MyISAM

   b) MyISAM only

   c) MyISAM and BDB

   d) InnoDB and BDB

5. If CHECK TABLE reports Table is already up to date

   a) you need to run REPAIR TABLE

   b) the storage engine is not supported by CHECK TABLE

   c) the table is fine

   d) none of the above

Exercises

Create a backup of your database using each of the methods in this chapter. Restore your database from each backup.

Answers

Quiz

1. b
2. a
3. a
4. b
5. c

Next

In the next chapter, "Securing Your MySQL Installation," we'll see how you can avoid the most common security pitfalls.

15

Securing Your MySQL Installation

In this chapter we'll discuss general security issues you should consider when running MySQL. Although we cannot be comprehensive in the space of a single chapter, we will give you a list of the most important don'ts. We will cover the following:

- How the privilege system works in practice
- Securing accounts
- Securing your installation files
- Filtering user data
- Other tips

How the Privilege System Works in Practice

In Chapter 11, "Managing User Privileges," we discussed user account creation, granting and revoking privileges, and the grant tables. We will begin this chapter by discussing how your MySQL server applies the privileges you have granted.

There are two stages to the privilege system. In the first stage, MySQL checks whether a user is allowed to connect to the server at all. The user table in the mysql database is used for this purpose. MySQL looks up your username and password as entered and the host from which you are trying to connect to see whether there is a matching row. If no row matches, you will not be able to connect to the server.

Because the user table supports wildcards in the host column, a user/hostname combination may match more than one row. MySQL determines which row is relevant by matching the most specific hostname first. For example, if there are rows in the table for test from host localhost and user test from host % (meaning any host), then the localhost row will be selected. Note that these two rows can have different passwords. This can cause a great deal of confusion. (We will look at an example of this in the section "Deleting Anonymous Accounts," later in this chapter.)

The second stage applies when you try to execute specific queries or commands. MySQL checks each query against the grant tables before it is executed.

If the query you are trying to execute requires a global privilege—such as doing a LOAD DATA INFILE or trying to use SHOW PROCESSLIST—the user table will be checked. For database-specific queries, the user table will be checked first. If the user has the privilege on all databases, this will be sufficient. If not, then the db and host tables are checked. If the user does not have the privilege at this level, then if any table- or column-level privileges are set, these will be checked last.

Securing Accounts

There are a few general security principles that apply to the management of user accounts in MySQL. We will look at these next.

Setting the Password for the Root Account

When you install MySQL, the root password is *not set by default*. You *absolutely* must set this password before using MySQL in anything other than a purely experimental environment. Without the root password set, anyone can log in and do anything he wants to your data. In virtually all cases, this is a very bad thing. If you have not done so already, set this password *immediately*.

Deleting Anonymous Accounts

When you install MySQL on Windows, it automatically creates some accounts for you. On Linux, this happens when you run the mysql_install_db script. Two of these accounts are anonymous; they represent the account you get when you don't specify a username. One has a host value of localhost and the other % (any other host, so effectively any remote connection). These accounts have no passwords set by default.

You can probably already see where we're going with this, but we strongly recommend that you delete these accounts. You can do this as shown here:

```
delete from user where User='';
delete from db where User='';
```

You will need to follow this with a FLUSH PRIVILEGES statement to flush the grant tables.

The second reason to do this is that these accounts can cause confusion when regular users try to log in. If you create an account for, let's say username laura at any host (%), then when laura tries to connect from localhost, the MySQL server looks for matching entries in the user table. It has laura@% and (anonymous)@localhost. Because MySQL matches the most specific hostname first, the matching row is (anonymous)@localhost. Note that although laura has supplied a username, this doesn't matter! The anonymous accounts don't require a username. This anonymous account is likely to have a different password from laura's account (by default, the password is blank, meaning the user should not supply one).

This means that when `laura` tries to log in with her username and password from `localhost`, she will get an `Access Denied` error for no obvious reason.

Again, the best way to avoid this problem is to delete these accounts and forget about them.

Dangerous Privileges

MySQL has a very fine-grained privilege system, as we discussed in Chapter 11. You must be very careful about to whom you grant some of these privileges. The specific ones to be most careful of are `FILE`, `PROCESS`, and `WITH GRANT OPTION`.

The `FILE` privilege allows users to `LOAD DATA INFILE`. This can be manipulated to load in files from the server (such as the password file /etc/passwd) or even database data files, effectively circumventing the privilege system.

The `PROCESS` privilege allows users to `SHOW PROCESSLIST`. This reveals the queries being executed at any given time, which may reveal confidential information about one user to another.

The `WITH GRANT OPTION` privilege allows a user to share his privileges with others. As long as you know this and understand the consequences, you can grant this privilege cautiously.

Passwords and Encryption

MySQL user passwords are encrypted. Before version 4.1, you could use the encrypted password as stored to log in. This has now been fixed and the password and login mechanism have been made more secure.

If you are writing an application that stores (non-MySQL) usernames and passwords, we recommend that you use something other than the `PASSWORD()` function to encrypt them. We recommend use of `MD5()` or `ENCRYPT()` instead. See Chapter 8, "Using MySQL Built-In Functions with `SELECT`," for a further discussion of these functions.

Securing Your Installation Files

In addition to setting up MySQL accounts securely, you must control access to the MySQL binaries, scripts, and data files. We will discuss some recommendations for this on your system.

Don't Run mysqld as Root

This is a recommendation for Linux and other Unix-like operating systems. Do not be tempted to run the MySQL server (mysqld) from the root user account. Just as you would if you were running a Web server, create a special user account for running the MySQL server. This way you can restrict the access privileges that the MySQL server has to the file system.

Access and Privileges Under Your Operating System

There is no point in spending time setting up user accounts in MySQL correctly if you cannot control file access in your operating system. You need to control user access to the MySQL binaries, scripts, and, in particular, the data directory. A common source of security holes involves users who have legitimate access to the machine where your MySQL server resides but not to, say, other users' databases. If these users can access the data directory, they can copy the data files and load them into another MySQL server.

Generally speaking, you want to ensure that the following safeguards are in place:

- Only appropriate users can run mysqld. You can restrict this to the user you have created for the purpose of running mysqld.

- Only appropriate users have access to MySQL's associated programs and scripts such as, for example, mysqladmin, mysqldump, and mysqlhotcopy. You may want to determine this on a program-by-program basis.

- Only appropriate users can access the MySQL data directory. If the server is running as user mysql, this user will need access to the directory. Any other users are optional and are therefore generally best denied.

Filtering User Data

Before passing on any user-entered data to MySQL, you should do some application-level error checking. Exactly how you go about this depends on the development platform you are using, but let's look at an example of why you should perform this error checking.

The problem may start with something as simple as a user entering his name—Patrick O'Leary—into your application. If you pass this data straight into MySQL, the apostrophe in O'Leary will cause a problem. In a more sinister context, users may try to enter MySQL commands into your application interface or Web forms. The steps you will need to take to check your data depend on your programming language, but some general guidelines can be found in the MySQL manual for a large number of languages.

Other Tips

We have covered the privilege system, looked at user accounts, considered the underlying filesystem files, and briefly mentioned filtering data. If you are concerned about the security of your network connection (which you probably should be with any external connection), MySQL allows you to encrypt transmissions with SSL. You should also give some consideration to physical security.

Using SSL Connections

If you want to avoid having crackers sniffing packets going between the MySQL server and clients, you can configure MySQL for secure connections. This means that all the data sent between the client and the server is encrypted using SSL (Secure Sockets Layer).

Setting up SSL requires that you install the OpenSSL library (available from `www.openssl.org`), start the server with the `--with-vio` and `--with-ssl` options, and do some setup at the command line. A good sample script of the work you need to do can be found in the MySQL manual; we have not reproduced it here.

After this is set up, you can restrict GRANT statements by requiring users to connect using SSL or to have an appropriate certificate. As a simple example, you can use the following GRANT statement:

```
grant all on employee.*
to testuser identified by 'password'
require ssl;
```

This creates (or modifies) an account for `testuser`, giving the user the password `password`. This user will be able to connect only via SSL. You can demand that all your users connect this way or perhaps all users logging in from anywhere other than `localhost`.

Securing Your Installation Physically

As a general guideline, if you are going to go to the trouble of carefully setting up user accounts in MySQL and the operating system and perhaps even requiring users to connect via SSL, then it is in your best interest to also secure your installation physically. If someone can take your server down by tripping over the power cable or steal your data by picking up the server and walking away with it, you have an obvious problem. Physical security is frequently forgotten, especially in small to medium-sized companies.

It may be less surprising for Windows, but even otherwise secure Unix/Linux systems are vulnerable when physical security is neglected. For example, with Linux it is trivial to alter a machine's root password when the user has physical access to the machine. Of course, with root access, all the data in your MySQL databases can be compromised.

Summary

Privilege System

- Stage 1: Check whether `user@host` is allowed to connect with this password.
- Stage 2: Check each query to see whether this `user@host` has sufficient privilege. Check the `user` and `host` tables first, then `db`, and then `tables_priv` and `columns_priv`.
- User table rows with more specific hosts are used in preference to those with less specific hosts.

Security Guidelines

- Make sure you set a root password for MySQL.

- Delete anonymous accounts; they allow access to strangers and may keep out legitimate users.

- Be very careful about granting the privileges FILE, PROCESS, and WITH GRANT OPTION.

- Encrypt application-level passwords with MD5() or CRYPT() rather than PASSWORD().

- Don't run mysqld as the Unix root user. Create a low-privilege user specifically to run mysqld.

- Limit access to mysqld to the MySQL low-privilege user.

- Limit access to programs and scripts as necessary to the user. Use the principle of least privilege: Give users access only if they really need it!

- Limit access to the data directory to the MySQL user.

- Never trust data directly from the user. Always filter it in your application-level logic.

- Turn on SSL connections if encrypted connections are required.

- Remember to watch the physical security of your MySQL server!

Quiz

1. Which table in the mysql database is checked to see whether a user may connect?

    a) tables_priv

    b) db

    c) columns_priv

    d) user

2. Which table is checked first to see whether a user may execute any particular query?

    a) user

    b) host

    c) db

    d) tables_priv

3. If MySQL finds multiple rows in the user table with the same username, which row is used for authentication?

   a) The row with the most specific host value.

   b) The row with the most general host value.

   c) Any row that has the right password.

   d) None of the above.

4. Which of the following privileges should you probably not grant to users?

   a) FILE

   b) PROCESS

   c) WITH GRANT OPTION

   d) All of the above

5. Which user should mysqld run as?

   a) A low-privilege user

   b) Root

   c) Either a) or b)

   d) Neither a) nor b)

Exercises

By referring to the sample setup in the MySQL manual, install OpenSSL for use with your MySQL server.

Answers

Quiz

1. d
2. a
3. a
4. d
5. a

Next

In Chapter 16, "Replicating Your Database," we'll see how you can set up two database servers to serve the same data. This spreads load, increases robustness, and makes backup creation easier.

## 16

Replicating Your Database

One of the advanced features included in MySQL is replication. Using this feature, you can have multiple servers storing the same data. You might do this for performance reasons, for reliability, or for ease of backups. Additionally, you might choose to make use of replication simply to spread your database load across multiple servers you already own, instead of one (new) large server.

Replicating a database can provide fault tolerance. If your master server fails, a slave can be treated as a hot backup and immediately be turned into the master.

In a system in which most operations involve reading data, but not writing data, replication can improve performance by routing queries to a number of machines. You might be trying to reduce load by performing queries on lightly loaded machines, or you might be trying to reduce network transmissions by sending queries to a geographically nearby machine. If your database queries are mainly fairly simple, even a simple rotating load-balancing algorithm can spread the load effectively. If some of your queries require extensive processing, you will probably have to investigate more sophisticated application-level load balancing.

A related use of replication to assist performance is in making backups. As mentioned in Chapter 14, "Backup and Disaster Recovery," backups can take a long time for a large database. Using replication, you can stop a slave and generate a backup of its data without affecting performance for other users.

Replication Principles

Replication can take various forms. The MySQL implementation is a directional master-slave relationship. One server is called the *master*. One or more other servers are called *slaves* to a particular master. The master controls what data is stored in the system while the slaves try to mirror that content.

The replication process relies on the binary log on the master. This log stores details of every query executed on the server since logging was enabled. Slaves are sent queries from the master's binary log to apply to their own stored data.

You would generally perform all write operations directly on the master and share read operations among all the slaves or even the master and the slaves. This is usually achieved by designing this logic into your application.

It is important to note that if you are adding replication to an existing database with stored data, the binary log may be incomplete. Binary logging is not enabled by default, so the server may not have been logging when you began adding data to the system. To start replicating, you need all slaves to have the same data that the master had when binary logging began. We will look at this subject in more detail later in this chapter.

After being started with consistent data, the slaves connect to the master and apply any changes appearing in the master's binary log to their own data. A thread on the slave connects to a thread on the master and requests new events. These are stored in a *relay log* on the slave. A separate thread on the slave reads events from the local relay log and executes the queries on the local mirror of the data.

Because the master and slaves can start at different times (because new servers can be added to the system while queries are being performed and because network connections can fail or become a bottleneck), slaves need to be able to keep track of where they are in the log of updates to be performed. It is important that atomic transactions are honored and updates are performed in order. For most applications, as long as the database moves from one consistent state to another, it is less important if the data being read is a few seconds or minutes out of date.

If you are considering using replication, you need to understand how it works. Updates are asynchronous and do not happen in real time. Queries sent to different servers can give different results for some time after an update is made. This can be seen as a negative, but the positive side is that if you have a slave running on a portable device or an unreliable network, it will happily operate for long periods between updating data from the master.

A Note on Versions

Replication was added in a fairly recent version of MySQL (3.23.15). It is therefore a feature that still improves with nearly every version that is released. If you intend to use replication, it would be a good idea to be using an up-to-date version of MySQL on all machines.

It is possible to have some combinations of versions running in master-slave relationships together, but this adds an extra level of uncertainty and is best avoided where possible. You can run into problems in which functions, such as PASSWORD(), have changed between versions if you try to make different versions work together.

If you really need to have different versions on the same system, a matrix of combinations of master and slave versions that can work together is available in the documentation here:

www.mysql.com/doc/en/Replication_Implementation.html

Setting Up and Configuring for Replication

Most replication systems use multiple machines on one internal network. If you are using machines connected via the public Internet, think carefully about the security implications. As a practical starting point, make sure that the port you are using for MySQL is accessible for any machines you need to connect through a firewall (3306 is the default port).

Assuming that you have a recent version of MySQL installed on your machines and one or more databases you want replicated, the following steps are required to set up a single master with one or more slaves.

Create a Replication User

It is good practice to create users with only the permissions that they need for their tasks, rather than using the root user for everything, as we discussed in Chapter 1, "Installing MySQL." You therefore need a user for replication activity on the master server.

If you are going to populate your slaves initially by using LOAD TABLE FROM MASTER or LOAD DATA FROM MASTER, your replication user needs a special set of permissions. The following GRANT statement (run on the master) will create a user with the permissions required for the startup tools to connect:

```
grant replication slave, reload, super, select
    on logs.*
    to replication@"%" identified by 'password';
```

(Note that this example uses the logs database. You should change this to the name of your database, and obviously you should change the password to something more secure.)

After the initial copy from master to slave is complete, the replication user will not need so many permissions. If you are populating your slaves from a backup or reducing the user's permissions after the initial copying is complete, the user needs only the replication permission, so the following query will create a user named replication that can connect from any of the slave servers (and any other machines):

```
grant replication slave on logs.* to replication@"%" identified by 'password';
```

The syntax for GRANT queries was covered in Chapter 11, "Managing User Privileges." The permission replication slave was added to MySQL 4.0.2 and is specifically for this purpose. For older versions of MySQL, use the permission file.

The query as shown will allow access only to the database named logs. If you want all databases on this machine to be able to be replicated, use *.* instead of logs.*.

Check Master Configuration

Your master server needs to have binary logging enabled. If you have read the installation instructions in this book, you have hopefully already enabled it because it has other uses beyond replication. To check that it is on, you can run a SHOW VARIABLES query. You can simply type

```
show variables;
```

to get a complete list, but for concise output, type the following:

```
show variables like "log_bin";
```

If binary logging is off, add `log-bin` to your options file as shown in the example in Listing 1.1. The options file will be named `my.ini` or `my.cnf`, depending on which operating-system conventions you have followed.

Edit your `my.ini`/`my.cnf` file to give your master server a unique id. At a minimum, your options file should now look like this:

```
[mysqld]
log-bin
server-id=1
```

The `server-id` is a unique identifier for each of your MySQL servers. It must be a positive integer, but the choice of `1` here was completely arbitrary.

If you have edited your options file, you will need to restart the server for changes to take effect.

Create a Master Snapshot

To start replication, you need three things:

- A complete, consistent snapshot of the current database
- The name of the master server's binary log file
- The offset into the binary log where the server is currently

Exactly how you grab these will vary a little depending on whether you are using MyISAM or InnoDB tables and how averse you are to stopping access to the database for a period.

For MyISAM tables, you can grab a snapshot after you start each slave. See the section "Start Slaves," later in this chapter. This method is not very efficient, though, particularly if you have a large amount of data and many slaves. For each slave, the LOAD DATA FROM MASTER query will obtain a lock on the master's data and hold it until a complete copy has been transmitted. You can lock the databases for a much shorter time by making the snapshot manually via the file system. This will also allow you to use one snapshot to start as many slaves as required, reducing time when the server is locked.

For InnoDB tables, you do not have the option of running a LOAD DATA FROM MASTER query. You can make a file-system snapshot or buy the hot backup tool.

If you are making a file-system snapshot, you first need to make sure that the stored data is consistent and up-to-date by running the following query:

```
flush tables with read lock;
```

This will also lock the table, barring any writes until you unlock it.

You can get the current binary log file and offset from the following query:

```
show master status;
```

The output should look something like this:

```
+------------------+----------+--------------+-----------------+
| File             | Position | Binlog_do_db | Binlog_ignore_db |
+------------------+----------+--------------+-----------------+
| server-bin.000007 |     211 |              |                 |
+------------------+----------+--------------+-----------------+
```

You need to record the contents of the first column (the binary log file name) and the second column (the offset into the binary log). If these are empty, you will be using an empty string for the filename and 4 for the offset.

To create a snapshot of a MyISAM table, simply copy the directory that contains the data using an archiving program. On Unix, type something like this to get a snapshot of our logs database:

```
tar -cvf /tmp/snapshot.tar /path/mysql/data/logs
```

On Windows, use WinZip or a similar archiving tool to grab a copy of the directory C:\mysql\data\logs.

After the copy is complete, you can re-enable write access to the database by typing this:

```
unlock tables;
```

The employee table we have been using throughout this book (like most tables the authors use on projects) is an InnoDB table. If you have purchased the (commercial) InnoDB hot backup tool, it is perfect for this task. It is available from Innobase Oy at

```
www.innodb.com/hotbackup.html
```

Without this tool, the safest approach is to flush and lock the database with the following queries. Use

```
flush tables with read lock;
```

and then display and record the binary log file and offset (as for MyISAM):

```
show master status;
```

Without unlocking the database, shut it down and make a copy of the directory that relates to that database inside your MySQL data directory. For InnoDB tables, you will also need to copy across the data files and logs. After the snapshot is complete, you can restart and unlock the database.

Configure Slaves

Each slave needs a unique server id. Edit your options file (my.cnf/my.ini) to add a line like this one to each:

```
server-id=2
```

The id must be a positive integer, but as long as no two are the same, it does not matter what you choose. If you are going to have more than a handful of servers running, an escalating sequence is probably your best hope of keeping them unique.

If you are working from a file-system snapshot, you need to copy the files into the appropriate places on the slave server. If you are working with more than one operating system, remember to consider filename capitalization.

Editing your options file or copying across InnoDB files will require you to restart your slave server.

Start Slaves

To start a slave that was set up as described here, you will need to run the following queries:

```
change master to master_host='server',
                master_user='replication',
                master_password='password',
                master_log_file='server-bin.000007',
                master_log_pos=211;
start slave;
```

In this example, the word `server` is the hostname of the master server. The word `replication` is the username of the user we created to do the replication tasks. That user's password should go in place of `password`. The binary log file name and offset fill out the parameters required.

The `START SLAVE` query launches the slave's replication threads, causing it to try to connect to the master and collect updates.

If you have copied a snapshot via the file system, you should be able to run some matching queries against the master and slave to check that the replication is working correctly. Make a small update to the master and check that it is mirrored on the slave.

If the tables you are replicating are relatively small MyISAM tables, you can create and populate them via a query like

```
load table logs.logJan2003 from master;
```

to copy a single table or

```
load data from master;
```

to copy all tables onto this slave.

After you have replication working, entering queries manually to configure replication is not practical, even if you restart only occasionally. The same information can go in your options file with a slightly different syntax.

Your slave's `my.ini` or `my.cnf` file could look something like this:

```
[mysqld]
server-id = 2
master-host = server
master-user = replication
master-password = password
replicate-do-db = logs
```

Advanced Topologies

The most common use for replication is load balancing in a system in which there are large numbers of reads and a relatively small number of writes. Most replication setups involve a single master and a small number of slaves, but in some situations, more complicated installations are justified.

If you plan a large number of slaves or have machines spread over many locations, it might make sense to have a cascading system in which one server acts as master for some of your slaves. One or more of the slaves then acts as a master for a further set of slaves. Figure 16.1 shows a single master (machine number 1) acting as a master to machines 2 though 6. Some of these slaves, in turn, act as masters to other sets of slaves.

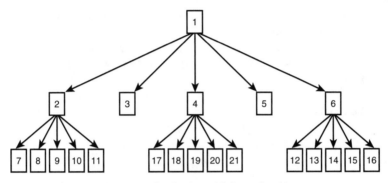

FIGURE 16.1   Replication with Cascading Masters

An arrangement like this saves load on the main master server and reduces network traffic on the links that lead to that machine. Depending on the ratio of reads to writes in your application, this can provide a great deal of scalability without much complexity.

It is fairly straightforward to have any number of slaves and even to have multiple masters, as long as each machine is a master in one relationship and a slave in another. As long as you build your application knowing that there will be times when some servers are missing recent updates, you can treat the system much like you would a single database server.

Things get more complicated when you have a circular relationship in which multiple servers are accepting write queries and updates are being replicated in more than one direction. The simplest circular relationship is a pair of machines, both acting as masters and both acting as slaves. Changes can be made to either machine and replicated to the other. You need to be very careful when writing an application for this sort of system.

Because changes are applied asynchronously, you can end up with conflicting auto increment fields, clashing unique ids, and inconsistent data. In some applications, this arrangement may work well. For instance, a data logging application with few relationships between tables that requires high throughput and availability may be willing to sacrifice consistency.

Replication Future

The current replication features are very robust. The features are bundled in the standard distribution (unlike most commercial databases) and have been used extensively in high-volume environments. Users you will have heard of include Slashdot, Yahoo!, and Google.

Having said that, the features are still relatively new, and there are some rough edges. As you have already seen, the process for setting up a new slave with a snapshot is not very user-friendly. The treatment of MyISAM tables and InnoDB tables is not consistent.

In general, you need to approach replication with a degree of care. The feature works and works well, but can be tricky to initially set up because different systems and setups vary. We generally recommend that you use the newest available versions of MySQL.

Some of these problems will be solved when MyISAM gets a hot backup tool like InnoDB's. Other features planned for future MySQL versions include multimastering—the capability of a slave to mirror two masters and resolve conflicts—and built-in failover and load-balancing features. Currently, you need to handle failover and load balancing in your application or buy a third-party clustering tool, such as Emic Application Cluster from www.emicnetworks.com.

There are some replication-related settings in the options file that are currently unimplemented. These include options for setting up SSL connections between slaves and masters. If your replication is done over a public network, this will make operating securely easier. Currently, if you want to make secure connections, you need to use another product, such as Stunnel.

Summary

- Replication is not suitable for all occasions, but if you have a busy application with a high read-to-write ratio, it can be an excellent scaling tool.

- Remember that updates are not applied to slaves in real time. Each copy of a table should move from one consistent state to another, but reads from different servers may give dated results while a slave updates.

- The most useful replication-related queries are START SLAVE, LOAD TABLE *name* FROM MASTER, LOAD DATA FROM MASTER, SHOW MASTER STATUS, SHOW SLAVE STATUS, and SHOW SLAVE HOSTS.

Quiz

1. MySQL replication can be used to
   a) create a development server to test and benchmark new code on real data without risk
   b) improve performance
   c) make backups less disruptive
   d) improve availability
   e) all of the above

2. The binary log file
   a) is created by default
   b) is useful for replication and backup recovery
   c) is an SQL dump file renamed
   d) all of the above

3. Read and write operations are usually performed on
   a) reads on slaves, writes on slaves
   b) reads on slaves, writes on masters
   c) reads on masters, writes on slaves
   d) reads on masters, writes on masters
   e) none of the above

4. The design of MySQL replication means that
   a) all data is up-to-date all the time
   b) servers need to be connected via a reliable network and if any server is unavailable, all others need to wait for it to be brought back online
   c) updates are fast but can take time to propagate to all slaves
   d) updates can be made to any server, and they will be sent up to the master and down to all the other slaves

Answers

Quiz

1. e
2. b
3. b
4. c

VI

Optimizing MySQL

17   Optimizing Your MySQL Server Configuration

18   Optimizing Your Database

19   Optimizing Your Queries

17

Optimizing Your MySQL
Server Configuration

In this chapter, we'll look at some options for speeding up your MySQL server. Server tuning is a huge topic and is something of a black art. In this chapter, we only aim to give you an introduction to the basics of tuning your server setup. We will cover the following:

- Compiling and linking for speed
- Tuning server parameters
- Tuning other factors

The key thing to remember when making any server tuning changes is that you will need to do it empirically. Try one change at a time, and measure performance before and after the change. Only then will you know whether your changes are actually improving performance.

If you are really trying to benchmark correctly, you may want to log a period worth of queries (an hour, a day, or some average period) and then replay those queries with the new server configuration.

Compiling and Linking for Speed

In Chapter 1, "Installing MySQL," we covered only installation from binaries (specifically RPM under Unix). When you're learning how to use MySQL, this is by far the easiest way, especially if you are not used to compiling your own software, as is the case for many Windows users.

You may be able to get a performance improvement from your server by downloading the source version and compiling it yourself. Specifically, if you have a Pentium-based machine and run Linux, you will be able to get a significant performance increase by compiling MySQL with the pgcc compiler, which optimizes for Pentium only. (These executables are not compatible with AMD chips, hence the binary available from MySQL is compiled with plain gcc.) MySQL AB says that you can get an extra 10% to 30% faster server if you compile it yourself with the right compiler and options on—see the manual for further details.

Another improvement you can make over the MySQL-supplied binary is available by compiling MySQL with support for only the character set(s) you need. The downloadable binaries contain support for all the character sets. (You can find more information on character sets in Chapter 12, "Configuring MySQL.")

The MySQL manual contains suggestions for optimizing user-compiled binaries for various operating systems. You can also find many operating-system and compiler-specific issues discussed on the MySQL mailing lists. The archives are at

```
http://lists.mysql.com
```

Tuning Server Parameters

You can tune your MySQL server parameters to try to optimize your configuration.

As a reminder, you can check the current values of server parameters with this:

```
show variables;
```

You can see the effects of your server configuration by looking at the output of this:

```
show status;
```

Another useful tool for monitoring what is happening with your server at any given time is Jeremy Zawodny's `mytop` Perl script.

This tool acts as the equivalent to the Unix top command and shows what processes are active, the process state, the time spent, and so on. Additionally, it allows you to drill into a MySQL process and see the actual query being executed.

You can download this from

```
http://jeremy.zawodny.com/mysql/mytop
```

All of these tools will allow you to keep track of the changes you have made and the effects they have.

There are so many server parameters in my.cnf options files that you may well wonder where to begin. Most versions of MySQL come with sample `my.cnf` files, typically in the support-files directory of your installation. There are four suggested `my.cnf` files in this directory: `my-huge.cnf`, `my-large.cnf`, `my-medium.cnf`, and `my-small.cnf`. You can choose one as a starting point for your system.

The key parameters you will tune have to do with how MySQL uses memory. For any database server, more memory is a good thing, but it's important that this memory is available to the database server and that it is allocated appropriately between tasks.

MySQL has a set of internal buffers and caches. You can control how much memory is allocated to each of these. The two most important parameters to control are the `key_buffer_size` and the `table_cache`. These two are shared across all the threads running on the server, and they have a huge influence on performance.

The *key buffer* is where MyISAM indexes are stored in memory. As index blocks are used, they will be loaded into the buffer. Each time a query is issued, if the relevant index block is in the buffer, it will be read from there. Otherwise, the index block will need to be loaded from the disk into the key buffer, which is obviously slower. Generally speaking, with the key buffer, bigger is better.

When considering what value to set for the `key_buffer_size`, you should look at how much memory you have overall, whether or not the server is a dedicated MySQL server, and how big your index data is (that is, how big your .MYI files are in total). Jeremy Zawodny, renowned MySQL tuning expert at Yahoo!, recommends setting this value to somewhere between 20% and 50% of the total memory on a dedicated server. If you are using a shared machine, it should obviously be a smaller amount. It should also be a smaller amount if your index data is small. If you have only 20MB of index data, there is little point in allocating 128MB to the key buffer.

Note also that the key buffer is only for MyISAM tables. Other table types have their own separate parameters for tuning. There is no point in greatly increasing the size of the key buffer if you are using only InnoDB tables, for example. In this case, the parameter you need is called `innodb_buffer_pool_size`. The InnoDB buffer pool stores both index and table data. (You can find more information on InnoDB configuration in Chapter 12 and in the MySQL manual.)

The second really important parameter is the *table cache*, controlled via the `table_cache` option. This limits the maximum number of tables that can be open at once. With MyISAM tables, each table and each index is a separate file on your operating system. Opening and closing files is slow, so these files are left open until they are explicitly closed, the server shuts down, or the total number of open tables exceeds the `table_cache` parameter. Increasing the `table_cache` value will be helpful if you have a large number of tables on your server. Your operating system will impose an upper limit on the number of open files or the number of files opened by a single process or user, so check this for your system before resetting the `table_cache` value.

Besides these two global memory pools, there are various chunks of memory allocated on a per-thread basis—for example, the *sort buffer* and the *read buffer*. The value is the same for each thread, but each thread can have this amount of memory allocated to the specified purpose.

The read buffer size, controlled by the `read_buffer_size` parameter, is used when a full table scan is performed to store the table data. The more table data that can be stored, the fewer disk reads that will need to be performed; however, if this value is set too high, the set of read buffers for each thread can become a memory hog. (You may want to note that this parameter was previously called the record buffer and was controlled by the `record_buffer` parameter.)

The sort buffer, controlled by the `sort_buffer` parameter, is used when you run queries containing ORDER BY clauses. It is used to sort the data. If you are sorting large datasets, make it bigger, but the same riders apply as to the record buffer.

Tuning Other Factors

Finally, there are a few tips that may help with your physical setup.

With regard to your operating system, MySQL recommends Solaris for getting the most out of multiple CPU machines. Although MySQL is used across various operating systems, development and initial testing are done on Solaris, so this would logically be the most optimized platform.

If you have access to multiple disks, you can improve performance by putting different databases on different disks. You can also use RAID—RAID 0 will improve reading and writing performance, and RAID 1 or 5 will improve reading performance. You will also get better performance from SCSI drives than IDE drives.

You may also consider the use of a journaling file system, such as Reiserfs or XFS. These may give a performance gain.

Obviously, a large and basic gain can be made by having fast networks between clients and servers and between masters and slaves when using replication.

Summary

There is an entire book's worth of material on MySQL optimization, so be sure to continue reading and researching for yourself.

- You may obtain a performance gain by compiling the MySQL binary yourself, especially if you are running Linux on a Pentium machine.
- Tune server parameters for a performance boost, particularly those relating to memory usage. More physical memory is always a good thing, but allocating it is more important. These are some particularly important parameters:
  - `key_buffer_size`: Amount of memory used for storing MyISAM indexes.
  - `table_cache`: Number of tables that can be open at once.
  - `read_buffer_size`: Amount of memory used to store data from full table scans.
  - `sort_buffer`: Amount of memory used to store table data to be sorted for `ORDER BY`.
- Tune hardware with more memory, use of RAID, use of a journaling file system, and a fast network between clients and servers and masters and slaves.

Quiz

1. The parameter that controls how much memory is used to store indexes for InnoDB is
   a) `key_buffer_size`
   b) `innodb_buffer_pool_size`
   c) `innodb_key_buffer_size`
   d) `read_buffer_size`

2. The parameter that controls how much memory is used to cache table data for InnoDB is
   a) `key_buffer_size`
   b) `innodb_buffer_pool_size`
   c) `innodb_key_buffer_size`
   d) `read_buffer_size`

3. The parameter that controls how much memory is used to cache table data for MyISAM is
   a) `key_buffer_size`
   b) `table_cache`
   c) `innodb_key_buffer_size`
   d) `read_buffer_size`

4. The parameter that controls how much memory is used to cache index data for MyISAM is
   a) `key_buffer_size`
   b) `table_cache`
   c) `innodb_key_buffer_size`
   d) `read_buffer_size`

5. The `read_buffer_size` parameter should not be made too large because
   a) if many threads are performing full scans, you will have a problem
   b) it is always possible to add more indexes so that MySQL will never need to do a full table scan
   c) it wastes disk space
   d) none of the above

Exercises

Experiment with using benchmarking programs to measure performance while setting the parameters discussed in this chapter to various values. Can you find an optimal value for each parameter on your system?

Answers

Quiz

1. b
2. b
3. d
4. a
5. a

Next

In the next chapter, "Optimizing Your Database," we will look at how to optimize your database schemas, how to index for optimization, and how to optimize individual database tables.

18

Optimizing Your Database

In Chapter 17, "Optimizing Your MySQL Server Configuration," we discussed how you can set up your server for optimal performance. In this chapter, we'll look at how you can optimize your database tables.

Common database design guidelines and normalization usually improve performance. There are also other choices you can make when working with your database design that will make the end product faster or slower. In this chapter, we will review these choices.

We will cover the following:

- What's slow in MySQL databases?
- Making the right design choices
- Using indexes for optimization
- Using OPTIMIZE TABLE

What's Slow in MySQL Databases?

Having read the preceding chapter on server optimization, we can now turn our attention to database optimization. In the next chapter, we'll look at specific query optimization.

If you have optimized your server (and perhaps thrown some hardware at the problem), you can next consider whether any of the following issues apply to you:

- *Not using enough indexes.* The number one cause of poor performance is using tables that have no indexes or that are without indexes on columns you are searching. This doesn't mean that you should have as many indexes as possible because that can cause the next problem on this list.
- *Using too many indexes.* Updating a lot of indexes as data is inserted or updated takes time. If you are retrieving data, indexes are good. When you are inserting new rows, updating rows, or deleting rows, indexes are no longer your friends. When you update data, the indexes need updating too, increasing the amount of overhead you have to deal with.

- *Using table- and column-level privileges.* If you use table- or column-level privileges for any resource, MySQL must check table and column privileges every time a user runs a query.

- *Making the wrong database design choices.* There are ways to design the actual structure of your database to make it faster to query.

We will discuss database design for speed and indexing in the next two sections.

Making the Right Design Choices

There are various design choices you can make that will help to speed up your database performance. They are as listed here:

- Use the smallest type that data will fit in. For example, if you are storing numbers from 1 to 10, don't use INT; use TINYINT instead. The smaller your rows and tables are, the quicker they will be to search. The smaller your data is, the more rows can be cached in memory.

- Use fixed-length records where possible. If all rows in a table are the same length, it's faster for MySQL to access rows in the middle of the table. To get fixed-length rows, all the column types you use must be of fixed length. This means no VARCHAR, no TEXT, and no BLOB.

  If you need to store TEXT and BLOB, you might consider denormalizing your schema to break the TEXT or BLOB fields out into a separate table.

  If you are using only VARCHAR, you can consider replacing them all with CHAR. This is something of a trade-off because CHAR will occupy more space on disk, going against our first suggestion in this list.

- Declare as many columns NOT NULL as possible. If your data logically requires NULL values, then obviously you should use them. However, note that you are paying a small speed and storage space price for these, so use NOT NULL wherever possible.

- Choose the table type on a table-by-table basis. Non–transaction-safe tables (for example, MyISAM) involve a lot less overhead and are therefore faster than the transaction-safe types (InnoDB and BDB). MySQL allows you to have a mixture of table types in the one database. Choose the fastest one that can do each job. (You can find more information about the different types in Chapter 9, "Understanding MySQL's Table Types.")

- Choose appropriate indexes. We will cover this topic in detail in the next section.

- In extreme cases, you may even consider denormalization of tables to reduce the number of joins made for common queries. Because this can make your database a nightmare to maintain, it is not generally recommended.

Indexing for Optimization

If you have been following along in this book, you should have a database that contains primary keys. This will ensure that you have at least one index per table because indexes are automatically created by MySQL for columns that are declared as PRIMARY, KEY, or UNIQUE.

If you are trying to optimize an existing database, it is worth checking whether the database has any indexes. It is a common design flaw to leave them out. The SQL command DESCRIBE will tell you what indexes a table already has.

So, what's an index, and what is it used for?

An index is like a lookup table that allows us to find specific rows in a table quickly. If an index is created on column X, we can search for particular values of column X in the fast-to-search index. The index will tell us where in the table the row containing that value can be found, so we can go directly to it.

If you do not have an index on a table, the entire table will be scanned to find rows you are looking for. Imagine trying to find a topic in this book by starting at the beginning and reading every word on every page. It is much faster to look up a topic in the index of this book and turn directly to the page you need.

Indexes in MySQL are stored as b-trees (binary trees), a data structure that is very fast for searching.

Indexes can be on a single column or can span multiple columns (just like keys). An index will be used when running a query, if the search is being performed on the following:

- A single column that has a single-column index—for example, if we index departments on departmentID and perform a query like SELECT...WHERE departmentID=n.

- A set of columns that forms a multicolumn index—for example, if we have created an index on the employee.assignment table on (clientID, employeeID, workdate) and we perform a query like SELECT...WHERE clientID=x AND employeeID=y AND workdate=z.

- A column or set of columns that forms a subset of a multicolumn index, as long as there is a *leftmost prefix* of the index columns—for example, with the assignment table as before, with an index on (clientID, employeeID, workdate), indexes would be used for these types of queries:

  SELECT...WHERE clientID=x
  SELECT...WHERE clientID=x AND employeeID=y

  But, they would not be used for this type:

  SELECT...WHERE employeeID=y AND workdate=z

The moral of the story is that is if you will be making frequent queries based on a column or set of columns that does not fit the preceding criteria, you should consider running a CREATE INDEX statement to create an appropriate index. Note that MySQL can use only one index per table in a single query. It cannot combine existing indexes automatically.

We will look further at this issue in Chapter 19, "Optimizing Your Queries," when we look at the EXPLAIN statement.

ANALYZE TABLE

We can use the `ANALYZE TABLE` statement to review and store the key distribution in a table. MySQL stores this information and uses it to decide how to execute joins. You can run this statement by typing

```
analyze table tablename;
```

Using OPTIMIZE TABLE

Finally, we should mention the `OPTIMIZE TABLE` command. It has the following, very straightforward syntax:

```
OPTIMIZE TABLE tablename;
```

This is the MySQL equivalent of defragmenting your hard disk. As you work with the database, the files that store the data end up with fragments of space within the data where records were deleted or where records had to be moved because an update made them larger. This scattered space is inefficient.

You should use `OPTIMIZE TABLE` periodically when you have deleted a lot of data from a table or if you have inserted, deleted, or updated a lot of rows and your rows are of variable length. It will tidy up the table's disk storage, re-sort the index, and update statistics for the table.

This command works only on MyISAM and BDB tables at the time of writing.

Summary

- You can optimize your database structure by keeping data a small and fixed size, by indexing appropriately, and by choosing an appropriate table type.
- Indexes are used to find records quickly according to the index column value.
- An index will be used in a query when the query is based on the index column or columns or a leftmost prefix of the index columns.
- `OPTIMIZE TABLE tablename;` performs housekeeping similar to defragging your disk.

Quiz

1. Which of the following statements about indexes is true?

    a) Indexes take up too much space on disk and should not be used.

    b) Not having any indexes can make your queries run slowly.

    c) You should index as many columns as possible.

    d) None of the above.

2. When choosing data types for columns

    a) use the same ones throughout a database because this will make the database more efficient

    b) use variable-sized ones wherever possible to optimize disk usage

    c) use fixed-sized ones wherever possible to speed up access to data

    d) none of the above

3. When choosing storage engine types for tables

    a) always use InnoDB or BDB because they are transaction safe

    b) always use MyISAM because it is the fastest

    c) use a mix of types depending on what you need in a table

    d) none of the above

4. An index will *not* be used if a query

    a) uses a leftmost prefix of the index columns

    b) uses all the index columns in a different order than in the index

    c) uses all the index columns in the same order as in the index

    d) uses a rightmost prefix of the index columns

5. Use OPTIMIZE TABLE

    a) when you have just created a table, to improve its structure

    b) when using InnoDB tables, to reduce overhead

    c) after a lot of SELECT statements have been run on a table

    d) after a lot of DELETE statements have been run on a table

Exercises

Which of the following queries on the employee database would use indexes? (You can check Chapter 4, "Creating Databases, Tables, and Indexes," for the exact structure of the database. Or, if you have it installed, use `describe` to see which columns are indexed.)

a)
```
select *
from employee
where departmentID=128;
```

b)
```
select employeeID
from assignment
where clientID=1;
```

c)
```
select skill, count(skill)
from employeeSkills
group by skill;
```

If these three queries were going to be run frequently, what additional indexes would you create?

Answers

Quiz

1. b
2. c
3. c
4. b
5. d

Exercises

Only b) uses an index.

You could consider indexing `employee.departmentID` and `employeeSkills.skill`.

Next

In the next (and final) chapter, "Optimizing Your Queries," we will discuss how to work out when particular queries are running slowly and why, as well as how to solve the problem.

## 19

Optimizing Your Queries

MySQL allows us to analyze individual queries to see how long they take and exactly how they are executed on the database. By looking at this information and armed with an understanding of how MySQL tries to optimize your queries for you, you can sometimes improve performance. In this chapter we'll look at the following:

- Finding slow queries
- Benchmarking your queries
- Using the slow query log
- Using EXPLAIN to see how queries are executed
- Understanding MySQL's built-in query optimization
- Optimization tips

Finding Slow Queries

To optimize any application, you must first find out which parts of it take up the most execution time. There are a few ways to do this:

- *Observation:* Frequently, the reason we notice that optimization is needed is that one particular query runs at the speed of continental drift.
- *Benchmarking:* Test your application to see which parts of it are slow.
- *Slow query log:* This log tracks slow queries, as you might expect from its name.

After a slow query has been identified, you can work out how it is being executed by MySQL by using the EXPLAIN statement and can take steps to optimize the query.

It is not usually necessary to attempt to speed up all queries in an application. Generally, only a small portion of your code takes up most of the execution time. Unless your system is very, very busy, the programming time spent attempting to accelerate parts that do not take much time is wasted.

Benchmarking Your Queries

In any kind of programming optimization problem, benchmarking is useful. By bench-marking, we mean specifically timing how long your queries take. This is best done by running a query many times and seeing how long it takes on average. A single execution of the query will be subject to load issues, so it may give unpredictable results. You will also find that the second time you run a query, it should be quicker because the query is cached.

You can, of course, use external scripts or programs to run queries multiple times. For an example, download the source distribution of MySQL and look at the benchmarking code that is included in the sql-bench directory.

You can also test the speed of evaluation of any expression (including a query) in MySQL by using the built-in BENCHMARK() function. For example:

```
select benchmark(1000000, 6*9);
```

This will produce something similar to the following results:

```
+------------------------+
| benchmark(1000000, 6*9) |
+------------------------+
|                      0 |
+------------------------+
1 row in set (0.25 sec)
```

The function takes two parameters: the number of times to evaluate the expression (in this case, one million) and the expression we want to evaluate (in this case, six times nine).

We do not really want to see the result of the SELECT query. The BENCHMARK() function always returns zero. What we are interested here is the time the query took to execute. In this sample output, you can see that evaluating 6×9 one million times on my system took a quarter of a second.

You can also pass BENCHMARK() a query, for example:

```
select benchmark(10000000,
  'select employee.name, department.name
  from employee, department
  where employee.departmentID=department.departmentID');
```

Using the Slow Query Log

The slow query log can be used to track which of your queries is running slowly. You define what is meant by "slowly," but it must be measured in whole seconds.

You can turn on slow query logging with the --log-slow-queries=*filename* option when starting the MySQL server or in your configuration file. If you also turn on the --log-long-format option, all queries that run without using an index are also logged. This can help you to see where you should be targeting your optimization efforts.

You can define what is meant by a slow query by using the long_query_time variable. You can set this in your configuration file or by using the SET command. This variable is in seconds.

You can read the slow query log manually because it's just a text file. You may find it more useful to view a summary of the queries that are running slowly. You can do this by running the `mysqldumpslow` script (in the scripts directory of your MySQL installation). This is a Perl script, so Windows users note that you will need to install Perl if you do not already have it. (Get it from www.activestate.com.)

One current limitation of MySQL is that you cannot configure it to log slow queries that take less than one second. On systems that process a large number of relatively simple queries, one second would be very, very slow. The administrator might want to be informed when queries take more than one-tenth of a second or some other fraction. This will be addressed in a future version.

Using EXPLAIN to See How Queries Are Executed

The EXPLAIN command tells MySQL to explain to you how a query will be executed. As a very simple example, we might type this:

```
explain
select e.name, d.name
from employee e, department d
where e.departmentID = d.departmentID;
```

As you can see, we have simply prefixed an unremarkable query with the word EXPLAIN. This will not actually execute the query, but will instead return some information about how MySQL plans to execute the query. You should see some results similar to the following:

```
+----+-------------+-------+--------+---------------+---------+---------+-----------------+--
----+-------+
| id | select_type | table | type   | possible_keys | key     | key_len | ref             |
rows | Extra |
+----+-------------+-------+--------+---------------+---------+---------+-----------------+--
----+-------+
|  1 | SIMPLE      | e     | ALL    | NULL          | NULL    | NULL    | NULL            |
5 |       |
|  1 | SIMPLE      | d     | eq_ref | PRIMARY       | PRIMARY |       4 | e.departmentID  |
1 |       |
+----+-------------+-------+--------+---------------+---------+---------+-----------------+--
----+-------+
2 rows in set (0.00 sec)
```

What does this all mean? You can see at a glance that there is one row in the result set per table in the query. (You can see which table is being discussed in the index column.) The order of the rows shows the order in which the tables will be joined.

The columns in this table are as listed here:

- id   This is a sequence number. If there is more than one SELECT in a query—for example, if you are using a subquery—each SELECT is numbered.

- select_type   This is the type of SELECT statement being performed. Most of the time this will be SIMPLE as in the preceding example, meaning that it's a plain vanilla SELECT.

If you are using subqueries, the outer query will be marked
PRIMARY and the inner queries will be marked SUBSELECT or DEPENDENT
SUBSELECT for correlated subqueries.

- table   This is the table this row is about.

- type   This is one of the most important columns for optimization. It tells you how
  the table is being joined to the other tables in the query.

- possible_keys   This tells you which indexes could have been used in the query. It will
  be NULL if there are no relevant indexes.

- key   This tells you which index was selected for use in the query. It will be NULL if no
  index was selected.

- key_len   This is the length of the index MySQL decided to use.

- ref   This is the value being compared to the key to decide whether to select rows.

- rows   This is an estimate of the number of rows from this table MySQL will read to
  generate the results of the query. You can work out how many rows will be read overall
  by multiplying the rows' values together. This gives a basic benchmark for how fast the
  query will run.

- Extra   Additional information may be given in this column. For example, the
  comment Using index means that MySQL can retrieve the result of the query
  completely from an index without reading data from the table.

So in this case, what is the output telling us?

The join type ALL for the employee table tells us that all rows will be scanned in this
table. This is obviously going to be slow if the table has a lot of data in it. In fact, the join
type ALL is the worst possible result. You will get this typically if a table has no useful index.
The obvious optimization here is to add an index. We'll look at this in a moment.

The row for department has join type eq_ref, which means that a single row will be read
from the department table for each row in the employee table. This is one of the best types.
The only better values for type are system and const, meaning that the table has only one
matching row and can effectively be treated as a constant. This part of the join we are pretty
happy with.

These are the other possible values for type:

- ref   All rows with matching index values will be read from the table. This is the next
  best option after eq_ref and represents situations in which you are dealing with non-
  unique keys.

- range   This is not as good as eq_ref or even ref. It means that all rows in a particular
  range will be read from the table.

- index   This is better than ALL, but worse than the other types mentioned previously.
  Seeing index means that the complete index will be scanned. This is preferable to
  scanning the complete table, but is far from ideal.

Next, let's look at the values of the `possible_keys` and `key` columns. The department table has one option—`PRIMARY`, the primary key, which is the one used. The employee table has the value `NULL` in both of these columns, meaning that there's no key to use and therefore no key will be used. Again, this is a pretty strong hint that we should be adding another index!

Based on this information and assuming that we're going to execute this query reasonably frequently and therefore would like it to be faster, we'll create another index as follows:

```
create index ename_did on employee(name, departmentID);
```

If we then rerun `EXPLAIN`, we get the following output:

```
+----+-------------+-------+--------+---------------+-----------+---------+------------------+------+-------------+
| id | select_type | table | type   | possible_keys | key       | key_len | ref              | rows | Extra       |
+----+-------------+-------+--------+---------------+-----------+---------+------------------+------+-------------+
|  1 | SIMPLE      | e     | index  | NULL          | ename_did |      85 | NULL             |    5 | Using index |
|  1 | SIMPLE      | d     | eq_ref | PRIMARY       | PRIMARY   |       4 | e.departmentID   |    1 |             |
+----+-------------+-------+--------+---------------+-----------+---------+------------------+------+-------------+
2 rows in set (0.00 sec)
```

You can see that there are some changes. The type for employee is now `index` because we now have an appropriate index to refer to. The new index is listed as a possible key, but it is not actually being used. Under `Extra` you will see that only the index for this table is used, rather than the table itself. This should be slightly faster.

The most basic use of `EXPLAIN` is to see where you can make better use of indexes to speed up your queries, but you might discover other approaches to speed up a query.

Understanding MySQL's Built-In Query Optimization

MySQL applies many optimization rules to queries.

MySQL uses its estimated number of rows (as shown in `EXPLAIN`) to work out the best order in which to join tables. If you notice that its estimate is off, you may want to experiment with using a `STRAIGHT JOIN` to force the table order. Benchmarking before and after cases will tell you whether you are helping or hindering.

To choose an index, MySQL looks for the most relevant index that spans less than 30% of the rows. If it can't find an index fitting these criteria, the table will be scanned instead. (This was what happened in the `EXPLAIN` query we looked at earlier, after we added the new index.)

Expressions in `WHERE` clauses are optimized in a similar way to the way many programming compilers optimize expressions. For example, unnecessary parentheses in expressions are removed. This is one reason you should feel free to make your queries more readable with parentheses.

If a query can be resolved wholly from indexes, it will be done without any reference to the actual rows in the table. Evaluation of `COUNT(*)` is also evaluated without reading or counting the rows in a table because this data is stored separately.

A more comprehensive list of the optimizations MySQL performs is in the manual, so we have not reproduced it here. But even that list is incomplete. You can read through the source code if you are interested in more information about how the query optimizer works.

Optimization Tips

There are three main things you can do to optimize your queries:

- **Add indexes.** If you have a frequent query on an unindexed column, add an index. For more information about how MySQL uses indexing, refer to Chapter 18, "Optimizing Your Database." Remember though that although an appropriate index might speed up operations that need to find data in the table, keeping indexes up-to-date increases the time required to write data. Do not add indexes that will not be used.

- **Use ANALYZE TABLE.** (See Chapter 18 for syntax.) This updates the information MySQL stores about key distribution. This information is used to decide the order in which tables are joined. If MySQL seems to be joining your tables in a strange order, try ANALYZE TABLE.

- **Use OPTIMIZE TABLE.** (See Chapter 18 for syntax.) This defragments the table storage, sorts the indexes, and updates the table statistics as used by the query optimizer.

Summary

- Find slow queries using BENCHMARK() or the slow query log.
- See how queries are executed using EXPLAIN.
- Speed things up by adding indexes and recheck with EXPLAIN.
- ANALYZE TABLE and OPTIMIZE TABLE will help the MySQL query optimizer to do its job well.

Quiz

1. The BENCHMARK() function returns

    a) the result of the benchmarked expression

    b) the time taken to execute the benchmarked expression

    c) zero, regardless of the parameters

    d) none of the above

2. You run EXPLAIN on a query and it tells you that the type for one of the tables in the join is ALL. This means that

    a) only one row will be read from the table

    b) all the rows with matching index values will be read from the table

    c) all of the index will be scanned

    d) all of the table will be scanned

3. You run EXPLAIN on a query and it tells you that the type for one of the tables in the join is eq_ref. This means that

    a) only one row will be read from the table

    b) all the rows with matching index values will be read from the table

    c) all of the index will be scanned

    d) all of the table will be scanned

4. You run EXPLAIN on a query and it tells you that the type for one of the tables in the join is index. This means that

    a) only one row will be read from the table

    b) all the rows with matching index values will be read from the table

    c) all of the index will be scanned

    d) all of the table will be scanned

5. The output of EXPLAIN tells you that MySQL is joining two tables in a suboptimal order. You should

    a) run ANALYZE TABLE on the two tables

    b) force the join order using STRAIGHT JOIN

    c) either a) or b)

    d) neither a) nor b)

Exercises

Consider the following query:

```
select department.name
from client, assignment, employee, department
where client.name='Telco Inc'
and client.clientID = assignment.clientID
and assignment.employeeID = employee.employeeID
and employee.departmentID = department.departmentID;
```

Use BENCHMARK to time this query over a large number of executions, and use EXPLAIN to see how it is executed. See whether you can increase the speed of execution by adding an index and rebenchmarking.

Answers

Quiz

1. c
2. d
3. a
4. c
5. c

Index

Symbols

+ (addition) operator, 112
* (asterisk), 112, 118
\ (backslash), 67
^ (carat) character, 118
/ (division) operator, 112
$ (dollar sign), 118
= (equality) operator, 113
> (greater than) operator, 113
< (less than) operator, 113
; (semicolon), 45
- (subtraction) operator, 112

Numerics

1NF (first normal form), 32-34
2NF (second normal form), 34-35
3NF (third normal form), 35-36

A

abs() function, 120
access, securing, 208
accounts. *See also* privileges
    anonymous, deleting, 15, 206-207
    creating for basic use, MySQL installation, 15-16
    security
        anonymous accounts, deleting, 15, 206-207
        dangerous privileges, 207
        encrypted passwords, 207
        root passwords, 206

ACID compliance, transactions, 153-154
activestate.com Web site, 241
adddate() function, 121
addition (+) operator, 112
administrative database activities
    caches, clearing, 186-187
    database information, retrieving, 183-184
    grant and privilege information, viewing, 185
    log files, 187
    MySQL server, starting up and shutting down, 181-182
    mysqladmin option summary, 188
    process information, viewing, 185
    server status and variables, viewing, 184
    table information, viewing, 185-186
    threads, terminating, 186
    variables, setting, 186
administrator-level privileges, 164
aliases, SELECT statement, 84-85
ALL keyword, 104
ALL privilege, 164
ALTER privilege, 164
ALTER TABLE command, 54-56
ANALYZE TABLE command, 234, 244
AND operator, 114
anomalies
    deletion, 31
    insertion, 31
    update, 32

anonymous accounts, deleting, 15, 206-207

ansi option, MySQL configuration, 176

ANY keyword, 104

applications, error-checking, 208

arithmetic operators, 112

asterisk (*), 118

attributes, database tables, 29

AUTO INCREMENT keyword, 49-50

autocommit mode, transactions, 151

avg() function, 125

AVG ROW LENGTH option, table optimization, 50

B

backslashes (\), 67

backup and restoration
BACKUP TABLE command, 198
FLUSH TABLES command, 197
from binary log, 198-199
LOCK TABLES command, 197
locking table, 192
manual, 197-198
mysqldump script
—add-drop-table option, 195
—add-locks option, 195
advantages of, 196
—all-databases option, 196
—allow-keywords option, 196
—d option, 196
—databases option, 196
disadvantages of, 196
—extended-insert option, 196
—lock-tables option, 196
—no-data option, 196
—opt option, 192
—quick option, 195
sample output, 192-195

mysqlhotcopy script, 196-197
reasons for, 192
RESTORE TABLE command, 198
tables, checking and repairing
CHECK TABLE command, 200
myisamchk program, 200-201
mysqlcheck program, 201
REPAIR TABLE command, 200
techniques for, 199
techniques, 191-192
testing, 199

BACKUP TABLE command, 198

basedir option, MySQL configuration, 176

BCNF (Boyce-Codd normal form), 36

BDB (Berkeley) tables, 50, 138

benchmark() function, 123, 240

benchmarking, queries, 240

BerkeleyDB (BDB) tables, 50, 138

BIGINT integer column type, 52

bin directory, 18

BINARY keyword, 113

binary logs
database restoration, 198-199
discussed, 187
replication, 214

BLOB column type, 53

Boolean expression subqueries, 103-105

Boolean full-text searching, 136-137

Boyce-Codd normal form (BCNF), 36

b-trees, 138

buffers, 227

built-in functions/operators, 111

built-in query optimization, 243-244

C

caches, clearing, 186-187

candidate keys, 29

carat (^) character, 118

cascading masters, replication with, 219

CASE function, 115

case sensitivity, identifiers, 42

cast functions, 123

ceiling() function, 120

CHAR column type, 53

char command, 46

character lengths, identifiers, 43

character sets, MySQL configuration, internationalization, 178

CHECK TABLE command, 200

checking and repairing tables
    CHECK TABLE command, 200
    myisamchk program, 200-201
    mysqlcheck program, 201
    REPAIR TABLE command, 200
    techniques for, 199

CHECKSUM option, table optimization, 50

clauses
    DEFAULT, INSERT statement, 69
    DELAYED, INSERT statement, 68
    DISTINCT, SELECT statement, 87-88
    FIELDS, LOAD DATA INFILE statement, 74
    FROM
        derived table subqueries, 102
        joins, 96
    GROUP BY, SELECT statement, 88-89
    HAVING, SELECT statement, 89
    IDENTIFIED BY, GRANT statement, 163
    IF NOT EXISTS, 49

IGNORE
    INSERT statement, 69
    LOAD DATA INFILE statement, 74
    UPDATE statement, 73
LIKE, 49
LIMIT
    DELETE statement, 72
    SELECT statement, 90-91
    UPDATE statement, 73
LINES, LOAD DATA INFILE statement, 74
LOW PRIORITY
    DELETE statement, 72
    INSERT statement, 68
    LOAD DATA INFILE statement, 74
    UPDATE statement, 73
ON, GRANT statement, 162
ON DUPLICATE KEY UPDATE, INSERT statement, 69
ORDER BY
    DELETE statement, 72
    SELECT statement, 90
    table rows, 56
    UPDATE statement, 73
QUICK, DELETE statement, 72
RENAME, tables, 56
REQUIRE, GRANT statement, 163
TO, GRANT statement, 162
WHERE
    joins, 96-97
    SELECT statement, 85-86
    UPDATE statement, 73
WITH, GRANT statement, 163

clearing caches, 186-187

column_priv columns
    columns_priv tables, 169
    tables_priv tables, 168

column privileges, granting, 165

columns

  columns_priv table, 169

  database tables, 29

  date and time types, 54

  db table, 167

  host table

    privilege columns, 168

    scope columns, 167

  keys, superkeys, 29

  numerical types, 51-52

  selecting, 83

  string and text types

    BLOB, 53

    CHAR, 53

    ENUM, 53

    SET, 54

    TEXT, 53

    VARCHAR, 53

  tables_priv table, 168

  unique, 50

  user table

    privilege columns, 166

    resource limitations columns, 167

    scope columns, 166

    secure connection columns, 166

columns_priv tables, privileges, 169

comma-separated values, 74

commands. *See also* **statements**

  ALTER TABLE, 55-56

  ANALYZE TABLE, 234, 244

  char, 46

  CHECK TABLE, 200

  COMMIT, transactions, 151

  drop database, 45, 55

  DROP INDEX, 55

  DROP TABLE, 55, 198

  EXPLAIN, 241-243

  FLUSH, caches, clearing, 186-187

  FLUSH TABLES, 140, 197

  LOCK TABLES, 152-153, 197

  OPTIMIZE TABLE, 134, 234, 244

  REPAIR TABLE, 134, 200

  RESET, caches, clearing, 186-187

  SET

    autocommit mode, disabling, 151

    log files, turning on, 187

  SHOW, 20, 183

  START TRANSACTION, 151

  UNLOCK TABLES, 152-153

  varchar, 46

COMMENT command

  table optimization, 50

  transactions, 151

comparison operators, 112-114

compression

  concat() function, 116

  MyISAM tables, 133-134

configuring MySQL

  InnoDB options, 176-177

  internationalization configuration, 178

  installation, 13-14

  multi-install configuration options, 177-178

  mysqld, setting options for, 175-176

  options file approach, 173-175

connections

  MySQL, testing, 14-15

  server security, 205

  SSL (Secure Sockets Layer), 208-209

consistency, transactions, 153

control flow functions, 115

conv() function, 116

convert() function, 123

count() function, 125

crackers, security, 208

CREATE DATABASE SQL statement, 43

CREATE privilege, 163

CREATE TABLE SQL statement, 43, 48-51

CREATE TEMPORARY TABLES privilege, 163

creating

accounts, basic use, 15-16

databases, CREATE DATABASE SQL statement, 43

HEAP tables, 141

indexes, 54-55

snapshots, database replication, 216-217

tables

CREATE TABLE SQL statement, 43, 48-51

employee database example, 44-48

optimization options, 50-51

cross joins, 100

curdate() function, 122

curtime() function, 122

D

data, uploading, 73-75

Data Definition Language (DDL), 42

data directory, 18

DATA DIRECTORY option, table optimization, 51

Data Manipulation Language (DML), 42, 65

data types, float, 47

databases

administration activities

caches, clearing, 186-187

database information, retrieving, 183-184

grant and privilege information, viewing, 185

log files, 187

MySQL server, starting up and shutting down, 181-182

mysqladmin option summary, 188

process information, viewing, 185

server status and variables, viewing, 184

table information, viewing, 185-186

threads, terminating, 186

variables, setting, 186

analyzation, ANALYZE TABLE command, 234

backup and restoration

BACKUP TABLE command, 198

from binary log, 198-199

locking tables, 192

manual, 197-198

mysqldump script, 192-196

mysqlhotcopy script, 196-197

RESTORE TABLE command, 198

tables, checking and repairing, 199-201

techniques, 191-192

testing, 199

creating, CREATE DATABASE SQL statement, 43

deleting, 55

design principles

anomalies, 31-32

design considerations, 30

normalization, 32-36

NULL values, 32

redundancy versus loss of data, 30-31

entities, defined, 27

identifiers

character lengths, 43

quote characters, 42

reserved words, 43

indexes

creating, 54-55

deleting, 55

optimization

considerations for, 231-232

design choices, 232

indexes, 233-234

OPTIMIZE TABLE command, 234

relational database management system (RDBMS), 28

relationships
  defined, 27
  many-to-many, 27
  one-to-many, 27
  one-to-one, 27

replicating
  advanced topologies, 219
  binary logging, 214
  cascading masters with, 219
  failover features, 220
  fault-tolerance, 213
  future of, 220
  load balancing, 219
  master configuration, checking, 215-216
  multimastering, 220
  permissions, granting, 215
  principles of, 213-214
  security implications, 215
  slave servers, configuring, 217-218
  slave servers, starting, 218
  snapshots, creating, 216-217
  version specification, 214

schema, defined, 30

selecting, 43, 83-84

tables
  ALTER TABLE, 54
  attributes, 29
  BerkeleyDB (BDB), 50, 138
  Boolean expression subqueries, 103-105
  columns, 29, 51-54, 83
  CREATE TABLE SQL statement, 48-51
  creating, 43-48, 50-51
  deleting, 55
  derived table subqueries, 102
  functional dependencies, 30
  heap, 50, 141

indexes, 233-234
InnoDB, 50, 137-138
ISAM, 50, 132-133
joining, 96-101
keys, 29
merge, 50, 139-140
MyISAM, 50, 132-137
privileges, 165-169
records, 29
renaming, 56
rows, 29
rows, deleting, 70-72
rows, duplicates, 87-88
rows, grouped, 88-89
rows, inserting, 65-69
rows, replacing, 70
rows, selecting, 85-86
rows, truncating, 72
rows, updating, 72-73
selecting, 83-84
single-value subqueries, 102-103
structure of, altering, 55-56
transaction safe, 131-132
tuples, 29
uploading data, 73-75

datadir option, MySQL configuration, 176

date and time functions, 121-123

date column types, 54

DATETIME column type, 54

dayname() function, 122

db tables, privileges, 167

DDL (Data Definition Language), 42

Decimal column type, 52

DEFAULT clause, INSERT statement, 69

DEFAULT keyword, 49

defragmenting MyISAM tables, 134

DELAY KEY WRITE option, table optimization, 51

DELAYED clause, INSERT statement, 68

DELETE privilege , 163

DELETE statement, 70-72

deleting
anonymous accounts, 15, 206-207
databases, 55
indexes, 55
rows, 70-72
tables, 55

deletion nomalies, 31

derived table subqueries, 102

describe command, 48

design choices, database optimization, 232

design principles, databases
anomalies
deletion, 31
insertion, 31
NULL values, 32
update, 32
design considerations, 30
normalization
Boyce-Codd normal form (BCNF), 36
first normal form (1NF), 32-34
second normal form (2NF), 34-35
third normal form (3NF), 35-36
redundancy versus loss of data, 30-31

directory structure, MySQL, 17-18

dirty read transaction isolation level, 155

disk space, MyISAM tables, 133

DISTINCT clause, SELECT statement, 87-88

division (/) operator, 112

DML (Data Manipulation Language), 42, 65

docs directory, 18

dollar sign ($), 118

DOUBLE column type, 52

drop database command, 45, 55

DROP INDEX command, 55

DROP privilege, 164

DROP TABLE command, 55, 195, 198

dump files, 196

duplicated rows, 87-88

durability, transactions, 154

dynamic MyISAM tables, 133-134

E

Emic Application Cluster tool, 220

encrypt() function, 123

encrypted passwords, 207

entities, defined, 27

ENUM column type, 53

equality (=) operator, 113

equijoins, 100

error-checking applications, 208

error logs, 187

executables, MySQL, 18-19

EXECUTE privilege, 163

EXISTS keyword, 104

EXPLAIN keyword, query execution information, 241-243

extra value, EXPLAIN command, 242

extract() function, 122

F

failover features, replication, 220

fault-tolerance, replication, 213

FIELDS clause, LOAD DATA INFILE statement, 74

FILE privilege, 164, 207

files
dump, 196
log files, 187

filtered data, security tips, 208

first normal form (1NF), 32-34

FLOAT column type, 52

float data type, 47

floating point numbers, 47

floor() function, 120

flow control functions, 115

FLUSH command, caches, clearing, 186-187

FLUSH PRIVILEGES statement, 206-207

FLUSH TABLES command, 140, 197

FOREIGN KEY keyword, 50

found rows() function, 124

fragmentation, MyISAM tables, 133

FROM clause
    joins, 96
    subqueries, derived table, 102

full joins, 100

FULLTEXT keyword, 50

full-text searching
    Boolean full-text search, 136-137
    MyISAM tables, 135-136

functional dependencies, concepts and terminology, 30

functions
    abs(), 120
    adddate(), 121
    avg(), 125
    benchmark(), 123, 240
    built-in, 111
    CASE, 115
    cast, 123
    ceiling(), 120
    concat(), 116
    convert(), 116, 123
    count(), 125
    curdate(), 122
    curtime(), 122

    date and time, 121-123
    dayname(), 122
    encrypt(), 123
    extract, 122
    floor(), 120
    flow control, 115
    found rows(), 124
    grouping, 124-125
    IF, 115
    last insert id(), 124
    length(), 116
    LIKE, 117
    load file, 116
    locate(), 116
    lower(), 116
    MATCH, 117
    max(), 125
    md5(), 124
    min(), 125
    mod(), 120
    now(), 122
    numeric, 120-121
    operators
        arithmetic, 112
        comparison, 112-113
        logical, 114
    password(), 124
    power(), 120
    quote(), 116
    rand(), 120
    replace(), 116
    RLIKE, 117-119
    round(), 120
    soundex(), 116
    sqrt(), 120
    std(), 125
    STRCMP, 117, 119
    string
        string comparison, 117-119
        string processing, 116

subdate(), 121
substring(), 116
sum(), 125
timestamp, 122
trim(), 116
upper(), 116

G–H

global privileges
 granting, 164
 security, 206
Google Web site, 138
grant columns, tables_priv tables, 168
GRANT statement
 IDENTIFIED BY clause, 163
 ON clause, 162
 REQUIRE clause, 163
 TO clause, 162
 WITH clause, 163
 WITH GRANT OPTION clause, 163
granting permissions, for replication, 215
granting privileges, 162
 administrator-level, 164
 column, 165
 database, 165
 global, 164
 table, 165
 user-level privileges, 163
greater than (>), 113
GROUP BY clause, SELECT statement, 88-89
grouped rows, 88-89
grouping functions, 124-125

HAVING clause, SELECT statement, 89
heap tables, 50, 141
host tables, privileges
 privilege columns, 168
 scope columns, 167
Huffman coding, compression, 134

I

id option, EXPLAIN command, 241
IDENTIFIED BY clause, GRANT statement, 163
identifiers
 case sensitivity, 42
 character lengths, 43
 quote characters, 42
 reserved words, 43
IF function, 115
IF NOT EXISTS clause, 49
IGNORE clause
 INSERT statement, 69
 LOAD DATA INFILE statement, 74
 UPDATE statement, 73
IN keyword, 104
INDEX DIRECTORY option, table optimization, 51
INDEX keyword, 50
INDEX privilege, 163
index value, EXPLAIN command, 242
indexes
 creating, 54-55
 database optimization, 233-234
 deleting, 55
 leftmost prefix, 233
 multicolumn, 233
 optimization considerations, 231
 query optimization, 244
 single-column, 233

InnoDB configuration options, MySQL configuration, 176-177

InnoDB tables, 50
consistent nonlocking, 137
licensing agreement, 138
row-level locking, 137
transactions with, 147-150
    ACID compliance, 153-154
    autocommit mode, 151-153
    transactions isolation, 154-155
Web site for, 138

INSERT METHOD option, table optimization, 51

INSERT privilege, 163

INSERT statement
clauses, 68-69
general form of, 68
listing, 65-66
output example, 67

inserting rows into tables, 65-69

insertion anomalies, 31-32

installation files, securing
access and privileges, 208
application-level error checking, 208
do's and don'ts, 207
filtered data, 208
physical security, 209
SSL (Secure Sockets Layer), 208-209

installing MySQL, 9
accounts, creating for basic use, 15-16
anonymous accounts, deleting, 15
on Linux, 10
on OS X, 12
on Windows, 10-11
root password, setting, 15
system configuration, 13-14
testing, 14-15

Integer column type, 52

interfaces
MySQL Control Center, 19
MySQL monitor, 19-21
phpMyAdmin, 19

internationalization configuration, MySQL configuration, 178

ISAM tables, 50
limitations, 132-133
overview, 132

isolation levels (transactions), 153
dirty read, 155
phantom reads, 155
read committed, 155
read uncommitted, 155
repeatable read, 154
serializable, 154

J–K

joins
cross joins, 100
equijoin, 100
full joins, 100
LEFT joins, 100-101
multiple tables, joining, 97-98
RIGHT joins, 100-101
self joins, 99
two tables, joining, 96-97

key buffer, defined, 227

key_len value, EXPLAIN command, 242

key value, EXPLAIN command, 242

keys, candidate keys and superkeys, 29

keywords
ALL, 104
ANY, 104
AUTO INCREMENT, 49
BINARY, 113

EXISTS, 104
FOREIGN KEY, 50
FULLTEXT, 50
IN, 104
INDEX, 50
PRIMARY KEY, 49
ROLLBACK, 150
SOME, 104
TEMPORARY, 49
UNIQUE, 50
UNSIGNED, 52

L

last insert id() function, 124
LEFT join, 100-101
length() function, 116
lengths, identifier characters, 43
less than (<) operator, 113
licensing agreements, InnoDB tables, 138
LIKE clause, 49
LIKE function, 117
LIMIT clause
    DELETE statement, 72
    SELECT statement, 90-91
    UPDATE statement, 73
LINES clause, LOAD DATA INFILE statement, 74
Linux, MySQL installation, 10
listings
    backup and restoration, mysqldump script, 192-195
    databases, table creation, 44-46
    INSERT statement, 65-66
    MERGE tables, 139-140
    MySQL configuration, options file approach, 174-175
    MySQL installation, configuration options, 13-14

load balancing, replication, 219
LOAD DATA INFILE statement, 73-75
load file() function, 116
locate() function, 116
LOCK TABLES command, 152-153, 195, 197
LOCK TABLES privilege, 163
locking tables, 192
logging
    binary logs, 187, 214
    error logs, 187
    log-bin option, MySQL configuration, 176
    log-error option, MySQL configuration, 176
    log-slow-queries option, MySQL configuration, 176
    logging options, MySQL configuration, 177
    query logs, 187
    relay logs, 214
    rotating, 187
    slow query logs, 187
    turning on, 187
logical operators, 114
long query time variable (slow query log), 241
loss of data versus redundancy, database design, 30-31
LOW PRIORITY clause
    DELETE statement, 72
    INSERT statement, 68
    LOAD DATA INFILE statement, 74
    UPDATE statement, 73
lower() function, 116

M

manual backups and restoration, 197-198

many-to-many relationships, 27-28

master servers, replication, master configuration, 213-216, 219

MATCH function, 117

max() function, 125

MAX ROWS option, table optimization, 51

md5() function, 124

MEDIUM integer column type, 52

merge tables, 50, 139-140

min() function, 125

MIN ROWS option, table optimization, 51

mod() function, 120

multicolumn indexes, 233

multimastering, replication, 220

multiplication (*) operator, 112

MyISAM tables, 50
    compressed, 133
    compressing, 134
    dynamic, 133-134
    full-text searching, 135-137
    improvements to, 132-133
    overview, 133
    repairing, 134
    static, 133-134

myisamchk command-line tool, 134

myisamchk program, 18, 200-201

MySQL
    configuring
        InnoDB, 176-177
        internationalization configuration, 178
        multi-install configuration options, 177-178
        mysqld, setting options for, 175-176
        options file approach, 173-175
    directory structure, 17-18
    executables, 18-19
    installing, 9
        accounts, creating for basic use, 15-16
        anonymous accounts, deleting, 15
        on Linux, 10
        on OS X, 12
        on Windows, 10-11
        root password, setting, 15
        system configuration, 13-14
        testing, 14-15
    server
        process information, viewing, 185
        starting up and shutting down, 181-182
    server tuning, optimization
        parameters, 226-227
        RAID utility, 228
        Solaris utility, 228
        speed, compiling and linking for, 225-226
    user interfaces
        MySQL Control Center, 19
        MySQL monitor, 19-21
        phpMyAdmin, 19

MySQL Control Center, 19

MySQL monitor, 19-21

mysqladmin program, 18, 188

mysqlbinlog program, 18

mysqlcheck program, 201

mysqld, setting options for, 175-176

mysqldump script, 18
    —add-drop-table option, 195
    advantages of, 196
    —all-databases option, 196
    —allow-keywords option, 196
    —databases option, 196
    disadvantages of, 196
    —extended-insert option, 196
    —lock-tables option, 196

—no-data option, 196
—opt option, 192
—quick option, 195
sample output, 192-195
mysqlhotcopy script, 196-197
mysqlshow program, 18

N-O

normalization
Boyce-Codd normal form (BCNF), 36
defined, 32
first normal form (1NF), 32-34
second normal form (2NF), 34-35
third normal form (3NF), 35-36
NOT NULL value, table creation, 49
NOT operator, 114
now() function, 122
NULL value
comparison operators, 112-113
database design, 32
table creation, 49
numeric functions, 120-121
numerical columns, 51-52

ON clause, GRANT statement, 162
**ON DUPLICATE KEY UPDATE
clause, INSERT statement, 69**
one-to-many relationships, 27-28
one-to-one relationships, 27-28
OpenSSL Library Web site, 209
operators
arithmetic, 112
built-in, 111
comparison, 112-114
logical, 114

optimization
databases
considerations for, 231-232
design choices, 232
indexes, 233-234
OPTIMIZE TABLE command, 234
MySQL server tuning
parameters, 226-227
RAID utility, 228
Solaris utility, 228
speed, compiling and linking for,
225-226
queries
ANALYZE TABLE command, 244
benchmarking, 240
built-in query optimization, 243-244
EXPLAIN command, 241-243
indexes, adding, 244
OPTIMIZE TABLE command, 244
slow queries, finding, 239
slow query log, 240-241
table creation, 50-51
**OPTIMIZE TABLE command, 134,
234, 244**
**options files, MySQL configuration,
173-174**
InnoDB options, 176-177
internationalization configuration, 178
multi-install configuration options,
177-178
mysqld, setting options for, 175-176
OR operator, 114
ORDER BY clause
DELETE statement, 72
SELECT statement, 90
table rows, 56
UPDATE statement, 73
OS X, MySQL installation, 12

P

PACK KEYS option, table optimization, 51

page-level locking, BerkeleyDB (BDB) tables, 138

parameters, servers, optimization techniques, 226-227

password() function, 124

PASSWORD option, table optimization, 51

passwords
encrypted passwords, 207
root passwords, 15, 206

permissions, for replications, 215

phantom reads transaction isolation level, 155

phpMyAdmin interface, 19

pid-file options, MySQL configuration, 177

portability, MyISAM tables, 132

possible_keys value, EXPLAIN command, 242

power() function, 120

PRIMARY KEY keyword, 49

privilege columns
db tables, 167
host tables, 168
user tables, 166

privileges
FILE, 207
granting, 162
administrator-level, 164
column privileges, 165
database privileges, 165
global privileges, 164
table privileges, 165
user-level privileges, 163

PROCESS, 207
revoking, 165
securing
dangerous privileges, 207
FLUSH PRIVILEGES statement, 206-207
global privileges, 206
server connections, 205
tables, 165
columns_priv tables, 169
db tables, 167
host tables, 167-168
tables_priv tables, 168
user tables, 166-167
viewing information about, 185
WITH GRANT OPTION, 207

process information (server status), 185

PROCESS privilege, 164, 207

Q

queries
joins
cross joins, 100
equijoin, 100
full joins, 100
joining multiple, 97-98
LEFT joins, 100-101
RIGHT joins, 100-101
self joins, 99
log files, 187
optimization
ANALYZE command, 244
benchmarking, 240
built-in query optimization, 243-244
EXPLAIN command, 241-243
indexes, adding, 244
OPTIMIZE TABLE command, 244
slow queries, finding, 239
slow query log, 240-241

SELECT statement, 82

subqueries
    Boolean expression, 103-105
    derived table, 102
    single-value, 102-103
    types of, 101

QUICK clause, DELETE statement, 72

quote characters, identifiers, 42

quote() function, 116

R

RAID TYPE option, table optimization, 51

RAID utility, MySQL server, optimization techniques, 228

rand() function, 120

range testing, comparison operators, 114

range value, EXPLAIN command, 242

RDBMS (relational database management system), 29

read buffer, 227

read committed transaction isolation level, 155

read uncommitted transaction isolation level, 155

records, database tables, concepts and terminology, 29

recovery. *See* backup and restoration

redundancy versus loss of date, database design, 30-31

ref value, EXPLAIN command, 242

REFERENCES privilege, 164

regular expression matching, RLIKE function, 117-119

relational database management system (RBMS), 28

relationships
    defined, 27
    many-to-many, 27-28
    one-to-many, 27-28
    one-to-one, 27-28

relay logs, 214

RELOAD privilege, 164

RENAME clause, 56

renaming tables, 56

REPAIR TABLE command, 134, 200

repairing MyISAM tables, 134

repairing and checking tables
    CHECK TABLE command, 200
    myisamchk program, 200-201
    mysqlcheck program, 201
    REPAIR TABLE command, 200
    techniques for, 199

repeatable read transaction isolation level, 154

replace() function, 116

REPLACE statement, 70

replacing rows, 70

replicating databases
    advanced topologies, 219
    binary logging, 214
    failover features, 220
    fault-tolerance, 213
    future of, 220
    load balancing, 219
    master configuration, checking, 215-216
    multimastering, 220
    permissions, granting, 215
    principles of, 213-214
    security implications, 215
    slave configuration, 217-218
    slaves, starting, 218
    snapshots, creating, 216-217
    version specification, 214
    with cascading masters, 219

REPLICATION CLIENT privilege, 164

REPLICATION SLAVE privilege, 164

REQUIRE clause, GRANT statement, 163

reserved words, identifiers as, 43

RESET command, caches, clearing, 186-187

resource limitation columns, user tables, 167

restoration. *See* **backup and restoration**

RESTORE TABLE command, 198

REVOKE statement, 165

revoking privileges, 165

RIGHT join, 100-101

RLIKE function, 117-119

ROLLBACK keyword, 150

root passwords, 15, 206

rotating log files, 187

round() function, 120

ROW FORMAT option, table optimization, 51

row-level locking, InnoDB tables, 137

rows
database tables, concepts and terminology, 29
deleting, 70-72
duplicates, 87-88
grouped, 88-89
inserting into tables, 65-69
replacing, 70
selecting, 85-86
truncating, 72
updating, 72-73

rows value, EXPLAIN command, 242

RPMs, MySQL installation, 10

S

schema, defined, 30

scope columns
columns_priv tables, 169
db tables, 167
host tables, 167
tables_priv tables, 168
user tables, 166

scripts directory, 18

searching
full-text searching, 136-137
MyISAM tables, 135-136

second normal form (2NF), 34-35

secure connection columns, user tables, 166

Secure Sockets Layer (SSL), 208-209

security
accounts
anonymous accounts, deleting, 206-207
dangerous privileges, 207
encrypted passwords, 207
root passwords, 206
installation files
access and privileges, 208
application-level error checking, 208
do's and don'ts, 207
filtered data, 208
physical security, 209
SSL (Secure Sockets Layer), 208-209
privilege systems
global privileges, 206
server connections, 205
replication systems, 215

SELECT privilege, 163

SELECT statement
aliases, 84-85
columns, 83
databases, 83-84

DISTINCT clause, 87-88
GROUP BY clause, 88-89
HAVING clause, 89
LIMIT clause, 90-91
ORDER BY clause, 90
overview, 82
simple query example, 82
table creation, 51
tables, 83-84
WHERE clause, 85-86
selecting
databases, use statement, 43
rows, 85-86
select_type option, EXPLAIN command, 241
self joins, 99
semicolon (;), 45
serializable transaction isolation level, 154
servers
master, replication, 213-216, 219
MySQL
optimization techniques, 225-228
process information, viewing, 185
starting up and shutting down, 181-182
status of, viewing, 184
slaves
replication, 213-214, 217-218
starting, 218
Services window (Windows Administrative tools), 182
SET column type, 54
SET command
autocommit mode, disabling, 151
log files, turning on, 187
variables, setting, 186

shared-memory-base-name options, MySQL configuration, 177
SHOW command, 20, 183
SHOW DATABASES privilege, 163
show processlist statement, 186
show variables statement, 186
SHUTDOWN privilege, 164
shutting down MySQL server, 181-182
single-column indexes, 233
single-value subqueries, 102-103
Slashdot Web site, 138
slave servers
replication, 213-214, 217-218
starting, 218
Sleepycat Web site, 138
slow queries server value, 184
slow query logs, 187, 240-241
SMALLINT integer column type, 52
snapshots, creating, 216-217
socket options, MySQL configuration, 177
Solaris utility, MySQL server, optimization techniques, 228
SOME keyword, 104
sort buffer, 227
soundex() function, 116
speed, MySQL server, 225-226
sql-bench directory, 18
SQL statements
CREATE DATABASE, 43
CREATE TABLE, 43, 48-50
DELETE, 70-72
INSERT, 65-69
REPLACE, 70
SELECT, 82-91
TRUNCATE, 72
UPDATE, 72-73

sqrt() function, 120

SSL (Secure Sockets Layer), 208-209

START TRANSACTION command, 151

starting
  MySQL server, 181-182
  slaves, 218

statements. *See also* commands
  ALTER TABLE, 54
  DROP TABLE, 195
  FLUSH PRIVILEGES, 206-207
  GRANT, 162-163
  LOAD DATA INFILE, 73-75
  LOCK TABLES, 195
  ON, GRANT statement, 162
  REVOKE, privileges, 165
  SELECT, table creation, 51
  SET, variables, 186
  show processlist, threads, 186
  show variables, 186
  SQL
    CREATE DATABASE, 43
    CREATE TABLE, 43, 48-50
    DELETE, 70-72
    INSERT, 65-69
    REPLACE, 70
    SELECT, 82-91
    TRUNCATE, 72
    UPDATE, 72-73
  SQL CREATE TABLE, 43, 48-50
  UNLOCK, 195
  use, database selection, 43

static MyISAM tables, 133-134

std() function, 125

stop words, full-text searching, 136

STRCMP function, 117, 119

string and text column types, 53-54

string functions
  LIKE function, 117
  MATCH function, 117
  RLIKE function, 117-119
  STRCMP function, 117, 119
  string processing, 116

subdate() function, 121

subqueries
  Boolean expression, 103-105
  derived table, 102
  single-value, 102-103
  types of, 101

substring() function, 116

subtraction (-) operator, 112

sum() function, 125

SUPER privilege, 164

superkeys, 29

T

table cache parameter, 227

table value, EXPLAIN command, 242

tables
  ALTER TABLE statement, 54
  BACKUP TABLE command, 198
  BerkeleyDB (BDB), 50, 138
  Boolean expression subqueries, 103-105
  checking and repairing
    CHECK TABLE command, 200
    myisamchk program, 200-201
    mysqlcheck program, 201
    REPAIR TABLE command, 200
    techniques for, 199
  columns
    date and time types, 54
    numerical type, 51-52
    selecting, 83
    string and text types, 53-54
    unique, 50

creating
    CREATE TABLE SQL statement, 43, 48-51
    employee database example, 44-48
    optimization options, 50-51
database tables, 28
derived table subqueries, 102
DROP TABLE command, 198
FLUSH TABLES command, 197
heap, 50, 141
indexes
    leftmost prefix, 233
    multicolumn, 233
    optimization, 233-234
    single-column, 233
InnoDB, 50
    consistent nonlocking, 137
    licensing agreement, 138
    row-level locking, 137
    transactions with, 147-155
    Web site for, 138
ISAM, 50
    limitations, 132-133
    overview, 132
joining
    cross joins, 100
    equijoin, 100
    full joins, 100
    LEFT joins, 100-101
    multiple tables, 97-98
    RIGHT joins, 100-101
    self joins, 99
    two tables, 96-97
LOCK TABLES command, 197
locking, 192
merge, 50, 139-140
MERGE, FLUSH TABLES command, 140

MyISAM, 50
    compressed, 133-134
    dynamic, 133-134
    full-text searching, 135-137
    improvements to, 132-133
    overview, 133
    repairing, 134
    static, 133-134
privileges, 165
    columns_priv tables, 169
    db tables, 167
    host tables, 167-168
    tables_priv tables, 168
    user tables, 166-167
reference information, viewing, 185-186
renaming, 56
RESTORE TABLE command, 198
rows
    deleting, 70-72
    duplicates, 87-88
    grouped, 88-89
    inserting, 65-69
    replacing, 70
    selecting, 85-86
    truncating, 72
    updating, 72-73
selecting, 83-84
single-value subqueries, 102-103
structure of, altering, 55-56
transaction safe, 131-132
uploading data, 73-75
tables_priv tables, privileges, 168
TEMPORARY keyword, 49
testing
    backup procedures, 199
    MySQL installation, 14-15

text and string column types
  BLOB, 53
  CHAR, 53
  ENUM, 53
  SET, 54
  TEXT, 53
  VARCHAR, 53
TEXT column type, 53
third normal form (3NF), 35-36
threads, terminating, 186
threads connected server value, 184
time and date functions, 121-123
time column types, 54
TIMESTAMP column type, 54
Timestamp columns, columns_priv tables, 169
timestamp() function, 122
TINYINT integer column type, 52
TO clause, GRANT statement, 162
transaction safe tables
  BerkeleyDB (BDB), 138
  InnoDB
    consistent nonlocking, 137
    licensing agreement, 138
    row-level locking, 137
    Web site for, 138
  types of, 131-132
transactions
  defined, 147-150
  START TRANSACTION command, 151
  with InnoDB tables, 147-150
    ACID compliance, 153-154
    autocommit mode, 151-153
    transaction isolation, 154-155
trim() function, 116
TRUNCATE statement, 72
truncating rows, 72
tuples, concepts and terminology, 29
type value, EXPLAIN command, 242

U

UNION LENGTH option, table optimization, 51
UNIQUE keyword, 50
UNLOCK TABLES command, 152-153, 195
UNSIGNED keyword, 52
update anomalies, 32
UPDATE privilege, 163
UPDATE statement, 72-73
updating rows, 72-73
uploading data, 73-75
uppercase() function, 116
uptime server value, 184
USAGE privilege, 163
use statement, database selection, 43
user accounts, security
  anonymous accounts, deleting, 206-207
  dangerous privileges, 207
  encrypted passwords, 207
  root passwords, 206
user interfaces
  MySQL Control Center, 19
  MySQL monitor, 19-21
  phpMyAdmin, 19
user-level privileges, 163
user option, MySQL configuration, 176
user permissions, for replication, 215
user tables, privileges
  privilege columns, 166
  resource limitation columns, 167
  scope columns, 166
  secure connection columns, 166

V-W

VARCHAR column type, 53

varchar command, 46

variables

    setting values of, 186

    viewing, 184

version specification, database replication, 214

Web sites

    activestate.com, 241

    Google, 138

    InnoDB, 138

    OpenSSL, 209

    Slashdot, 138

    Sleepycat, 138

    Yahoo!, 138

WHERE clause

    joins, 96-97

    SELECT statement, 85-86

    UPDATE statement, 73

wildcard matching, LIKE function, 117

Windows, MySQL installation, 10-11

Windows Administrative tools, Services window, 182

WITH clause, GRANT statement, 163

WITH GRANT OPTION clause, GRANT statement, 163

WITH GRANT OPTION privilege, 164, 207

X-Y-Z

XOR operator, 114

Yahoo! Web site, 138

YEAR column type, 54

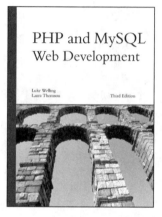
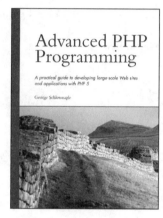
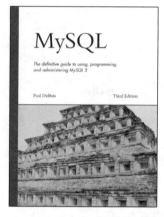

The definitive books on the world's most popular open-source database, written by the world's best authors

MySQL Tutorial

Luke Welling and Laura Thomson

ISBN: 0-672-32584-5 • $29.99 US

MySQL Tutorial is a clear, concise introduction to the fundamental concepts and techniques of working with MySQL. It teaches the beginning MySQL user how to create and administer powerful databases that can be used at home, work, and on the Web.

MySQL Certification Study Guide

Paul DuBois, Stefan Hinz
and Carsten Pedersen

ISBN 0-672-32632-9 • $49.99 US

MySQL Language Reference

MySQL AB

ISBN 0-672-32633-7 • $39.99 US

MySQL Administrator's Guide

MySQL AB

ISBN 0-672-32634-5 • $39.99 US